# THE ISLE OF FOULA

# THE ISLE OF FOULA

A SERIES OF ARTICLES ON BRITAIN'S
LONELIEST INHABITED ISLE

IAN B. STOUGHTON HOLBOURN

WITH A MEMOIR BY
M. C. STOUGHTON HOLBOURN

Birlinn

This edition published in 2001 by
Birlinn Limited
West Newington House
10 Newington Road
Edinburgh
EH9 1QS

www.birlinn.co.uk

First published in 1938 by Johnson & Greig, Lerwick

ISBN 1 84158 161 5

British Library Cataloguing-in-Publication Data
A catalogue record for this book is available
from the British Library

Typeset by Textype, Cambridge
Printed and bound by Antony Rowe Ltd., Chippenham

# CONTENTS

# ACKNOWLEDGMENTS

My thanks are due to Messrs. Johnson & Greig for their generosity in publishing this book; to the editors of *The Scotsman*, *The Edinburgh Evening Dispatch*, *Antiquity*, *Discovery* and *The Middle Border* for permission to reprint articles and for the loan of blocks; to Mr H. B. Curwen, Mr John Peterson, Mr L. G. Scott and Dr Hylas Holbourn for the use of photographs; and to all the people of Foula, without whose help this book could not have been compiled and upon whose good nature I rely to overlook all defects.

M. C. S. Holbourn
Penkaet Castle,
Pencaitland, December, 1937

# FOREWORD TO THE BIRLINN EDITION

It is now over a century—a century of immense change—since Ian Stoughton Holbourn bought the island of Foula. How he would react to the island now is hard to imagine. The material technological changes would be difficult enough for him, and he would most certainly be overwhelmed by the change in social attitudes. Like many landlords of his time he could respect many of his tenants on a one-to-one basis, but was steeped in the Victorian 'them and us' class attitude. What would he think of his own grandchildren having become crofters, living among the 'peasantry'?

Much of the Professor's working life was spent lecturing in the United States, where his image as the laird of a remote Scottish island had great appeal. To complement this picture he created his own Holbourn tartan, despite the fact that Shetland knew nothing of Gaeldom and the clans. The Professor's love of Foula comes across in the book, through which the reader is introduced to a romantic, dramatic and mystical place where life was harsh, strenuous, unyielding and difficult. Yes, that side of Foula is there and always will be, but there are other sides. It is also a place of calm and peace, where the sea lies still, the flowers scent the air, the grass ripples with a gentle breeze and the sky is patterned with summmer light.

Professor Holbourn's wife, Marion, was the instigator of this book. Perturbed that he had died leaving a huge body of unpublished writing on a vast range of subjects, she put together this volume with material either synthesised or lifted straight from his notes. She also contributed an informative memoir of the man herself. Although the book caused some anguish among the family when first published (those closest often see faults that others overlook), it is a unique record of a fascinating place, containing much of social and historical interest.

When Professor Holbourn died in 1935 he left Foula in trust among his three sons, Hylas, Alasdair and Phil, with his wife as life rentrix. With Marion outliving her husband by over forty years, Foula affairs occasioned much family discussion—not always very harmonious. When Alasdair realised that his mother would outlive two of her sons, he wrote in his will: 'As Foula is only a nuisance, I leave my share to Phil!' Perhaps this does not give an absolutely realistic impression—Foula's nuisance value, from a landlord's point of view, was more due to the Crofters Acts of the last half of the twentieth century than to the family trusts. These Acts turned the landlord/tenant relationship on its head. So perhaps the Professor would not be so upset at his descendants being crofters after all.

John G. Holbourn, eldest grandchild, June 2001

# FOREWORD

I am the wrong person to write an appreciation of this book: my knowledge of Foula is so complete and yet so scanty: the sixteen weeks which I spent there, struggling to make "The Edge of the World," were full of experience, but it was experience directed towards one end, to tell my story and to present to the world the most complete picture that I could of its background—Foula.

Two things came out of those weeks in 1936: our film, which, I think, will yet make Foula one of the best-known places in the world, instead of the least; and the other is a love for the island and its people.

So perhaps I have a right to this page, after all.

An island has a personality of its own, the more remote, the more insistent. Why has an island an irresistible appeal to us all?

I think that the answer is because it is complete. We can see it as a whole. Other places have the same appeal, that we can feel at the first visit, but not in such an intimate, such a *concentrated* form. A lonely island throws its spell over the traveller as soon as he sets foot on its smallest rock.

So it was when I first saw Foula. On a still night in June we neared the little lights of Ham Voe at midnight. We were six

hours out from Scalloway in a motorboat. The five peaks of the
island lay black against a violet sky. A few fishermen were out
under the cliffs. On the port bow the moon shone across the sea
and on the starboard the setting sun was shining, and the two
glittering paths met and broke in our wake. I have never
forgotten it.

My film tells the tale of the defeat of a people. It was
created and brought to life by the help of the people of Foula.
They one and all proved more helpful, more sympathetic and
more truly intelligent than any men and women with whom I
have worked.

Whatever the critics say, the real star of my film is the
lonely island of Foula—and the real makers are its people.

MICHAEL POWELL
London, 1937

# 1
## GEOGRAPHICAL AND PERSONAL

All islands have a charm; but Thule, Fughley or Foula is among the most fascinating in existence. Tudor says that it is, for its size, undoubtedly one of the most interesting islands in the British seas—perhaps the most interesting. Yet Tudor did not see some of its best scenery, and apparently knew nothing of its interesting history—the Thule of the ancient world; the Iona of the North, and the source of Christianity; its udal tenure and its line of petty kings; its folk tales and quaint survivals, and its remnants of mediæval poetry recently discovered—not to mention that it is an ornithologist's paradise, and even boasts a variety of mouse (*Mus Thulensis*) peculiar to itself.

The island lies a hundred miles to the North of Scotland and twenty-seven miles West of Scalloway in Shetland, lat. 60° 8′ N, long. 2° 5′ W; or a little further north than Cape Farewell in Greenland and about the same longitude as Aberdeen.

It is three and a half miles long and two and a half miles wide, and its area is somewhat over 4,000 acres, or about six times the size of Hyde Park and Kensington Gardens together, or five times the size of the Central Park in New York.

The journey averages about four days from Edinburgh. The simplest way is to take the steamer from Aberdeen to Lerwick and, after spending a day in Lerwick, as the boats do not fit very conveniently, cross the Mainland of Shetland to the little village of Walls—a 27-mile drive through delightful scenery. The mail-boat to Foula runs once a week in summer, weather permitting, but in those boisterous seas one is lucky if it is not more than a day or so late.

To cross the twenty-mile stretch of ocean one passes down the beautiful Sound of Vaila and then the great hills of Foula break into view on the horizon, and gradually grow up with their ever-changing beauty of colour and light and shade. Only a frequent visitor to the isle can know these amazing differences of colour and tone, ranging from a pale jewelled green to deep purple. One day the isle rises dark against the sea, the next it is bright and the sea is sombre. Sometimes the land is full of light and shade and modelling, or again it looks as flat as if cut out of cardboard. Occasionally the island seems transparent as though made of a coloured jewel. Some of the cloud effects are magnificent. Perhaps the most delightful is when a thin sheet of white cloud, looking like a fall of snow, clings to the outline and surfaces of the hills and pours over the edges as a white foaming waterfall.

Foula's splendid hill line is best when viewed from nearly north-east at some four to four and a half miles from the shore, with the peak of the Sneug rising in the centre flanked by those of Hamnafjeld and the Kame, and with Soberlie to the north and the rounded top of the Noup away to the south. The form of the isle varies greatly according to aspect, and the view from the south has the character of a gigantic fortress or tower, while on the west one can picture Lucifer falling from the dizzy ramparts of the walls of Heaven. These are the highest sheer cliffs in Great Britain, a vast wall of absolutely vertical rock 1,220 feet high. "As a group these precipices stand unrivalled in the British isles," says Professor Heddle in the *Mineralogical Magazine*. The Faroes alone can match their grandeur. They are equally impressive from above or below. Gazing upward from the sea one feels as though the mountains would indeed fall on us and the hills cover us, as the prophet phrases it. Never in all my travels have I seen anything that gives quite such a sensation of toppling mass and overwhelming awe. If we climb the hills and come at the cliffs from the top the effect is equally impressive. I have seen people fling themselves down on the ground at a considerable distance from the edge and refuse to look over. A glorious sight rewards those who creep to the edge. The great gulls four feet six across the wing, fly down and down till they look like a swarm of midges and eventually disappear altogether. Or perhaps a fulmar petrel will fly past at a distance of some eight feet, and remain absolutely motionless in the air for five or six seconds, and then sweep round in a great curve and return to repeat the performance.

A stone thrown from the top of the cliffs helps to give an impression of their height. For some reason, presumably the resistance of the air and the fact that the stone has to be thrown outward to clear the fallen rocks at the foot, it takes eleven seconds to reach the sea. I have frequently given people some idea of the distance by asking them to imagine the stone thrown when I say "now," and that it reaches the bottom when I say "splash." The reader should amuse himself by timing it on a watch, as most people's notion of a second is nearer to half that time.

The landing-place is on the east side at Ham Voe, except for the Admiralty, who use a very awkward landing at the south end and have it marked on their charts because Noah, or some other early navigator, once drifted ashore there. Being a government department it is quite useless to point out the fact to them, although I have done so repeatedly for a quarter of a century.

Until recently the only way to get ashore was to clamber up the natural rocks, a proceeding not unattended with risk, particularly in a heavy sea. But this only added to the charm and inaccessibility of the place. Even in calm weather the Voe was often the scene of small mishaps. Most of the laird's family have had a wetting at some time. His lady was on one occasion stepping into a boat when the boat and the land parted company. It is not the man alone who hesitates that is lost; and when it was too late to put both feet either aboard or ashore, five feet of water was the only alternative. "And you can't swim, can you?" said the laird's brother calmly, as he leaned over to observe the figure in the sea. When after a scramble and a hasty change the two arrived at the yacht, the laird merely remarked coldly: "What a time you have been! Now we have missed the tide." It is a hard and unfeeling world! But the laird had his own turn later, when standing out on the bobstay of his yacht to do some repairs at the end of the bowsprit. The bobstay broke, and on hearing a splash a man rushed forward shrieking, "My God! Can you swim?" "Yes," was the reply, "but it's beastly cold. Throw me a rope!" And after some delay a rope was procured. Alas for those who go down to the sea in ships!

In 1914 a grandmotherly and extravagant government provided a pier when a simple landing-place would have been cheaper and more satisfactory. It ends in a jagged sunken skerry as a trap for unwary vessels. The romantic approach is completely spoiled, but this is what we call progress. One of its achievements has been nearly to prove the death of the laird's youngest son, who was so lacking in circumspection as to fall off it. There was no scrambling out this time as the pier is vertical, and had he not been towed ashore by his ten-year-old brother's fishing rod he would undoubtedly have been drowned, as he was only five years old and had not yet learned to swim.

Many a scene of danger and bravery has been enacted in the Voe when bringing in the mailboat in stormy weather. Sometimes lines have been stretched across the Voe to drag her in; oil has been poured on the water, and not on one occasion alone have the islanders rushed into the Voe at the risk of their lives to save her from the furious seas.

The east side of the island is low with cliffs varying from 80 to 120 feet, and there are only three possible landing places. The land is pierced by numbers of caves—a source of delight to holiday explorers. Perhaps the best of those on the east side is the Hesti Geo at the south end. A boat can enter for a distance of about two hundred feet before the roof lowers, though the channel probably goes through to the west side. By far the finest is a cave with intersecting galleries at the north end, but years may pass before the sea is smooth enough to permit entrance to be made. On the east side are spouting caves or "shooting geos," which may be heard booming according to the direction of the wind. The three near the Ha' act as weather prophets. When the northernmost is sounding it foretells a north-east wind; the midmost foretells a south-east and the southernmost a sou'-wester. The extreme north and south points are on the low ground—the Ness, by the Freyers, and the South Ness or "the Lady's Ness."

Nearly as far north as the Ness is the Strem Ness, where a furious tide-race or strem runs. The view from each is unique, and alone worth travelling a hundred miles to see. The view of the Noup from the South Ness resembles that of the famous South Stack near Holyhead, but is finer, while that from the Strem Ness is even more beautiful, with the mountain range of Foula spread out behind the lovely bay, and the great stacks of the Freyers to the north. When there is a sea running, as there generally is in these wild parts, the chasm between Strem Ness and Muntaavie Stack is particularly grand. The view from the Freyers is of the great stacks themselves. A low vault runs through the Brough, on which are the remains of a Pictish brough, but the glory of the three is the Gaada Stack (*gaad* = a hole). This looks finest from the sea where its two great arches between its three pillars rise straight out of the water like a titanic castle. This is perhaps the grandest stack on the British coast.

There are a number of lochs on the lower ground, ths largest, the Mill Loch, being about one sixth of a mile in length. As its name implies, this was the source of power for turning one of the three horizontal watermills in which the corn used to be ground. So active was this particular mill that its use was restricted to two hours grinding per croft at a time, and even then it frequently ran dry. Masses of yellow irises grow along the principal burn. A few trout were recently introduced and are rapidly increasing in spite of the attentions of the kittiwakes, who cluster on the bridge and pounce upon the fish as they pass.

The highest point on the low ground is Kruger, 200 feet above sea level, where Pictish remains have been found, and there is a grave not yet excavated.

In the middle of the isle are grouped the high hills. Hamnafjeld in the centre rises 1,126 feet, with a steep face, from the back of Ham and the Mill Loch. It is a mountain of mystery, for, somewhere near the top, is the famous Lum o' Ljorafjeld mentioned by Sir Walter Scott in *The Pirate*. The exact position of this uncanny feature has been lost, probably intentionally, but it is too well authenticated not to exist, although we may not credit all the tales about it. The lum, or chimney, is a hole in the ground going down to an enormous depth. It was supposed to be bottomless, and was inhabited by the trolls or trows inimical to mankind, and from its depths ascended mephitic vapours. The islanders believed that it was a fatal place for strangers, although after three weeks one would become more or less immune. Indeed it was considered rash for any visitor to go up into the hills at all until after some weeks. It is recorded that two men of the island went with a dog to gather sheep on the hills when two sheep and the dog disappeared down the lum, and their bodies were afterwards found in a sea cave at the entrance to Ham Little. It is continually recorded in literature. We are told that "a

Dutch shipmaster visited the spot and let a barrel of lines down the lum, some say two barrels, which is very wonderful considering that a barrel of lines is reckoned to be several, some say nine, miles of length," and yet he could not reach the bottom. (*Old Lore Miscellany of Orkney and Shetland, Pightland Firth and Caithness Saga Book of the Viking Club*). At a later date we are told that the laird himself (presumably one of the Scotts) went to the place and let dawn twelve bolts of line with a weight on the end and yet did not reach the bottom; so he decided that it was too dangerous and had the opening covered in with flagstones.

The weirdest story is that of three strangers who visited the isle and were determined to see the lum, and who, in spite of the warnings of the islanders, went straightway up to the hills. They lifted the flag from the mouth, and one of them fell dead upon the spot; the other two fled precipitately down the hill with the trows after them, and one of them died on the east side of the Mill Loch and was buried where he fell, and the site of his grave is still pointed out; and the third managed to reach the Ha', where they were lodging, but was raving mad. He jumped into his boat, put to sea, and was never heard of more. Although some people refuse to believe in the lum there can be little doubt of its existence. Such potholes are very common, especially in limestone districts—though Foula is old red sandstone. Moreover the name Ljorafjeld means "chimney-mountain," of which fact the islanders seem unaware, and the name is older than these legends. It seems certain that some such pothole gave the name to the hill. There is nothing incredible in the story of the sheep and the dog; Gaping Gill Hole in Yorkshire comes out at Ingleborough Cave, a distance greater than this would be.

In his *Art Rambles in Shetland* John T. Reid states that he visited the lum and removed the flag which covered it. He was a plain matter-of-fact man with no superstitions, and he jokes about the fact that he had a bad passage home as a punishment. The tale is obviously bona fide. The secret unfortunately is lost, but it should be rediscovered. The information one can gather is not very clear. It is generally said that it was on the Moor of Ljorafjeld, and considering the significance of the name one may assume that local tradition is correct. But what is the exact location of the Moor of Ljorafjeld it is difficult to discover. It lies south of the summit of Hamnafjeld and the descriptions seem to point to the hollow ground in a south-westerly direction to the east of Tounafjeld. The following direction was given to me by an islander: "Follow the ridge from the dyke and posts towards the southern cairn, a little more than half-way, where there is a flat place with moss rather than stones." There is another piece of evidence. About a hundred yards west of the cairn at the top, over in a straight line to the Smallie are the remains of a little house which a boy built, perhaps in order to watch the sheep and kye lest they fall over the steep face of the hill, as I have seen a cow do, or perhaps as a refuge from his father, who is said to have treated him unkindly. The house is said to have been built on the very top of the lum. On the whole the older generation of islanders are averse to discussing the position of the lum.

On the west side of the island at the head of the valley of the Daal is a most wonderful feature which few tourists have seen. This is the Sneck of the Smallie, a great cleft in the ground going down 219 feet and 8 or 10 feet in width, with absolutely vertical sides as though built of masonry. It is both beautiful and awe-inspiring, and one of the finest things of its kind in the British Isles. It is in two stages, and the lower is reached through a hole under a large boulder which is jammed in the cleft. The climb down is not exactly difficult but it is dangerous on account of rocks falling from above and still more from the uncertain nature of the foot hold. A few skeletons of sheep and birds strewn on the bottom are unpleasantly suggestive.

Another magnificent sight is the Kittiwakes' Ha', a natural arch forming a lofty hall into which a boat with a forty-foot mast can be taken and still show the vaulted roof soaring nearly another 100 feet above, although when John Manson, our best cragsman, was young a man could not stand upright in the opening—so rapid is the destruction wrought by the waves. This arch is the headland of Easter Hoevdi, some 275 feet high, and behind is the most beautiful, though not the highest, range of cliffs in the island, with an 800-foot drop, sheer, and in some places actually over hanging.

Under the top of Soberlie in the face of the cliff is the so-called Carbuncle. Rays of bright light can be seen radiating at night from the dark face of the rock. The cause is not known.

For its size, therefore, Foula has its full share of nature's wonders. The finest cliffs in Britain, probably the finest rock-cleft, and perhaps the finest stack, is a considerable share for one small island.

Not least among the attractions of Foula is the charm of its inhabitants. The writer has travelled over a million miles in some thirty different countries, and except in the less frequented parts of Norway has never met a community to compare with it for courtesy, intelligence, genuine kindness and honesty. Doubtless there are black sheep even in Foula, but the place where none are to be found has yet to be discovered.

The population, which was 240 at the beginning of this century, is now only about half that number. The people live by crofting, fishing and knitting, but now that the trawlers have spoilt the fishing by destroying the spawning beds, and the introduction of machine spinning and knitting has reduced the demand for hand-made shawls and hosiery, the island is much less prosperous than it once was, since the lack of a safe harbour and the general inaccessibility of the place make it almost impossible to dispose of farm produce. But this very inaccessibility has produced a remarkably intelligent and skilful race of people, for where there are no specialised tradesmen it naturally follows that each man must be able to build his own house and his own boat, and make his own furniture, clothes and boots. If he desires anything from a frying pan to a fiddle he sets to work to make one for himself. But in addition to being able to turn a hand to anything many islanders excel in their own particular line. For example one is famous as a seaman, another as a mason; this man is the best boat-builder, and that the best smith; some are musical, with fine voices and a remarkably accurate sense of pitch; while it goes without saying that the younger men are interested in machinery. They are exceptionally clever in repairing articles which the townsman would throw away, and when we smashed a cherished 'cello we sent it to a Foula man who repaired it perfectly although he had never seen such an instrument before.

A naive tribute to the honesty of the folk may be seen in the following anecdote. One of our islanders, who happens to be an expert on birds, is fond of accompanying visitors to the hills. Two men came to see the island, and "Tammie" took them along the banks to Hodden Geo. They climbed down the cliffs to see the birds' nests. One of them had a pair of ivory opera or field glasses and, after starting his descent, he put the glasses in his pocket and threw the case up over the banks as he thought it would encumber him. Later on, when they came to North Veedale he remembered the case, and Tammie, who had noticed where it had fallen offered to go back for it. The gentleman replied that the case was worn out and of no value, but Tammie decided to go back and, on picking it up, noticed that something rattled inside the case. He mentioned this when he returned it to its owner, who on opening it found that it contained his purse. "I should have been a poor man today if I had lost that!" he exclaimed. It was full of gold, as he kept his silver in his pocket. He took out a sovereign and offered it to the finder, but, as Tammie remarked, "I told him that what I had done was of no consequence as someone would certainly have found the purse before long and returned him his gold."

Kindliness and courtesy are very much in evidence. The

same man, after spending hours in carrying up our three months' supply of luggage and provisions, for which service he stoutly refused payment, remarked, "Naebody minds carrying till (towards) a house: it's carrying awa' that's bad." Perhaps the prettiest compliment we ever received was from a woman who said, "When the birds go south and you go south it is as though all the clocks had run down."

One of the most perfect gentlemen it has been the writer's lot to meet was not one of the old British aristocracy, although they are very hard to beat, but the skipper of the Foula mail-boat, who died in 1913. He was a man of eighty-four, a superb seaman still handling with splendid skill the open sailing boat, only some twenty-five feet over all, that carried the mails through twenty miles of the stormiest seas in the northern hemisphere. He was a man of strong personality, to whom others instinctively looked for leadership, and he took his responsi-bilities very seriously. He never allowed the chance of making a passage to slip by, and many a morning before the first streak of dawn, he would send his crew wading up the burn in their sea-boots, feeling for stones to serve as ballast for the little vessel. He suffered from a disease which kept him in constant pain, yet he was never anything but cheerful.

Magnus Manson was a small man with a noble head and a singularly beautiful face through which his fine character shone. His dark locks curled about his neck, and his clear eyes wore the expression of a mariner whose gaze was habitually fixed upon the far horizon. His manners were absolutely natural, as he had never been anywhere to learn them, but to see him take off his hat to greet a lady, or hand her into a boat, was a lesson in perfect deportment from which any young aristocrat might profit. He was a deacon at the little chapel and a spiritual inspiration to the whole isle. The language of his theology may have been old-fashioned and narrow but his heart was broader than his theology. Like Enoch, he was a man who walked with God, and when, as occasionally happened, the minister asked him to lead the congregation in prayer, it was a revelation. A grand old man if ever there was one!

Even although a motor has now been fitted to the mail boat, housekeeping is apt to be an anxious business, and it was still more so when the boat was dependent upon a dipping-lug sail and six pairs of oars. One Sunday morning when the mail-boat had been detained on the Mainland by bad weather for many weeks, two children called at Magnus' house. They came from opposite ends of the isle but both had the same tale to tell—there was no flour or meal in the house. As skipper, Magnus was in rather a better position than some of the others and could bring in his supplies in larger quantities. With characteristic island generosity, Mrs Manson went to her meal bag but found only a handful remaining. She parted the meal between the two children, and just as they were leaving she looked up and saw the little mail-boat returning. His nephew, Thomas Isbister, followed Magnus as deacon of the Church, and eventually became catechist, and was, like his uncle, universally beloved. "A good lad, Thomas," was the comment of an old woman, and perhaps this simple phrase sums up his character as well as any. Of medium height and wiry build; always smiling, kindly and thoughtful; trustworthy and generous; broad minded and of considerably wider reading than his fellows, he was one to whom all in difficulties of mind, body or estate instinctively turned for help and advice. For in addition to his faithful service of the Church, and his deep sense of spiritual realities, he possessed the versatility of the Shetlander in an unusual degree. A competent seaman, mason, and smith as well as a crofter, he was clever both with hand and head. Many a time he has helped me to mend something that I could not manage myself. But it was his spiritual influence which was most deeply felt, and this is what no mere words can convey, for he was "far ben."

No one has ever visited Foula who has not been entranced,

and such a visit is a liberal education in itself, geographically, historically, aesthetically and, last but not least, socially. A visit to Foula is a strong medicine, if not a cure, for that parochialism both in time and space that is the curse of the dwellers in our great modern cities, who but dimly realize that there is any epoch other than this somewhat shallow-brained one in which we live, or any place beyond the shriek of their trams, trolleys, and motor cars, or the cosmopolitan monotony of their banal hotels and sleek conventional suburbs.

# 2
## ULTIMA THULE

"The World's End"—the very name has a romantic sound! The claim of Foula or Fughley to be the Ultima Thule of the ancient world has been questioned. Nothing can be proved, but on the principle of elimination we venture to maintain that it is the only place that can make the claim. Let us marshal such evidence as we have found.

The island has been known by a number of different names. It is marked as "Thule" in maps of the sixteenth century. A Venetian map of 1339 marks an island *Tile* just beyond the north-west corner of Scotland. *Uttrie* is a name commonly found on old maps of the sixteenth and seventeenth centuries. *Fughloe*, *Fugloe*, and *Fughley* are found on many old maps, and the modernized form is "Foula." It is suggested that *Thule* is from *telos* meaning "an end." Vergil in the *Georgics* speaks of "Ultima Thule"—*Tibi serviat Ultima Thule*, is one of his compliments to Augustus—"To whom the World's End is subject." Tacitus also uses the phrase. *Uttrie* presumably means "outer" or "uttermost," or "outer" or "uttermost isle." In Icelandic or old Norsk *ut* is "out," and *uttrie* is "outer." *Ut*, *utter*, is the Anglo-Saxon form. In Icelandic *ey* is "island." *Uttrie* may therefore be either *utri* or *utri-ey*, meaning outer or uttermost island, and much the same as

"Thule"; in short a simple translation of the older word, or even of *ultima*.

As for the form *Fughley* or *Fugloe*—*oe* is the Danish and modern form of the Norsk and Icelandic *ey* (cf. Faroe). The local pronunciation is Fughley and not the modernized Foula. *Fouley* is often found in old maps. *Fugl* is the old Norsk for "bird"— English *fowl*. The Shetland pronunciation of fowl, which is still the ordinary word for bird, is as the English "fool." It is not impossible that the change of "th" to "f" was merely substituting a word that would be better understood, just as we find "land" as an Anglo-Saxon corruption substituted for the Keltic *llan*, e.g. "Pencaitland" for *Penkaetllan*. *Utri Fugley* would then mean "Ultima Thule." Or again the "f" may represent the Norseman's attempt to pronounce the difficult "th," just as "d" is substituted for this sound in Shetlandic dialect.

It is doubtful whether the name ever had a strictly geographical interpretation, for the end of the world tended to shift as knowledge widened. Iceland was called Thule in the Middle Ages. The earliest use of the name that the writer can find is that of Pytheas, the astronomer, geographer, and explorer, who is said to have set out from Marseilles about 320 BC. Unfortunately his works are lost, and Strabo, our chief informant, seems to have had a childish professional grudge against him. It is all very obscure, but apparently he went first to South Britain and then, following the usual method of the ancient mariner, who did not set out on a voyage out of sight of land, coasted along through the Skager Rack to the Baltic and afterwards up the west coast of Norway to the land of the midnight sun and was shown the legendary place "where the sun goes to bed." At some time he went along the British coast, but whether he actually went to Thule himself or only heard of it is not clear.

Before discussing the difficult problem of Pytheas it is better to begin with the simpler one of Agricola. An important point that has been overlooked is that in Tacitus' day the texts of Pytheas were complete, so that Agricola was not dependent upon the biased account of Strabo but could form his own judgment on the actual spot. If he said he saw Thule, he had good reason for doing so. That Virgil hails Augustus as including Thule in his rule does not count for much; but, so far as it is not mere rhetoric, it implies that Thule was somewhere whither the Roman arms had gone. In Chapter 10 of the *Agricola* Tacitus says:

> Hanc oram novissimi maris tunc primum Romana classis circumvecta insulam esse Britanniam adfirmavit, acsimul incognitas ad id tempus insulas, quas Orcades vocant, invenit domuitque. Dispecta est et Thule, quam hactenus jussumet hiems appetebat. Sed mare pigrum et grave remigantibus, ne ventis quidem perinde attoli, credo quod rariores terrae montesque, causa ac materia tempestatum, et profunda moles continui maris tardius impellitur Naturam Oceani atque oestus neque quoerere hujus operis est, ac multi rottulere: unum addiderim, nusquam latius dominare mare, multum fluminum huc atque illuc ferre, nec litore tenus adcrescere aut resorberi, sed influere penitus atque ambire, et jugis etiam ac montibus inseri velut in suo.

We may translate the portion of importance thus:

> The Roman fleet, after circumnavigating then for the first time this coast of a newly-found sea, proved that Britain was an island, and at the same time discovered and subdued islands, hitherto unknown, which they call the Orkneys. Thule too was seen, which was as far as it was told them to go, and winter was approaching. But they reported that the sea was sticky and heavy for rowers, and similarly not even raised by the wind . . . I would add but one word—nowhere is the sea more completely the master, it carries many of the

rivers to and fro, nor does it just flow and ebb on the shore but flows right into the land and surrounds it, and is even engrafted into the hills and mountains as though into their very selves.

Thule, then, was seen: he does not say that it was seen from the Orkneys, but, as Shetland is the only land visible from Orkney, when looking northward, one may assume that this was the case. Also Thule is distinguished from the Orkneys; that must be the force of *et*. From Fitty Hill, the highest point of the northern Orkneys, only three things can be seen, and those only in the clearest weather, namely the Fair Isle, Fitful Head, and Fughley, which is both the furthest and much the highest. If he actually made Shetland he could not fail to be struck by Fughley, with its high peaks all alone in the distance—Uttrie, the uttermost isle— and much the most impressive of either the Orkney or Shetland groups. To this day the Shetlanders regard it as the end of all things. If Shetland was Thule, Fughley was Ultima Thule even then.

The thick and heavy seas, and even the enigmatic remark about the winds confirm the story. The tides are some of the worst in the world and rowing is often impossible. The furious currents in the narrow channels between the hills will not be forgotten by anyone who has been carried down them willy-nilly for twenty-five miles, as has happened to the author; and the black oily swirl of the tides that lays the waves is another characteristic feature.

Agricola's Thule then may be considered as settled. Either it was Shetland as a whole, of which Fughley was the furthest and highest point that he saw, or it was Fughley itself.

The Thule of Pytheas is a more difficult problem. The three significant passages that we have been able to discover are three in Strabo and two in Pliny. The first is in Book IV, Chapter 5. 5., and is very indefinite. "Concerning Thule our historical information is still more uncertain on account of its outside position; for Thule of all the countries that are named is set farthest North." Then follows one of Strabo's numerous diatribes against Pytheas. The second is in Book II, Chapter 5.8: "Now Pytheas of Massalia says that the parts about Thule, the most northerly of the British Isles, are the most remote, and that there the circle of the summer tropic is the same as the arctic circle."

Strabo placed the terrestial tropic at 24°. If Pytheas did the same, the complement of this would be 66°. There is a margin of doubt here, as the latitude of Shetland is not quite 61°. But it is most improbable that it is more than a rough estimate, and we know that Pytheas was far out in his reckoning when he made Britain 20,000 stadia in length.

Pliny throws a further ray of light. He has been discussing the region where there is a six months' day and a six months' night, and continues:

> Quod fieri in insula Thule, Pytheas Massiliensis scripsit sex dierum navigatione in Septrionem a Britannia distante; quidam vero et in Mona quae distat a Camuloduno Britanniae oppido circiter ducentis millibus affirmant. [Which Pytheas of Hassilia wrote was the case in the isle of Thule, distant six days' sail north from Britain; but some affirm it is also so in Mona, which is about 200 miles distant from Colchester, a town in Britain.]

Mona presumably means Anglesey, for the Isle of Man is out of the question, but even Anglesey is more than 200 miles from Colchester. For either of these islands six months' day and six months' night is a wild exaggeration. However if they were so described, *a fortiori* could Fughley be. It is possible to read small print all night in summer in Fughley, and the crofts at the north end do not see the sun for six weeks in the winter. To a child of the Mediterranean, the winter in Foula would seem to be all night and the summer all day.

The other passage in Strabo is in Book I, Chapter 4, 2: "Then to the circle that runs through Thule (which Pytheas says is a six days' sail north from Britain, and is near the frozen sea)." Notice he does not say that it is in the frozen sea, and all the discussion upon that is beside the point.

Pliny (IV. 80) says: "A Thule unius diei navigatione mare concretum, a nonnullis Cronium appelatur. ["From Thule the frozen sea is one day's sail. It is by some called Cronium."] However, he is not necessarily quoting Pytheas. This is the only passage that at all contradicts the claims of Fughley. As any such island would not fulfil any of the other conditions even if we could find it, it does not suggest any rival.

Pytheas' Thule, then, was the most northerly of the British Isles. It had very dark winters and very light summers, in which respect it is curiously classed with Mona a long way south. Now, so far no one has raised any objections, and the only serious objection is that it was six days' voyage from Britain. This, the armchair geographers consider insuperable, which surely merely shows their ignorance.

Let us then make for ourselves a picture of the voyage of an ancient explorer, Pytheas or another, in those regions which we have known from our youth up. We will imagine that he has been coasting northward along the harbourless and inhospitable northern coast of Scotland; but Pytheas, or whoever he was, was obviously a rash man. His craft was probably sadly ill-adapted to those seas. We do not picture him in a war trireme or even a keles. It was customary to beach the boat at night, a precaution necessary for an ancient explorer in uncharted seas, and therefore she would not be burdened with a deck. The boat would probably be about the size of a large sixern, such as are still common in these northern waters, although they are fast disappearing. His would, however, be an inferior sea-boat. These old descendents of the Viking days are built for heavy seas and have a very short keel, a very pronounced sheer, with high stem and stern and both stem and stern pointed. They are the best rough-weather boats in the world; and they need to be. We are sorry for Pytheas, but he has to make the best he can of his Mediterranean tub.

He has reached Wick; and as he returned safely home, some local salt must have warned him of the perils, and that there is absolutely no shelter or landing on the iron-bound coast. Pytheas is anxious to start, but a wild north-easter is blowing and he has to wait. Presumably it is summer or the voyage would hardly have been accomplished. The weather-wise at last tell him he may go on; but he must not expect a slant, as they are rare occurrences, and he must look out for changeable weather. He starts at eight next morning with a north-west breeze; and, as he wishes to save his men, he beats north with a short leg and a long leg, but makes poor progress, as he cannot keep his craft close to the wind. He is much annoyed to see a local sixern leave him behind; but he perseveres. However, the slowness of his boat brings him an adventure upon which he had not reckoned. The local boat gets across the Pentland Firth in time; but he is caught by the ten-knot tide, an unprecedented experience. He rows, he sails, he exhausts his vocabulary, for the water certainly is thick and sticky; but all to no purpose, and by three in the afternoon he finds himself some thirty miles East of Duncansby Head with about as much chance of reaching South Ronaldsay as the moon. In his despair, he sacrifices to Poseidon, and a miracle occurs, and his boat begins to move the other way. This tide is not so fast as the other, and his position for the wind is now hopeless; but Pytheas is a lucky man, and by midnight, with the strenuous rowing of his exhausted crew he reaches South Ronaldsay.

Consequently next morning they "sleep in" and no start is made till midday. The explorer is told of the principal burgh of the Orkneys and, without further adventure, he arrives safely at the site of the later Vikings' Kirkwall in the evening. Pytheas manages to do a little business with the natives before retiring to rest and lays in a stock of provisions, as the outer islands are ill-supplied. He has not the least idea of where he is going, as he is not going anywhere in particular and possesses no chart; and the fact of not knowing a solitary word of the language makes a topographical conversation a difficulty. Probably Hermes intervenes, otherwise there will be no story of a six-day voyage. As he does not know what is beyond, he obviously cannot ask for it; and the local bookseller is out of charts. Our armchair gentlemen furnish no suggestions, so we suppose another miracle which enables him to make for the island with the highest ground in the north of the Orkneys, which cannot be seen from where he is.

Be that as it may, he is up betimes on the third day and by the aid of a local pilot makes his way through the excessively sticky water to Westray, where he can look around and see where he wants to go next. It is a glorious day, and in spite of the old inhabitant's contempt for his clumsy craft, and the conversational impasse, they make land at 5 p.m., and are on the top of Fitty Hill by seven, in time to see the magnificent view. But what interests Pytheas are two little spots in the far north-north-east and another more easterly not so far away. These are Fugley, Fitful Head and the Fair Isle. Nothing else can be seen.

Pytheas makes wild gesticulations implying a desire to get there. The pilot shakes his head and explains that it isn't done and adds that he will "nae gang" and that it is "gey unchancy." Pytheas does not understand, but decides to go by himself.

The further spots look the more enticing, and at four in the morning he is already at sea. One of our authorities tells us that everything gets mixed in this part of the world. It certainly gets mixed for Pytheas. In the first place instead of getting lighter it gets darker, the land seems to be swallowed up and the air grows thick so that nothing can be seen. At the same time a wind rises and it is a west-sou'-wester, and that means real business. The wind howls and the sea carries. Pytheas has never seen the sea carry, at least not as it does here. The swell that never dies down rises to the largest waves that he has ever seen in his life. The impenetrable thickness of the fog terrifies him. Mercifully the mast carries away at the first onset and so the story of Pytheas is able to continue. Then through hour after hour of black fear they bale the boat and do their best to keep her head-on to the sea.

They see nothing but a petrel, but are carried away past the Fair Isle. The meteorological station is not yet built, or he might know as he passes the north station that not a single calm day has been recorded in seven years, summer or winter. These are the worst seas in the northern hemisphere, but he does not know; and one recalls proverbs about fools rushing in and others about wind and shorn lambs. He envies his armchair rivals, but being a true seaman he gets a certain satisfaction.

As a matter of fact it is only a summer gale; but Pytheas has never seen anything like it. (The Fughley mail-boat, with a motor, and a far better sea-boat than that of Pytheas was unable to get out of the isle on a single day for eight successive weeks a few winters ago, in spite of all the local lore and consummate skill in handling a boat). The Sumburgh fog-tables are still two thousand years ahead; but they would not cheer him, as the records show an average of five hours fog per day in June for three years.

More miracles befriend him, and although he has to spend a night at sea he eventually struggles through the terrible Sumburgh Roost, the stormiest and worst of all the tide ranks, which has the peculiarity of never turning the other way, although it drops from ten to a single knot. At last he arrives at Scalloway where the Jarls later had their capital. Here he is fortunate in finding an interpreter, and is a little surprised to discover that Greek coinage is used in the islands, when such rarities as coins are used at all. The wonderful island with the great high peaks that he had seen as a spot in the distance from Orkney is still far oft, but he has seen it on his way up the west coast, and asks a little more cautiously this time how he can visit it—Uttrie, the Uttermost Isle.

Perhaps they tell him of the eleven-knot rank on the Hoevdi, and the danger of the landing. Certainly no pilot will take him. Perhaps the intrepid mariner makes the venture. Perhaps he is content to spend the sixth day in looking at it and in writing up his log.

If Pytheas on the sixth day actually reached Fughley, he was luckier than the laird's son, who, when his father was taken ill in Shetland, wanted a man to go back into the isle with him. Fughley is regarded with terror. The *Oceanic* was wrecked on the reef at the south-east of the island and its dangerous and only landing place is strewn with lost anchors, and it is surrounded by appalling tide races.

After trying all round the village of Walls among these expert seamen, all of whom refused to go, he at last found a man in an outlying croft who was willing. But when the man went "ben" to tell his womenfolk, the boy heard shrieks and imprecations dissuading him from doing anything so foolhardy and wicked; and the man yielded to the superior force of woman.

We ourselves go every year; and by the aid of a modern steamer, a motor car and a motor boat, it may, when Providence is kind, be done in three days. However we have sometimes waited three weeks to cross, and on one occasion never got across at all.

The only time the writer ever did it in his yacht, a decked fore-and-aft and a better boat than Pytheas is likely to have had, it took six days.

A hearty welcome and six days' entertainment by the laird awaits the armchair geographer who pays a visit in a craft analogous to that of Pytheas, and, unlike Pytheas, he may have a chart and compass and know where he is going. The account of his voyage will be interesting *if he ever arrives!*

## THE ISLE OF FUGHLEY

Who is it loves the sea,
And the salt sea-spray on his face?
Come let him sail with me
And flee from the land for a space.
Let us leave the long stretches of road,
Hemmed in by the hedges and walls,
And turn where the limitless tides have flowed
And the voice of the sea-bird calls.

Let us make for the queen of the deep,
The lonely isle of the north,
Precipitous, towering, and steep,
That over the waste looks forth
Wherever the eye may gaze,
Be it north, south, east or west,
There is naught to behold but the wide sea ways
And the ships on the ocean's breast.

It is there that we live in the seas—
No stretches of country behind,
Not a breath of a land-blown breeze,
Each wind is a sea-blown wind.
Far in the uttermost tide
Agricola saw her stand,
With the clouds on her faint far peaks that hide
Thule the ultimate land.

## 3

# THE IONA OF THE NORTH, AND
# THE VIKING CONQUEST

How early Foula was inhabited, or indeed any of the Orkney and Shetland groups, is very uncertain. Kist graves and pottery, a Pict's house and other fragments of the earliest civilizations of Shetland and Orkney occur in Foula, and there is no reason to suppose, as some have done, that its colonization occurred at a different age from the rest.

The theory that these groups were not inhabited at the time of Agricola's voyage I utterly reject. In the first place Tacitus distinctly states that Agricola "invenit domuitque"; if he subdued or conquered there was somebody to subdue.

I would call attention to an important piece of evidence that has been overlooked, and that is the Arthurian legends, in which King Lot of Orkney plays an important part. It is also significant as implying that the Arthurian and Orkney civilizations are one. Although it would be rash to argue too much from a single character such as King Lot, who might be a later interpolation as Lancelot was, there is no doubt that the Arthurian period was before the Christian era. The Arthurian civilization is what we call, rightly or wrongly, Celtic. We find in Shetland, and still more in Orkney, Celtic stones and also Celtic place-names. In Shetland the latter are all of a religious nature,

which point to religious settlements. One of the few Celtic
stones, of which there is a cast in Lerwick Municipal Chambers,
shows a hippopotamus and a Coptic headdress, clearly
indicating a Christian mission from Egypt. It is uncertain
whether we can go so far as to say that this proves a Celtic
occupation, or only Celtic religious settlements, which may even
have been in the otherwise uninhabited country. But it seems to
me that we are justified in taking Tacitus' statement to prove
inhabitants, whether Pictish (whatever that may be), Celtic or
Teutonic (and on the whole the Arthurian legend suggests that it
was not Teutonic), to whom came Christian missionaries,
possibly Celtic themselves, but very likely Copts who settled
amongst Celts.

The fact that Columba is said to have met in AD 565 a
Scandinavian chief of Orkney at the residence of Bridei, the
Pictish king, may be taken as another isolated scrap of evidence.
It points to a distinction between Pict and Teuton and to an
earlier date for the clash between these two than is generally
supposed. The name Pentland Firth signifies Pictland Firth, and
if Picts existed anywhere they existed round the Pictland Firth
(called Pightland Firth as late as 1701). Whether Picts and Celts
are the same is too thorny a problem to be considered here.
What, however, clearly emerges is a pre-Teutonic occupation
which we may call Pictish or Celtic, followed by a Scandinavian,
and a very early introduction of Christianity, which may even
have been due to St Columba himself.

This brings us to the first historic event after the sighting of
the island by Agricola. There is at Copenhagen, among the
ancient Norwegian documents, a record stating that at a very
early date there was a monastic settlement and collegium in
Foula, and that this island played the part of an Iona in the
Christianising of the north. This is said, somewhat doubtfully I
think, to be confirmed by the name "Freyars," or "Friars" as it
appears on some old maps. The word "freyers," however, is Norse

for "banks," and is therefore a mere coincidence. The local tradition that the ancient school at Northerhouse was connected with a monastery is more likely to be correct.

The remains of this early civilization are slight. There are the remains of a Pictish burial-ground at the north end of the island. An interesting kist grave was discovered about 1922 above Housabrecks Wick but was unfortunately broken up. A Pictish house is said to have been unearthed on Kruger, and there are remains of prehistoric kitchen middens. Whirley Knowe, that is Witches Hillock, until quite recently had the remains of its stone circle. It may have been the place of judgment and execution or perhaps the temple site. Excavation showed quantities of small stones or pebbles stained by black, greasy signs of fire and burnt animal fat, possibly indicating that sacrifices took place there.

There are various other stone relics. Holy water stones are Pictish and were used for washing the children, apparently a sort of baptism, and were broken by the Norsemen. There was a Pictish brough on the stack of that name at the North end, but within living memory the last of the stones were removed for ballast for the fishing boats. An earthenware vessel of an early type was found in the peat, and also an elaborately carved wooden staff which crumbled at a touch.

The custom of the Celtic Church was to plant their monasteries and missions on remote islands, such as Iona, Lindisfarne, the Farne islands, and Skellig Michael—and Foula is just the kind of position they would have chosen. Whether this was a Celtic mission, perhaps of the time of St Ninian, 320, or possibly of St Columba in the sixth century, or again what we might term a Coptic–Celtic mission from Africa, probably will never be known. It is interesting to think of this little island, the end of the world, playing so important a part in the spread of Christianity. The Norsemen extinguished Christianity when they conquered the island and set up the religion of Odin, and

Christianity was not again introduced until the time of St Olaf. It seems most likely that it was during the earlier period that Foula played the part of an Iona.

The second historic event is the landing of Guttorm, the Viking. The Norse poets relate that Harold Harfagra, chief of Westfold and some small petty Norwegian states which he inherited in 863, hearing of the transcendent beauty of the Princess Gida and believing all that was told to him, sent a noble to make her an offer of marriage. "The name of Harold is not sufficiently renowned," the haughty lady replied. "Never will Gida esteem the noble suitor worthy of her love until he has reduced all Norway under his power." Harold was not disheartened and vowed that he would neither comb nor cut his hair till this was accomplished, and as it was a matter of years his hair grew so long and thick that he was known as Harold Hinn Lufa, "Harold the Hirsute," "Shock-headed Harold." When he had achieved his goal and conquered all Norway, he was staying at Jarl Ragnvald's place in Möre. He took a bath, combed his hair and got Ragnvald to trim it for him. He looked so much the better for his toilet that Ragnvald surnamed him Harfagra—fairheaded—by which name he was afterwards known.

Before the end of the century Harold was king of the whole country and proceeded to establish a kind of feudalism, proclaiming that the udal lands belonged to the crown and that those who wished to remain in possession of their estates must pay a tax. As a result, those chiefs who valued their independence and sovereignty became sea rovers and made new homes for themselves in Iceland, the Faroes, Shetland, Orkney and elsewhere. It was probably at this period that the island of Foula was conquered. The Viking Guttorm or Guttern, in true Scandinavian fashion, was fleeing from the vengeance of blood and decided to make his home in this inaccessible natural fortress. He landed at the south end and overcame the Pictish inhabitants, but, according to local tradition, had a difficulty in making his way northward on account of the small trees and brushwood that then covered the island, and which afforded ambuscade for his foes (as in the memorable case of Sphakteria). He made his way after setting fire to it and burning it down.

It has been usual to discountenance the story of the trees in Foula although large roots are often found in the peat. We have planted thousands since 1899 in sheltered spots, but only a few remain and they have never attained any size, though they might do so if planted over a large area. But we must remember that, although Iceland is at present unwooded, we are told that Ingolf, who settled there about AD 880, found a country so thickly covered with forests of birch trees that he could only proceed by cutting his way before him. I may mention that when I was in Iceland I was told that I should ride through a wood, and after some hours I enquired when we were coming to it. "We passed through it some time ago," was the reply. "I forgot to call your attention to it." It consisted of dwarf trees some twenty inches in height. I have however seen in Iceland a wood of small trees some five or six feet high, but even these could only be regarded as scrub. The trees of Iceland and Shetland were probably destroyed for fuel long since, but that trees can grow in these countries is proved by those artificially planted at Akureyro in the former country and Tresta in the latter, and the tradition of the Foula trees is probably correct.

The grim horror of those early days looms through misty legends; and it is told how the Picts knew of a method of making the heather mead, a wine or spirit obtained from the heather roots (not the heather-berry wine still made). Only one old man and his sons held the cherished secret, and according to some traditions he was a priest, and therefore an early forerunner of the monks of Chartreuse. The victorious Norsemen, after slaughtering most of the inhabitants, tried to induce the old priest to divulge the secret by promising him and his sons life and freedom. The old man, fearing that his sons would be tempted to yield through love of life, replied that he himself was willing to disclose the mystery but that he feared the vengeance of his sons, and requested that they should first be killed. Guttorm slew the youths while the father turned away his head. He then laughed in their faces and taunted the hated conquerors with their impotence to discover the secret which now he alone knew. Naturally the victors slew him also and thus the recipe for the heather mead was lost for ever. The same tradition is found in several parts of Scotland, and it is possible that some such incident may have occurred more than once.

Guttorm made his abode at the south end of the island and the place was called after him, Guttrun or Guttern and has been continuously inhabited until 1913, when it was occupied by David Henry, who was almost certainly a lineal descendant of Guttorm. The island became a miniature kingdom under Guttorm and his successors. He was presumably Folkis Kongr, or Folk King, and also Godi or High Priest and Judge. The tenure of the island is Udal, or Odal, and is held not of the king or the State or of any man, but of God and the Sun. This raises a number of interesting questions regarding land tenure and Scandinavian society, which will be discussed in a subsequent chapter.

One other legend survives from these dim times. It is said that there were once three brethren who lived in Foula in the remote prehistoric past and that they quarrelled and killed each other just below the top of the Sneug and were buried where they fell. Tradition marks the spot, and when Sands, the archæologist, was in the island he excavated at the place indicated. Here he found obvious traces of burial having taken place, but no actual remains. The Oxna Gate, where the Sneug and the Kame join, was said to have been made by the oxen of a man who lived on Kruger in prehistoric times, or, as an islander phrased it, "about the time that Noah was getting to be an old man." The kye, which were kept on Kruger, were driven to

Wester Hoevdi by way of Oxna Gate.

The Norse of Foula was famous for its purity, and sons of the Scottish kings were sent to learn the language from the successors of Guttorm. The little ruined homestead of Northerhouse marks the school, and perhaps the abode, of royalty. There is an interesting confirmation of this fact. Andrew Manson, great-uncle of Thomas Isbister, the late catechist, was in the navy and at the siege of Gibraltar. There he found an old history of Shetland, or, according to another account, found it in the ship's library, wherein he read of the sons of the Scots' king going to Foula. He felt somewhat sceptical and noted that a well at Northerhouse was mentioned and the distance and direction from the house given. On his return home he carefully measured the distance, and on digging found a finely-built well on the very croft that members of his family had occupied for generations. His great-grandfather, who lived in Northerhouse, was a wealthy man for those days, possibly in consequence of the entertainment of royalty. He had several daughters and when he died he left each of them a mare and foal and fifteen yowes (ewes) with their lambs. This legacy of yowes and lambs was called "Lambo-tiende." It is said that "the daughters used to ride away on horseback to take home the peats and they span with the old distaff while sitting upon their horses."

This croft lies close to the kirkyard, and a weird tale is told in this connection. Like all the stories in this collection it was taken down verbatim from an islander and will be given with as little alteration as possible, although no attempt is made to reproduce the Shetland dialect. In the old days mould (earth) taken from a newly-made grave was said to cure all sorts of ills; for example it is good for the toothache. The folk of Northerhouse, which was a kind of a monastery then, had the privilege of distributing the mould. Somebody had taken some mould from a grave and, having used it, he returned it as was the custom to the man in Northerhouse. It was a wild night so instead of taking it back to the kirkyard the guid man just laid it on the wall-head above the door. Later on a most uncanny knocking came at the door, and the guid man's daughter rose to answer it. But her father sharply bade her sit still where she was. He put on his clothes and went forth. In about fifteen minutes he returned all wet and with a queer kind of look on his face. The girl asked him where he had been. He replied: "To the kirk—it was yon man come for his mould."

Norse continued to be spoken in the island until comparatively recently. Old David Henry in Guttrun, mentioned above, knew over a thousand words which were taken down by Dr Jakobsen, the philologist, on his visit to the island. David's father could speak the language fluently, and it is interesting to notice that it is the classical Norse, practically unchanged. William Henry, David's great-uncle, who also lived in one of the Guttrun houses, recited to Mr George Low (*Tour of the Shetlands*), thirty-five stanzas of a Norse ballad, describing the lives of the earl of Orkney and the daughter of the king of Norway. Mr Low did not know Norse and apparently took it down phonetically. It has since been restored by Norse scholars into modern Danish and Icelandic. I give two translations, together with Dr Hibbert's comments from his *Description of the Shetland Islands*, p. 258.

## THE FOULA BALLAD

Not longer ago than seventy years [says Hibbert], a number of popular historic ballads existed in Shetland, the last person who could recite them being William Henry, a farmer of Guttorm, in the island of Foula, who was visited in the year 1774 by Mr Low. "I do not remember," says this tourist, in a letter to Mr George Paton of Edinburgh, preserved in the Advocates' Library, "if I left you a copy of a Norse ballad. I wish you would try if Dr Percy could make anything of it. If you have no copy, I shall send an exact one, though I cannot depend on the orthography, as I wrote it from an honest countryman's mouth, who could neither read nor write, but had the most retentive memory I ever heard of. [True of Foula people today—IBSH.] He, I am afraid, is by this time dead, as he was then old and much decayed; but when I saw him, he was so much pleased with my curiosity—and now and then a dram of gin—that he repeated and sang the whole day." Some kinds of poetry, as the historical ballads and romances, which William Henry could recite, were, as he stated, never sung but on a winter's evening at the fireside. The subject of one of them, as explained by this aged and last minstrel of Hjaltland was "The strife of the earl of Orkney on account of his marriage with the king of Norway's daughter."

Hildina, the daughter of the king of Norway, was beloved by Hiluge, a courtier, whose pretensions to her hand, though supported by the approval of the crown, she discouraged. While this sovereign, accompanied by his favourite, was engaged in a distant war with some northern potentate, one of the earls of Orkney, in his rambles on the coast of Norway, met with the fair princess and became enamoured of her charms. Nor did his accomplishments obtain for him less favour in the lady's eyes, as she eventually gave her hand to this new lover, and fled with him to the shores of Orkney, in order to avoid the wrath of her sire.

When the king, on returning from the wars, had learned what had happened, the daring presumption of the earl in obtaining an unsanctioned alliance with the crown exasperated him to the greatest degree; while Hiluge felt no less wounded under the poignancy of slighted love. Both were impatient to gratify their revengeful feelings, and for this purpose, set sail with a strong force and landed at Orkney. By the persuasion of Hildina, the earl met her father unarmed and, throwing himself upon his mercy, eloquently besought from him a reconcilement to the nuptials. The monarch's affection for his daughter, which nothing could wholly subdue, made him relent; but no sooner had his son-in-law left him to communicate the joyful result of the conference to his spouse, than the courtier, by resorting to all the artful means he could devise by reminding the king of the affront committed against the royal dignity, succeeded in inducing him to recall his promise of forgiveness. Nothing, then, could prevent the dispute from being decided by the sword alone. Hiluge and the earl met arm to arm; their combat was desperate, but the contest proved fatal to Orkney's chief, who was cleft to the earth by his fierce and over whelming adversary. The victor cut off the head of the unfortunate bridegroom, and, bearing away this dreadful signal of his triumph, threw it, bedewed with blood, at Hildina's feet, accompanying the brutal act with the most sarcastic reproaches. The lady, after recovering from the horror with which she was struck at the sight, felt her injured pride return, and told the destroyer that great as was her affliction for the loss of her husband, the feeling was subordinate to the impatience that she felt under the cruel insult with which her feelings had been mocked.

Hildina, being compelled to return with her royal father to Norway, was again sought for in marriage by Hiluge, the renewed suit being importunately seconded by the king. The lady thus beset, gave a reluctant consent, requesting as the slightest of acknowledgments for her concession, that she might be allowed to fill the goblets with wine at her wedding dinner. The marriage was solemnized, the banquet prepared, and Hildina, after having secretly drugged the wine that was to be used, poured it into the cups and presented it to her guests; its narcotic qualities soon threw the company into a deep slumber and the lady then began to execute the work of deadly vengeance she had meditated. She first ordered her sleeping father to be conveyed out of the house to a place of safety, and, seizing a lighted brand, set the mansion in flames and invested it with her dependents to prevent escape. Hiluge, roused by the blaze, saw the treachery and piteously cried out for mercy. Hildina heard with horrid delight his supplication and, bitterly returning the taunts he had used while throwing her husband's head at her feet, left the wretched courtier to perish in the flames.

The following is the paraphrase given by Joseph Anderson (*Orkneyinga Saga*, 1873, introduction p. 114). It is interesting to notice the difference between this simple rendering and the appallingly stilted performance above.

> A young nobleman at the court of Norway made love to the king's daughter, Hildina, and was rejected by her, though her father supported his pretensions to her hand. When the king and Hiluge were away at the wars, an earl of Orkney came to Norway and found such favour with Hildina that she consented to fly with him to the Orkneys. When the king and Hiluge returned and discovered what had happened in their absence, they set sail, with a great host, in pursuit of the fugitives. Hildina persuaded the earl to go unarmed to meet her father and ask for his pardon and peace. The king was pleased to forgive him and to grant his consent to their union. But now Hiluge, by artfully working on the king's mind, stirs up his latent wrath against the earl, and induces him to revoke his consent. The result is that he decides that Hiluge and the earl shall meet in single combat, and fight it out to the death of one or other. Hiluge was victorious and, not content with the death of his enemy, he cut off his head and cast it into Hildina's lap with taunting words. Hildina answered his taunts boldly and conceived a bloody revenge. But she must now follow him to Norway, where he renewed his courtship. E'er long she seemed to relent and gave him her promise, but besought her father to grant her this boon—that she herself should fill out the first wine-cup at the bridal. Her request was granted, the guests came, the feast was set, and Hildina filled up the wine cups for them. The wine was drugged and

they were all cast into a deep sleep from which nothing could awake them. Hildina now caused her father to be carried forth and set fire to the house. Hiluge, awaking in the midst of the burning, cried out for mercy. Hildina replied that she would give him the same mercy as he had given to her earl, and left him to perish in the flames.

The same old man who recited "The Foula Ballad" also knew a song about the queen of Foula.

In his *Antiquities of Shetland*, Gilbert Goudie says that in 1770 Mr Low noted and has preserved the Lord's prayer in the Norn of the islands as remembered in Foula. An old man, Walter Isbister in Breckins, recited this and also the twenty-third Psalm to me in 1921.

The only building likely to date back to Norse times is the south-west corner of the Hametoun dyke, and even this, except for the foundation has probably been rebuilt. Norse tradition may be seen in the watermills, where the wheel is turned horizontally by the flow of the stream. The kollies (Norse *kola*, a lamp) although they resemble the Scots cruises, are Norse in form, having a deeper and smaller bowl, and a proportionately larger lip. The upper bowl was filled with home-made fish oil in which lay a piece of twisted rag to form a wick. They were in common use at the beginning of this century. The bysmar is an old Norse form of weighing instrument. It is shaped like a pestle with a hook on the smaller end. On the pestle are notches to show the point at which the fulcrum must be placed to give the various weights. There are several in the island but only one in constant use.

The Foula Reel is an ancient Scandinavian dance and the tune, like "The Fields of Foula" and a few others, is also Scandinavian. Words were fitted to it later by Miss Chalmers of Lerwick, called "The Shaalds of Foula." The dance was discovered by an English princess and introduced into London ballrooms at the beginning of the nineteenth century under the name of "The Swedish Dance." If the princess had only known she could have found the same dance within her own dominions.

The Henries of Guttrun were called the White Henries to distinguish them from the Black Henries, who were incomers. David himself was an interesting character. It was he who made, with no better equipment than a penknife and a resting-chair, the beautiful model of a Shetland sixern in the City Museum, Edinburgh. I allowed him to sit rent free because he had once lent seventy pounds at interest to a former factor and fish-curer, who failed and involved old David in the ruin. He also had a small sum of a pound or so stolen from his kist and used constantly to bemoan the fact to me. It was before the days of the old age pension and. like many others, David was extremely poor. On one occasion when I went to visit him I found him stripped to the waist mending his only shirt with a piece of an old canvas bag. He came out to see my wife, who was with me, struggling into his shirt from which a needle was hanging, and apologised saying that he was "doing a shift"—to hide the fact that he possessed only one shirt. We sent him some shirts later which gave him great joy. Like many of the older islanders he never addressed me in the second person but in the third, as this was felt to be more ceremonious, and would call me his master, asking, for example, "Has my Uaster been at the hills today?" He was extraordinarily active, and, when well over eighty, could run barefoot like a hare. As we have said, he was descended from the original Norse conquerers, and there is a gap of only two, or possibly three generations between the last known Henry descended from Guttorm and the earliest of the present Henries. It is conceivable that their descent from the kings of Foula may account for the possession of so large a sum of money and the prosperity of the family until so recent a date.

James Henry, David's uncle, was a remarkable man. In appearance he was a true Scandinavian, well over six feet, exceptionally handsome, fair-headed, with chiselled features, immensely strong, fierce-tempered, kind-hearted and a lover of justice. He fought in the battle of Trafalgar and at the taking of St Jean D'Acre, and served on the ship which conveyed Napoleon to St Helena. Although he was forty years at the wars he never received a scratch. At St Jean D'Acre the men were landed from the warship by running three abreast across two planks between the ship and the land. The men on either side of James were shot dead, but he was unhurt. On another occasion he was holding in the boat while the men jumped ashore. Shots were flying and men dropped around him like "nories," but no gun was fired in reply till all the men had landed. Then they planted a Union Jack in the sand and fought desperately till they won the day. One day, when left in charge of a boat, he was annoyed by a crowd of menacing natives, but scattered them by firing a big gun single-handed.

His most remarkable feat was the capture, unaided, of an enemy's ship in port. Three men had been left in charge; he killed one on deck and battened the others down below. For this exploit he was rewarded by a capful of sovereigns as prize money. He was remarkably reticent about his experiences and when pressed to recount his adventures would remark—"What good would it do you if I told you?" He inveighed bitterly against Napoleon, whom he regarded as a monster "raised up to scourge the people for their sins." Any injustice infuriated him. He objected to a nation enriching itself by means of war. When, after some victory, he watched waggon after waggon of gold bullion being carted over Westminster Bridge to the House of Commons, he demanded angrily what *they* had done to earn all that money.

When home for a short time after twenty years of service he found that the money due to his dependents had not been paid. A man called Scott in Burrafirth was responsible. James called at Scott's house and when the servant maid came to the door he asked if Mr Scott was in. "Yes," she said. "Then tell him that James Henry from Foula wants to see him." The maid went upstairs and returned with the message that Mr Scott was too ill to see anyone at all that day. James replied, "I'll either see him today or see him in hell," and stalking past her up the stairs he found Scott sitting at a table. Drawing out a large knife he asked if Scott had paid James' father the money that had been sent to him. Scott admitted that he had not. James stepped up to the table and sticking the knife into it said, "Pay me my money or I'll take your life." Scott immediately handed over the money. James did not tell the story himself but it was discovered, many years after by his nephew who, when taking a cow to be sold in Lerwick entered a wayside house to shelter from the rain. There was an old woman, nearly blind, sitting beside the fire, and some resemblance, probably in the voice, caused her to ask if he were a Henry. On hearing that he was, she then asked if he were related to an old man-o'-war's man named James Henry, and proceeded to relate the above story, adding that she was the maid at Mr Scott's house when James called.

On his way to Quebec with the Wolfe expedition James* was sailing in a transport ship which had at some time been a timber vessel. They got into a blow and suffered considerable damage to the spars and rigging. The soldiers on board were told off to assist the crew in repairing the damage when a dispute arose between James Henry, who was the boatswain, and a

---

*It has been pointed out that if James Henry served on the Wolfe expedition of 1759 and also conveyed Napoleon to Saint Helena in 1815 he must have been still serving in the navy when well over seventy. Though this is improbable it is not impossible, as we have had Foula men in the merchant service at that age. James maintained that he was a long way past a hundred years old before he died, but the islanders did not take him seriously. The story was pieced together from several different sources and it is quite likely that in handing down verbal traditions the scene of one or other of the incidents has been confused with some other event. Possibly we may in time discover further clues.

young artillery officer who was in command of the soldiers. According to one story James protested that a halyard that was to be used to hoist a spar was not strong enough. The officer refused to listen to the more experienced old salt, and ordered the spar to be hoisted, with the result that the rope broke and the spar killed a man in its fall. "I told you so!" exclaimed the enraged boatswain and, lifting a hand-pike, he killed the officer with a blow. Whatever the cause, all accounts agree that James lost his temper and felled the officer. He was arrested, but there was some hitch in regard to his punishment, since it involved the question of military as against naval discipline. Meantime he was placed in irons, with two men to guard him, in the f'rard 'tween decks. While the question of procedure was being debated James remarked to his guards that it was a pity that they should be sitting there when he had a bottle of Jamaica rum in his chest if he could get at it. At his suggestion they removed his irons and one of the guards accompanied him to the fo'castle to fetch the spirit. They were so keen on the rum that they were careless enough not only to get drunk but to neglect to replace the prisoner's irons. At this time the ship was sailing up the St Lawrence and James could see the land quite near. As has been mentioned, the vessel was a timber ship and therefore had a timber port in the bow, used for loading the baulks. He slipped out through the port and hung in the chains while he heard men running hither and thither in search of him. When it grew dusk and the land was only some three miles distant, he slipped into the water and swam for the shore. It is said that he had thirty changes of linen which he had to abandon, but he was wearing a belt containing a large sum of money. As he neared the shore he felt his strength giving out so he unbuckled his belt and lightened himself of his load of wealth. He reached the shore, and somehow found a friend who assisted him. In time he became possessed of a schooner and traded up and down the American coast. Eventually he returned to Lerwick, where his wife was living. She was a very beautiful but inconstant woman. On his way to rejoin her after his long absence he saw her coming towards him down the Lerwick street carrying a young baby. Without a word he turned and fled from her, and did not stop till he reached his native isle. Here he took up his abode in the deserted and partially ruined chapel at the foot of Hamnafield. The building had been thatched, and the boys (who will be boys all the world over) used to roll down stones from the steep face of the hill on to his roof for the pleasure of seeing the old man come out and rage at them. He was entirely dependent upon the charity of his neighbours, who themselves had not much to give. He used to meet the boats when they came in from the fishing and they never failed to give him a few fish. There was one old woman who never passed him without saying, "Ah, poor body!" and she asked why he never came to her house. One day, when almost famished, he took her at her word; but when he came to her house he saw her hiding from him. Stung to the quick he went away in tears.

When Laurence Gray, late skipper of the mail-boat, was a little boy, he and his sister were sent to take the old man a kettle of beast, i.e. the first thick milk which a cow gives after calving, and which, when boiled, is considered a great delicacy. The children had to crawl on their hands and knees through the door, which had been barricaded up. "I see him still," said Laurence, reflectively, "as clearly as I see you. It was a poor hole of a house. I remember his lamp; it was just an ink bottle with a piece of rag in it. Well, he was very happy to see us and supped away at the milk. He was not fit to sup it all and put the remainder into some can that he had. Then he gave us back the kettle, saying 'and now, may the Lord bless the boars' [cow's teats]. Then he suddenly added, 'Have you any tedders?' As we did not understand, he repeated the question. He spoke rather indistinctly. I thought he meant tethers. 'Yes,' said I, 'We have four.' He laughed and took our kettle and filled it with tatties. Then I knew he meant 'tatties' and not 'tedders'."

One thing haunted him to his death. During a battle he boarded an enemy's ship and took part in the work of slaying. He pursued one very beautiful youth who fled from him. He said it was the most beautiful face he had ever seen, but he was hasty and angered, and hunted the young man till he climbed up the rigging. James followed him and just as he was going to strike, the youth prayed very earnestly for mercy, but James hardened his heart and never till his dying day forgot the death of the beautiful youth.

In the days before the Protection Acts, when the great skua or bonxie, whose sole breeding place then was in Foula, had become almost extinct, a party of tourists landed on the island to shoot these rare birds. The infuriated James attacked the visitors and there was a battle royal so that the tourists were thankful to escape in safety to their boat. They happened to travel south on the same steamer as old Scott of Melby, then laird of Foula. He listened with interest to their impressions of Shetland. They expressed themselves as delighted with everything they had seen with the exception of the island of Foula, which they described as being inhabited by savages amongst whom it was unsafe for civilized people to land. "Indeed," asked Melby, in some surprise, "what did they do yo you?" The strangers enlarged upon the rough usage that they had received at the hands of the barbarians. "I am grateful to you for telling me," remarked Melby, "I happen to be the laird of Foula, and I shall reward the people handsomely for the treatment they gave you. My only regret is that they did not serve you even worse." Personally, I think James deserved another capful of sovereigns. If this fiery, tender-hearted old Viking had been born a ruler of men, who can say what new saga might have been added to the world's literature.

## THE MONKS OF FUGHLEY

Christ was born i' Bethlam,
    And He was Ane o' Three;
But for the gain of a' His pain
    He hangit on a tree.

The monks sailed frae Egypt,
    And sailed upo' the main,
As month and twa month,
    Till the mune cam roun' again.

Ance our fair Father, Christ
    Sailed o'r Galilee;
And thought He gar'd [made] the waves be still
    He hangit on a tree.

The main mast was siller [silver],
    The tap-mast was gowd [gold];
Three month and four month
    Mune and mune row'd.

Whither did the monks gang?
    What gar'd them flee?
Tae tell the North the tidings
    That He hangit on a tree.

They cam till the warld's end
    Where the black tides drift;
The tap o' the lone isle
    Was far i' the lift.

They cam till the warld's end;
    They ca'ed it Thule,

And louted doun and thanked Him
    Wha hangit on a tree.

A stane kirk they biggit [built]
    Abune [above] the iron strand,
For Christendoun o' Northmen
    Thorough Hjaltland.

In Orkney and Caithness
    And far Suderey,
Frae Thule the North kenned
    Wha hangit on a tree.

The stane kirk has fa'en doun
    Lang years syne [since];
But the geste [exploit] that the monks did
    The years canna tyne [lose].

Still soughs [sighs] the West wind,
    Still moans the sea—
Wha cam tae heal the warld's dool [grief]
    Was hangit on a tree.

## THE HEATHER-MEAD

'Twas far away on a far off day
    That Gudrun sailed the sea:
And he set his course for Thule's Isle,
    Wi' a gudely galaxy.

"Pull hard, pull hard!"—the Viking cried,
    "And cleave the rising faem [foam];
Pull hard, pull hard against the tide,
    Or I wot we'll ne'er see hame."

O white, white was the seething rank [tide-race],
　　And the wet wind hissed and blew;
And white, white were their faces a’
　　Afore they gat her through.

He’s landed on the bonnie isle
　　Wi’ three score men and mair;
And they hae reached the Hametoun dyke,
　　Biggit [built] sae strang and fair.

And syne [afterwards] they cam till Quinister,
　　And mony a carl [countryman] hae slain.
“O wha can mak the heather mead?”
　　But answer gat they nane.

“Gin ye would mak the heather mead
　　Ye’ll get nae answer here;
For ye maun gang [go] to Soberlie,
　　It’s there that ye maun speir [enquire].”

They hae cam through blude till Northerhouse;
　　But deid men canna speak;
And they maun gang till Soberlie
　　To get the thing they seek.

O hard the fecht [fight] at Whirlie Knowe,
　　Breckins and Hamnabrek;
Naught, naught they learned at Mogill
　　And naught at Ljorabeck.

And a’ the nicht they lay them doun
　　In Gravins’ ruined stead,
And a’ the nicht they heard a bairn
　　That grat [wept] his mither dead.

By day death lurked in every tree
    And half his men lay still;
So they set the forest in a lowe [blaze]
    And fought their way uphill.

And never, never, never mair
    Did birk or rowan graw;
And bleak the haugh [flat ground] and bleak the muir
    And bleak the airts [direction of wind] that blaw.

North, North they strade tae Harrier
    And ower Skjordar's hecht;
And they brak the doors o' Mucklegrind
    Jist at the fa' o' necht.

They slew the carline [old woman] in her bed
    And her dochter at the fire;
But they maun gang till Soberlie
    Tae gain their hairts' desire.

Till Soberlie they cam at last;
    "Noo yield ye," Gudrun cried,
"Or we'll pu' the roof about your lugs
    And winna be denied."

"O wha be yon wad scale the wa'
    And thunners at the yett [gate]?
The reek may blaw across the Isle;
    But in ye sall na get."

" 'Tis Gudrun thunners at the yett,
    'Tis I the trees hae brent [burned];
Gin ye na open wide the door
    I trow ye sall be schent [confounded]."

They brocht a log tae burst the bars
    And swung it strang and straight:
For the first strake o' the sturdy aik [oak]
    They had na lang tae wait.

At the neist [next] strake o' the Norroway aik,
    The door began tae strain:
At the third strake o' the michty aik
    The door was burst i' twain.

"Noo yield the secret o' the mead,
    The heather mead tae me,
The secret thou thy lane [alone] dost ken [know],
    And I will set thee free."

"O it's I wad tell the secret fine
    And I that wad be free;
But it's I that fear ma twa braw sons
    And the deith they'd gar me dee.

"O gin ye slay ma twa braw sons
    And each a corse [corpse] is laid;
It's then we'll drink the heather-mead
    And need na be affrayde."

'Tis Gudrun and his seven men,
    His seven henchmen a'
Hae taen the auld [old] Pict's twa braw sons
    And pinned them tae the wa'.

The father through the wind-eye keeked [window peeped]
    And turned awa his heid;
And when he turned again he spak—
    "I wot that they are deid.

" 'Twas nane wha kenned the heather-mead
    But them and me oor lane,
And noo that baith o' them are deid
    I trow ye sall hae nane."

O lude he leuched [laughed] and lude he cried!
    "There's nane wha kens but me;
Ye ne'er sall drink the heather-mead
    Whate'er the deith I dee.

"But wae, wae for ma bonnie sons
    Tae gang afore ma day!
And wae, wae for the auld man
    That he suld see them gae.

"O wae, wae for ma bonnie sons!
    And wha sall tell we're gane,
When the cauld airts blaw and the cauld caavies snaw [snow
    showers]
    Abune the cauld hearth-stane?"

'Twas Gudrun swung his battle-axe
    And swung it high in air,
And syne the secret o' the mead
    Was lost for ever mair.

## 4

# THE END OF THE DANISH DYNASTY

The Norse udallers continued in a direct line from Guttorm, without a break in the family until the beginning of the sixteenth century. Although the island had become Scots, they kept up a connection with Denmark until the last. Latterly, at any rate, they lived for most of the year in Denmark and only came for a season to their island home. One may hazard a guess that their close Danish connection was of a much later date than the original Norse settlement, possibly the result of a Danish marriage when the island was part of the Scandinavian dominions. The homestead of the udallers was at some time changed from Guttrun, for at the close of the sixteenth century the Ha' was certainly at Quinister. The rent was paid in kind— butter, eggs, mutton and stockings. It was customary to delve during the first half of the day and, during the latter half, to sit at the doors, knitting stockings, both men and women, and looking out to sea, watching for the arrival of the Danish boat bringing the udaller.

The last male of the line of Norse udallers died about AD 1580, from an accident on the crags when fowling, a not uncommon cause of death in those days. The Norse line ended in his daughter queen Katherine, known according to the island tradition, as Katherine Killoch or Kinloch, but possibly more correctly Katherine Asmundder. She was an infant when her father died and seems to have been born in 1568, and succeeded to the property on coming of age. It seems to me just possible that we have here the explanation of the two versions of her name and that her guardian's name was Killoch or Kinloch. She was known as the queen of Foula. She resided mainly in Denmark, as her forebears had done, until she was of some age, visiting the island each year. Queen Katherine's visits, however, seem to have grown longer until we find her taking up her abode entirely in the island. At some time she abandoned the old Ha' at Quinister and built for herself a house outside the Hametoun dyke, the site of which has always been known as Katherine's Crue or Kreug Katrine. The mound was excavated by Sands, who found what had undoubtedly been a human habitation. Fragments of pottery, limpet shells, ashes and the bones of birds were unearthed. It lies between the Baxter Chapel and the dyke, and the remains of the enclosure can still be traced. Her story is a romantic one and by far the fullest piece of connected incident of which we have any record until quite recent times. In addition to the local tradition, there is a very full account in Danish literature, the source of which I have not been able to trace. The story was published, but with the names changed, in the *Shetland Times* of 13 January, 1873. On 27 December 1897, a very full account appeared in *The Scotsman*, but how far it is a translation and how far a free rendering one can only guess. It is, however, best to insert it verbatim. As it has been known in the island for some time it is impossible to distinguish the local tradition from it, but the Foula version certainly gives a few important points not contained in this account.

## THE LAST NORSE LANDOWNERS OF FOULA
(Republished by kind permission of *The Scotsman*)

The year 1590 was a most unfortunate one for Shetland. November of the previous year came in accompanied with severe snowstorms, which continued with an occasional interruption till the following June. In eight months 30 severe storms swept across the island. For three months the snow lay several feet on the ground and no outside work of any kind was done till Summermill day (14th April, Old Style). A few weeks of milder weather which then set in enabled the people working at their harvest to cultivate their small farms or tacks and then a succession of storms ensued.

To the surprise and delight of everyone midsummer day dawned calm and beautiful. The sea was smooth, the sky clear, the sun shone brilliantly, the air was vocal with the screams of sea birds and life and bustle suddenly sprang up in every household. Every man who could pull an oar in the whole Shetland group was in active preparation for the first trip of the season to the haaf. The sudden change from a dull despondency observable everywhere to one of joyous animation would have perplexed a stranger unacquainted with the cause. Nowhere would this have been witnessed to greater effect than in Foula, an island on the West coast of Shetland. After a morning of busy excitement among the inhabitants there, every one preparing and everyone ordering, whole families left their home and repaired to the beach as if they were about to leave the island, and there occurred a scene of congratulation on the change of weather and of kissing, each one calling his neighbour "My brother" ("The common appellation to all acquaintances is 'brother.'"—*Low's Tour*, 1774), such as can scarcely be realised at the present day. One or two of the oldest and most experienced men shook their heads, hinted at the change being too sudden and advised the men not to be too venturesome. They were laughed at, told that they themselves were not so cautious 30 years ago and that the sudden change meant utterly exhausted storms.

On one of the boats more than ordinary interest was centred. The skipper was Hakon of Guttorm, an athletic, powerful looking man of 25 years, and the crew consisted of, besides himself, his father, an elder brother, a brother-in-law, an uncle and a cousin. As a rule it was the cool experienced, middle-aged man who was chosen skipper. But Hakon was a precocious youth, had given evidence of superior abilities and for his coolness in danger, his abilities in managing a boat and his success in everything he undertook, he had been chosen skipper of the new boat the crew built and that was his first trip in command. He was the best crags-man, the swiftest runner, the best fencer, best dancer at balls and weddings and was the pride and boast of the island. In addition to these, he was to be married at the close of the season. The people had higher expectations of Hakon's success than of the others, although the hopes of all were high. When all were ready the crews, with a parting cheer, turned their boats with the course off the sun (it is contrary to island custom to turn a boat widdershins) and pulled out to sea.

There was only one little creek in the island that would shelter boats, and as they passed out of it there stood on the furthest rock a young woman, fresh and fair as the morning and before whom the crews rested on their oars for a moment as they bade her good-morning and good-bye. The people reburned home when the boats floated, but the woman stood there immovable and shading her eyes with her hand she watched the boats until they appeared like specks in the distance. She then turned with a sigh and slowly wended her way to her house, which stood on the Southern part of the island and in size and construction still retained traces of ancient habits and customs.

Katherine Asmundder, the young woman mentioned, was the last descendent in a direct line of Guttorm, a Norwegian rover, who, together with his family, settled in Foula towards the close of the tenth century, claimed the island as his own, and since that period the island had remained in the possession of his family. His homestead still bears the name. Katherine's father died from an accident in the crags when fowling when she was an infant, and on coming of age she succeeded him in the property. On the morning we first saw her she was barely twenty-two years, and was the handsomest woman, not only in Foula, but on the west coast of Shetland. Her beauty of face and figure was such that she attracted attention wherever she went, and she was often spoken of in places she had never seen. The descendents of Guttorm, the rover, seemed of two distinct races, one dark and the other fair. Among them were men and women particularly handsome, and others were noted only for their plainness. Katherine was the last of her house and of her race in the direct line, and nature seemed to have lavished on her all the personal attractions of the fair or blonde side of her family. She was tall, slender, and lithe. Her face inclined to the oval, her features were regular. Her eyes were of the deepest blue, and expressive of every emotion. Her yellow hair fell in waving curls over her shoulders. Her voice was low and musical, and her every movement was easy and graceful. She was thoughtful and contemplative, loved to saunter along the cliffs and listen to the song of the sea and the screams of the wild birds, and to form theories of her own as to all she heard and saw. She did not feel her life a lonely one, she had her own duties to perform, all that interested those around her interested her, and if she knew nothing of the gaieties of life she knew nothing of its sorrows. All the songs and sagas of her people she knew by heart, and her gentle manners and winning ways won her the esteem and confidence of all.

The inhabitants of Foula often visited the mainland to sell their produce and purchase what they required, but except when the boats of the mainland were driven to Foula by storms, no one ever thought of visiting it. The islanders, in consequence, lived a very secluded life, lived, and thought, and acted as their fathers had done for centuries, with but little variation or change. It chanced, however, that when Katherine approached womanhood the haaf became the playground of storms which were felt nowhere else, and there was scarcely a week in summer that a boat's crew of young men was not driven to Foula. Every parish and island had its own haaf or fishing ground, and boats from the West Coast haafs and those of Fethaland, Yell, and Unst found their way to Foula, all driven by storms that the Foula people had not felt. Very often the boats had a supernumerary hand on board, the son of the laird of the district to which the boat belonged, and Katherine not only had admirers by the score, but jealousy and feuds sprang up among the visiting crews. She was attentive to the wants of all, but to none of them did she give even a stray thought. Hakon and she had been engaged for some years, and he alone absorbed her whole mind and thought.

The weather on that midsummer day continued fine and beautiful, and the people on shore, whose every glance was towards the sea and sky, congratulated themselves on their changed prospects. Even the children were interested, and danced with delight when they thought of the pleasure they would experience in meeting and welcoming home the crews of the haaf boats. Towards evening an ominous-looking cloud appeared on the horizon, and the sun went down in a dense mass of clouds surrounded by a corona of fiery streaks. The boats were expected with the morning tide, but a little after sunrise a heavy shower of snow fell, and an hour or two afterwards a severe winter storm was raging. The people rushed to the top of Ljorafield, the highest peak in the island, in the hope of seeing the boats in the offing, but, after waiting for hours, not a speck could be seen amid the spindrift and foam to seaward. Foula is surrounded with strong currents, and since the boats did not return in the morning, they could not, had they been near the land, have reached the island till the afternoon, owing to the strong tidal streams, or ranks as they are called, which extend from the island far into the ocean, and in which the waves roll like breakers. To cross such tidal streams except in certain states of the tide and near the shore is extremely dangerous.

As the day wore on the storm increased, and the anxiety of the people became intense. All work was suspended, the hill tops were covered with people—aged men tottering on their staves, women with infants at their breasts, old and young were there, each and all straining their eyes seaward, and mistaking every speck in their strained vision for a returning boat. Evening came, but no tidings, and the storm raged with exceeding fury. Night was spent on the hill tops. The people could not return to their dwellings, but took shelter under rocks and in caves which the winds and waves of untold ages had scooped out. Morning brought no relief, and as it was believed impossible that an open boat could live in such a sea, all hope was at last abandoned. The scene was indeed one of lamentation and mourning. In every house one or more were absent, and in several cases all the grown-up male members of the family had perished. Before leaving they all gathered around old Olav, a kind hearted aged man. Removing his cap, he said in a voice quivering with emotion, "the hand of the Lord is heavy upon us this morning, my bairns," and looking upwards he offered up a prayer such as has never been heard since. It had neither beginning nor end nor middle, was without order or arrangement, was, in fact, simply a cry wrung from the old man's heart and directed to a being whom he believed saw, heard, and could help them. Scarcely had he finished when a boat with her sail torn and partly hanging in shreds, was observed approaching the island. The sight of her was like the sight of one from the dead. There was a rush to the sea shore and her every movement was watched with the keenest interest. The waves were running so high that she was often long hidden from view, and fears were as often entertained that she had foundered; but she was managed with superior skill and breasted the billows with buoyancy of a sea-bird. "It is Hakon," cried a dozen voices at once. "None but he could manage a boat like that in such a storm and sea," and turning to Olav they asked what he thought. "No, boys, no," Olav replied, "it is not Hakon. The boat is a stranger and is taking the rank at the wrong place and at the wrong time. Heaven have mercy on her." Scarcely had the words passed out of the old man's mouth when the boat rose on the crest of a towering billow, the torn sail shook and fluttered for a moment and then disappeared. "She is in the rank and has gone," the old man cried, and a yell of despair which seemed to cleave the air arose from the lookers on. In an hour or less, as time in such cases cannot be measured, the boat, contrary to all hope or experience of the kind, emerged from the rank and slowly made towards the creek. The boat was indeed a stranger from the island of Papa Stour. She had been out the whole of the storm, and after making superhuman exertions to reach her own shores, had that morning as a last resource stood for Foula. On rising on the crest of the wave, as seen from the shore, the hal'ards got foul, the sail would not lower, and in a moment the men were sitting up to their waist [sic] in water. They were stunned by the suddenness of the disaster and were rendered incapable of exertion. The only man who retained his presence of mind was Hind Eunson, the skipper. He bounded out of the stern, cut the hal'ards, drove in the end of the blaand keg with his foot, and before the crew had recovered from their stupor, he had the boat partially emptied. Their condition was indeed pitiable, there was a wild look in their eyes, and their faces wore a mingled expression of exhaustion and terror. Their hands were swollen and skinless, and they themselves were so worn out that, with the exception of the skipper, they had to be helped out of the boat. They had, however, the welcome news to convey that they had seen five boats under the lee of the island, which they doubted not were Foula boats. "Five boats," the people all at once exclaimed, "where is the sixth?" but no answer could be given.

The storm moderated, and the boats arrived at the creek, Hakon's boat was missing, and all that was known of her was that she had left her companion boats on the inner haaf and proceeded to the bank in the hope of finding more fish there. Hakon's crew were given up as lost, and all but Katherine Asmundder believed it. The other boats had returned, she thought, the Papa Stour boat had been at sea during the whole of the storm, and had reached land. Hakon's boat was new, his crew good, he himself was inferior to none, and until news had been received from all the stations on the mainland she would not mourn but hope.

More than thirty years passed; hope had died in the heart of Katherine Asmundder; another generation had arisen, and the remembrance of Hakon and his crew lingered only as a tale, when one April day, a Walls boat delivered a letter to a Foula boat on the Shaalds, addressed to the chief magistrate of the island. The letter was delivered, and the people flocked to the house of the Ranselman to hear it read. Katherine Asmundder (tradition says she could neither read nor write), now only the remains of her former self, went also. The letter which was from Guttorm Plantation, Jamaica, and dated two years before, read as follows:

> SIR,—My father, Hakon Magnusson, was born in Foula, and spent the first twenty-five years of his life in your island; in the prosecution of his calling as a fisherman he was one day overtaken by a storm, was picked up by a passing ship, carried to the West Indies, and he and his crew were sold to the planters on a neighbouring island as slaves.
>
> My grandfather and uncle died a few months after their arrival, and the remaining three men survived them only a few years.

From the first my father was more fortunate than his companions. His master—a humane man—treated him kindly, and in gratitude for an important service, he gave my father his liberty, and a sum of money to enable him to commence business for himself.

He removed to this island, purchased a small property, married, became a successful planter, and died last year on the anniversary of the day he was picked up on your northern seas.

My father never forgot his early home and friends, but as all his efforts to gain intelligence of them had failed, he left instructions with me to try and communicate with them, tell the particulars of his life, and forward through Messrs. Finch & Company, our London correspondents, £300, one third to be given to Katherine Asmundder, the friend of his youth, and the remaining two-thirds to be equally divided among the surviving relatives of his father's family. On hearing from you I shall remit the money, and advise you.

With moistened eye and quivering lip, Katherine listened, and when she heard her name mentioned she sank on the floor, saying, "Amidst all his trials and all his prosperity he thought of me to the last. He has now gone home. I will soon follow and meet him there," and covering her face with her hands, she sobbed like a child. She was shortly afterwards seized with a desire to sell the island and leave it, and in the following November, when on her way to negotiate a sale with the fishcuring owner who had used the island for some years as a fishing station, she was drowned, and as she was the last of her house, and the maxim of government in those days was "he shall take who has the power," the man to whom she was going quietly annexed the island to his property.

(The foregoing is an extract from *The Scotsman*,
27 December 1891)

There are a few errors in the account, which although very
correct in many particulars, show that the writer was not familiar
with the island. Ljorafield is not the highest point, nor does it
command a view of the west. That the islanders did not know of
the boats taking shelter is rather incredible. Even under ordinary
circumstances their knowledge of the least thing on any side is
amazing, and under such conditions, when everyone was on the
*qui vive*, it is out of the question. They probably discovered the
news independently of the Papa boat, though a stranger might
well have surmised that the Papa boat was the informant. The
story differs from the island tradition in many respects. The
following version was written to me by one who left the isle as a
youth and who had not seen *The Scotman*'s account.

> Katrine must have been a very saintly woman. When her
> lover went away that day she watched him from the Head
> of the Baa, well knowing that he would never return, for she
> had heard the Fjulgie song from the song. [The Fjulgie
> resembles the Greek Siren except that it is never seen. The
> song is of surpassing sweetness and foretells the death by
> drowning of the hearer or the hearer's dearest friend.] The
> grief of Katrine does not overwhelm her nor make her
> despondent. On the contrary it shed a kind of halo around
> her and she became so gentle and good that the wild birds
> came to her hand and were not afraid. She became the
> refuge and help of every afflicted and suffering bird and
> animal as well as of the Islesfolk. Hence the name "Kreug
> Katrine." [*Kreug* means shelter, and we used to kreugen
> when sheltering from the magnificent snow showers of
> Foula. She never tried to sell the isle. This is how she was
> drowned.] A French ship anchored off the Hame Banks,

the crew being entertained by Katrine in the manner of the times. The captain, a very dashing sailor, fell in love with Katrine whose gentle resistance of his overtures infiamed his passion out of all bounds. He resolved to kidnap Katrine and invited her aboard the ship with that intention. Rowing out of Lady Geo, on a beautiful, still day, the boat was suddenly engulfed and she, poor lady, drowned. There was nothing in sea or air to account for the disaster. It was, of course, Hakon who took her away beside himself to save her from the outrage of capture. Katrine never grew old, but looked just as young as on the day that Hakon sailed away.

Foula tradition records that the ship that captured Hakon was a Russian vessel. This is not improbable as the Shetland fish trade was for a long time mainly with Russia. Another point in the island tradition is that Hakon belonged to the family of David Henry, who was, as we have seen, at one one time in possession of seventy pounds, which may indicate that he inherited some of Hakon's money. Hakon is said to have been the son of a William Henry in Guttrun.

The fishcurer, who is referred to in the preceding account as having annexed the island on the death of Katrine, may, through his business, have established a lien over the property. Indeed, tradition says that Hakon's money came at an opportune moment to enable Katrine to free the island from encumbrances, and that she was setting out to transact the business when she met her death. But the times were certainly lawless, and the Danish heirs who, being foreigners, would have difficulty in establishing their claim undoubtedly lost their little kingdom. Thus Thule ceased for 300 years to be an independent property, nor did the lairds reside there regularly, even for a part of the year, until the days of the present Udaller.

# 5

# UDAL PROPERTY AND THE KINGS OF FOULA

W e have mentioned that Fughley is Udal property, and, as is
the case with a considerable part of Shetland, has never
recognised any overlord, not even the crown. As late as the
seventeenth century the possessor of the island was known as
Queen—Queen Katrine. My belief is that the Crofters' Acts of
1886 and subsequently were all of them *ultra vires*.

To follow the whole and exceedingly complex story of
social development and land tenure from early times would be
too lengthy a business, but the essential thing to remember is
that when the islands were pledged to the Scottish crown in
1468 it was stipulated as a condition that the old laws and
customs should be retained. Although local rulers, and
particularly the infamous Stewart earls, have repeatedly violated
law and custom, and these infringements have become
established, yet the Scottish crown has never abrogated the
original treaty, and on many occasions (one only a few years ago)
has admitted the fundamental Scandinavian law, where no
definite contrary custom has been established.

Properly to understand the situation it is necessary to go
back a long way. Scandinavian society seems to have borne no
little resemblance to that described by Homer. It was pre-

eminently aristocratic. What has caused the popular but entirely unfounded illusion to the contrary is a mystery. The most casual perusal of early Scandinavian literature makes this absolutely clear. Society rested upon slavery or serfdom, and even the lowest class of freeman played but a comparatively minor part in the state. My own estimate is that the aristocrats were at the most in the proportion of one to six, and probably not more than ten per cent of the population, and possibly as low as five per cent. As in Homer there were great leaders of men, but nothing resembling absolute sovereignty, still less the faintest suggestion of over-lordship of land or property. Homer's Agamemnon had no rights even over personal property. Indeed the whole plot of the *Iliad* arises from an illegal attempt to assume such rights. As for land, the bare thought had never entered their heads.

The earliest picture of Scandinavian or Teutonic Society is that in the famous *Eddas* of Saemund Vigfusson. These *eddas* (or "tales of a great-grandmother") were probably gathered from oral tradition by Saemund, who set them down and edited them. They go back to a period long before his time—before the northward movements of Teutonic society took place. The *Volundar-kvida* is cognate with the *Nibelungenlied*. Both come from a common source and give the same story, but the Icelandic version is incomparably the finer. They are among the greatest literature of the world and at their best rank with Homer. Indeed I consider that there are few more magnificent things in existence than Saemund's *Lay of Atli*. The society represented is one directed by powerful aristocratic families and their masterful heads.

In addition to these pictures we have a very curious and interesting poem, The *Rigsmal*, which is a sort of social–economic poem explaining in a mythological way the structure, organisation and occupations of the social classes. Nothing could be clearer or more definite. Rig or Heimdall, the warder of Heaven or the Sun, the life-giving, fructifying power, comes to the earth and visits the house of Ai and Edda (the great-grandmother). By his power this couple produce a son called Thraell, Thrall—serf or slave. It is curious to notice that he is dark of skin, of hideous countenance and with protruding heels. (I have wondered whether by any chance the early Scandinavians knew of the Negroes.) He also has a shrivelled skin, a hunched back and knotted knuckles. To express the aristocratic contempt for this lowest class his daughters have such names as Smoky-nose, Tear-clout and Lazy-body. The occupations are menial—binding bast, carrying faggots, manuring fields, making fences, tending swine and cutting peat. Rig continues on his journey, and at the next house Amma, that is grandmother, bears a son Karl, that is Churl. He becomes the progeniture of the second class of society. They are red-haired and florid, and good-looking, for their daughters bear such names as Pretty-face, Blyth-speech, Chatterbox, and so on. (Here again there may be a racial distinction which we cannot discuss; great-grandmother and grandmother may well represent older and later race-stocks). They are represented as clean and well dressed, and seem to be engaged in weaving, carpentry, and the occupations of the artisan. They are also the farmer class, for whom the thralls toil ceaselessly so that they, the churls, can provide enough to maintain the jarls in splendour. Jarl (i.e. noble) is the son born by Modi (mother) at the third house visited by Rig. This appears to be the god's own son, which I infer the others are not. From him is descended the aristocratic class, with fair hair, a clear complexion and fine, piercing eyes. (Again this seems to be racial. No one, so far as I am aware has called attention to the point, but it seems to me that here we may have a clue to the vexed ethnological question of the North, and particularly the British Isles. First what, for want of a better name, we may called the Picts—hunched and dwarfish, the oldest race [v. the Dwarfie Stane in Shetland]; secondly, the so-called Celts, the second wave; thirdly, the Teutons).

This last aristocratic class spends its time in deeds of prowess and elegant accomplishments, to the admiration and astonishment of the churls. The aristocrats, it is clear, are the lords of the soil, which is given to them by Rig or Heimdall, the sun-god. No one in the course of this discussion seems to have noticed the important lines which I therefore quote verbatim:—

Heimdall or Rig gives his own name to Jarl, recognises him as his son and gives him the udal land and property.

THAN HAD HANN EINATZ
ODAL VOLLU
ODAL VOLLU
OC ALDNARBYGDIR

His own name he gave him
and his son declared him
whom he bade possess
his allodial fields ⎤ sic
his allodial fields ⎦
his ancient dwellings

These three divisions of early Scandinavian society—thrall, churl and jarl—are very sharply marked.

The next important picture that we have is in the sagas, including the *Orkneyinga Saga*, which are historic. The fundamentals are essentially identical. Society is still purely aristocratic and the land is still udal. The only differences are that customs are stereotyped and legalized in a regularized system. It is from the sagas that we obtain specific details of practice. To understand the social system we must first consider the problem of udal tenure.

## UDAL TENURE

The vagueness of some writers, at any rate in English, with regard to the nature and meaning of udal tenure is amazing, and the nonsense talked is beyond belief. One would imagine that they had read no early Scandinavian literature at all. In the first place the land is as we should phrase it allodial; that is, it is held of no man and no human society or state but *de sole et deo*—of the sun and god. This is made perfectly clear by the *Rigsmal* that we have quoted above, and it is interesting to notice the repetition of the words ODAL VOLLU: ODAL VOLLU, as though to emphasize the fact, the buildings—"the old-time buildings" are included. These are given by the sun-god to the aristocrat who even then holds as the heir and not in any form of tenancy. These lands and buildings are not given to the others, and I emphatically reject the suggestion that the karls were odal born or udallers. We are so obsessed by mediaeval feudal notions that we cannot think of anyone holding land or possessions apart from the state or the king. But we must remember that in early Northern society (as in Greece and among the Jews and probably everywhere) the king was the leader of the people, the king of the people, and in no sense the king of the country or lord of the land. (That was still so in Germany. The emperor was strictly the emperor of the Germans, not of Germany.) The idea of the king or the State owning the land is comparatively modern. Land, therefore, was allodial, held in entire independence of any overlord, as indeed it is still in Norway today. The title to land (to use a modern phrase) was undisputed de facto possession.

In the early days the immigrants to a new country such as Iceland and Shetland (Hjaltland), simply took possession of such land as they wanted, subject to the similar desires of their fellow immigrants. Later the established custom was to light fires along the boundary so as to mark off the portion claimed

(*Landnama* V, Chapter 1). The fires had to be lighted within a single day. It inevitably followed in a primitive state of warlike society that if one could wrest the land from another by force of arms and hold it, it became one's own. Conquest was recognised, and the custom of wager by battle grew up. This does not seem to have been very prevalent, but there is an instance in the *Eyrbyggia Saga* where Thorolf Baegifot in this contemptible manner gained the estate of the aged Ulfar who, though really too old to fight, preferred death to dishonour. When the combatants, however, were equally matched it seems in early days to have been considered more honourable than purchase (as most people seem to consider today in the case of countries) and regarded as a gift from Thor. In short, udal tenure is simply the tenure by which a state or a people hold land today. Nevertheless, purchase gradually came to be the usual method and the purchaser became a udaller with the same absolute right in the soil.

The custom of succession, however, which must next be considered, affected the question of purchase. It was the rule, at any rate in theory, that the land should be divided equally between the sons and daughters of the deceased owner. It is generally stated that the law of progeniture did not hold, but this is not entirely correct. In the first place the dignity of position and the office of godi, for example, descended to the eldest son. The daughters, moreover, seem usually to have been given the outlying parts of the estate. But most important of all, the eldest had the right to buy out the others. In other words, although the total value of an estate, real and personal, was divided equally the eldest had a very distinct first claim upon the real estate. What is more remarkable is that this claim was valid at least as far as the second generation.

There is an example in the *Eyrbyggja Saga*. Thorstein had two sons—one who died young leaving a son, Snorro, and another, Borko. Snorro compelled his uncle Borko to sell him at a valuation the share that had belonged to his deceased father. He then, while still a minor, assumed the priesthood which had been held by his uncle. It would appear that some at least of these priesthoods were attached to the land. It was possible for anyone who could prove relationship to the original owner to buy out the purchaser—even to the third generation—by paying the original price, plus the cost of improvements. Further, before a sale could take effect it was necessary to obtain the consent of the heirs, and even then the purchaser was very much in the position of a younger member of the family.

Such, then, is udal property. There is no need to discuss Hibbert's ridiculous contention that the term was in contradistinction to scattald. For one reason amongst many others, scat was not introduced until the time of Harold Harfagra (AD 880) whereas the *Rigsmal* refers to a period before the north migrations. Moreover, the sales and charters mention arable and pasture, minerals and seaweeds. It is worthy of note that udal property extends to the lowest spring tide. Seaweeds, which belong to the foreshore, are expressly mentioned in sales and charters.

An interesting case in this connection came up recently in Shetland. In 1903 the Lerwick Harbour Trustees claimed a piece of ground which had been part of the foreshore but which they had drained and converted into dry land. Under Scottish law the foreshore belongs to the crown but under udal law, which is still the law in Norway, it belongs to the owner of the land opposite the shore. In this case the udaller claimed the ground which was of considerable value as a building site. The case went into court and eventually to the Court of Session, where the crown lost the case owing to the knowledge of udal tenure and of the conditions under which the islands were pledged to the Scottish crown, on the part of Mr, afterwards Lord, Salvesen, who is of Norwegian extraction. The history of the gradual stealing of udal rights and the conversion of udal to feudal lands would take us too long to discuss. Suffice it to say that a considerable amount of land in Shetland is still udal.

Passing now to the social conditions, we find in historic times that the three classes of the *Rigsmal*—Jarls, Karls or Churls, and Thralls—have been increased to four by the addition of a class of freedmen. The four classes, recognised by law, are known as the free, the unfree, the freedmen and the thralls, and the line of division is sharp and distinct. The term jarl, or noble, gradually came to have a more specific meaning, and free is a better generic term. The unfree are the old second class, the karls or churls. The freedmen appear always third in order, which would imply that they were thralls raised to the status of churls. But in that case the term freedmen (after all only an English translation) is confusing.

These were the distinctions in law; but socially there were others, certainly in the class of the free. Among the freemen or nobles we naturally find leaders or chiefs, who occupied a closely analogous position to that of the Greek chiefs or kings in Homer. Corresponding to the little states of Greece with its isolated valleys, peninsulas, and detached islands, we find the same in Norway, Shetland, and Iceland. These divisions in Scandinavia at the time of Harold Harfagra were known as herads, and though they might be subdivisions of a larger entity, they were mainly separate independent states. We find the same independence in the early days of Iceland and Shetland, and the island of Fughley, which we may liken to that of Ithaca in Homeric Greece, seems to have retained that independence until a late date, probably to the seventeenth century.

The chief of these petty states was generally known as hersar, but when of any size or importance, he bore the title of Fulkis-Kongr. Fulki signifies a district and is derived from the word folk, which is the same as in English. Kon was the name given by Rig to the son of Jarl, and in old Norse it meant a man of high birth. All the descendants of Rig were Konung. The term seems to have been exactly analogous to the Homeric *basileus*, and very loose in its application. It seems to have been more or less a courtesy title, and as in the case of *basileus* only to have come to hold the more specific meaning that we associate with it after contact with the strict monarchies of other lands. The Fulkis-Kongr, although of course a udaller, was primarily a king not of land but of the people, and was somewhat analogous to a Highland chief. It is clear, however, from the story of the colonization of Iceland that these petty kings on taking possession of a district, assigned lands to their free, or noble, followers. The king may have had the right of reversion, but that would merely place him in the position of any other heir, and be in accordance with udal tenure. In practice the family would rarely become completely extinct. Nevertheless, the power of the Fulkis-Kongr, in distributing land and settling property disputes, would place him in a position somewhat resembling a land-king. There were, however, kings who possessed no land. A host-king was a ruler of warriors, and a sea-king a commander of a ship. "There were many sea-kings who ruled over many men, and had no land. He only was thought to deserve the name of sea-king who never slept under a sooty rafter and never drank at the hearth corner." (*Ynglinga Saga*, Chapter 34.) "As soon as Olaf got men and ships, his warriors gave him the name of king, for it was the custom that host-kings who went on Viking expeditions, if they were king-born, should be given the name of king, although they ruled over no land." (*St Olaf's Saga*, Chapter 4). Kings were as plentiful in Scandinavia as in Homeric Greece, for the son of a king bore the same title as his father, as with German titles of the present century.

Scandinavian society, although aristocratic, was very definitely anti-monarchic. The term "monarchy," that is "single rule," is to some extent relative. A father may be the single ruler of a family, and the kings were to some extent single rulers within their own sphere, but society as a whole was aristocratic, and the aristocrats among themselves were in a measure even democratic, which has doubtless given rise to the mistaken views of many writers. On the whole, however, they were oligarchic, and it was a comparatively small number that exercised any real power—men of the status of Snorro or Njal or Olaf Pa. They were firm in their objection to monarchy, and it was this objection that caused the communities of Iceland and of Orkney and Shetland to come into being. It was the revolt of the landed aristocracy against the new kingship of Harold Harfagra, established about AD 880, that made these old aristocrats seek new homes, and found colonies in Iceland, Faroe, Shetland, Orkney, Caithness and the Hebrides. Their ideal was an aristocratic republic, recognising no single overlord or monarch.

The depredations of these Vikings, and presumably to some extent even their independence, roused Harold, and he fitted out a great fleet and conquered the Hebrides, Orkney and Shetland, in 875. Caithness, Orkney and Shetland he formed into one earldom, and offered it to Ronald, count of Merca, who resigned the gift in favour of his brother Sigurd, who thus became the first earl of Orkney. Hibbert remarks in a note: "It is certain from the Norwegian historians that the largest division of property in the Earldom of Orkney was originally possessed by the Earls themselves." The Shetland islands were ruled by Scandinavian Jarls until 1231.

At first the Viking chiefs of Iceland remained absolutely independent, as presumably did the Shetland chiefs, and almost certainly the little king of the remote and isolated island of Fughley, but eventually the endless feuds and dissensions with no central authority to control them resulted in the formation of a semi-republican institution, which in Iceland was accomplished at the end of a generation by Ulfliot in 928, who three years before had been selected to find a remedy for the troubles of that country.

In the year 1379 there was a failure in the male line of the jarls of Orkney, and Henry Sinclair, the nearest heir, succeeded to the earldom, which remained in the hands of the Sinclairs for a century.

The crown of Denmark and Norway had tried unsuccessfully to enforce the annual payment of 100 marks which Scotland had agreed to give for the cession of the Western Isles. After much controversy the matter was settled by a marriage between the Princess Margaret, daughter of the king of Denmark, Norway and Sweden, and the seventeen-year-old son of James III. Orkney and Shetland were pledged to James for 58,000 florins as part of the dower of the princess, one of the conditions being that the natives of the islands should retain their ancient laws and customs. Denmark has never relinquished the right of redemption. Subsequently the then Lord Sinclair bartered to James III his whole title to the earldom in exchange for Ravenscraig Castle and lands, and James, in 1530, granted the royal estate of Orkney and Shetland to his natural brother James, earl of Moray.

Fughley, or Uttrie, the Uttermost Isle, was certainly never a part of the earldom of Orkney, and more than probably was never, except in the loosest sense, included in the earldom at all. The name itself may be taken as implying this, possibly, as well as referring to the geographical situation and to the tradition of Ultima Thule. The outer isles appear to have been outside any clear ecclesiastical system till comparatively recent times, which points to the same conclusion.

In Fughley Guttorm established a miniature kingdom on the lines of the small independent kingdoms of the old country, and from the remote and inaccessible situation of the harbourless and impregnable isle, a score of miles over the turbulent seas from the nearest other land, he and his successors seem to have remained in a little independent world apart, free from the turmoils and strife that disturbed the other communities. Little is known of the history of the island for six hundred years, but the dynasty of Guttorm preserved its ascendancy during all that time. Its absolute isolation and consequent complete independence would doubtless give the island an importance far beyond that warranted by its size and wealth. Its imposing appearance set in full view of the whole long line of the Shetland group has tempted a modern novelist, who knows nothing whatever about the past history of the island, to write a novel called *The King of Foula*.

In early times the local kings presided in the triple capacity of military commander, priest and judge. The priest-king was known as *godi* (plural: *godir*) literally a god. He marks the summit of the aristocratic class and was distinguished from the *stormenn*, or great men, the other wealthy landed proprietors who likewise assigned land to their "free" followers. When these priest-kings had taken possession of a district, and allotted the land, they erected a temple and administered justice and religion as at home. The place of justice was a circular ring of stones. One of the stones was set apart as the stone of Thor on which victims were broken. In the *Eyrbyggja Saga*, we read that Thorolf erected a temple to Thor, and reserved to himself the office of godi. The isolation of Fughley would render it necessary for Guttorm to assume the office and perform the duties of priest and judge as well as military commander. Although the godi was originally elected, the office had become hereditary in the earliest days of colonisation; it was also saleable, and in that case descended to the heirs of the purchaser. In the *Gragas*, the Norwegian law-book, we find, "If a man has bought a godiship or it has been given to him, then it shall be inherited (by his heirs)." Njal, for example, obtained a priesthood for his foster-son in order that he might marry the haughty and ambitious Hildegunna. (This is fortunate for me as I cannot claim to be a descendent of the Foula kings! But I have in some measure aspired to the office of godi, as I frequently take services and have even officiated at funerals and the sacrament.)

In Fughley, as we have seen, Whirly Knowe was the place of justice or the temple site. The government of the herad, or petty state, in Norway resembles that of Homeric Greece. It lay in the hands of a general assembly or Thing, presided over by the chief or king, and was composed of the free-born, who were the landed proprietors of the herad. Their sons or relatives were permitted to appear only if they themselves possessed lands. The karls were not Thingsmen, and for this and other reasons I emphatically reject the common view that the karl is the typical udaller. Even apart from the very clear statement in the *Rigsmal*, it is obvious to me that only the freeman could own udal property. That in course of time some of the others may have attained to udal possession is quite possible; but thereby they pass into the class of the free. There was no other possible tenure for the noble or free but udal tenure. Whatever other people were the noble or free were udallers and certainly owned most, and probably at first all, of the land. The judges and doomsmen had their expenses to the Thing paid by means of the Thingfaring tax levied upon the inhabitants of the district, mainly, it would appear, on the unfree. Judging from later enactments, the judge received payment as well as a proportion of the fines. There were also temple payments to the priest. The power of these chiefs is illustrated in the *Eyrbyggja Saga*, where Thorolf sneeringly remarks to Snorro, whose assistance against his son he is endeavouring to obain, "I wot well the cause of thy regard for Arnkill, thou thinkest he will pay for thy support in the Thing more freely than I."

Independent as these chiefs were amongst themselves, their relation to their followers was distinctly feudal in nature. They rarely went out unattended not merely by retainers but by armed followers, who were odal-born, and who rendered returns both in service and kind to the chief or king who had allotted land to them. Even the wealthier udallers were clearly in some way dependent on these powerful priest-kings. For example, in

*Kormak's Saga*, we read that Bersi, as Thingsman of Olaf Pa, had to attend his booth at the local Thing and found it already thronged by others on a similar errand.

Leaving the aristocratic class we may now turn to the others—the karls, thralls, and freedmen. The *Rigsmal* significantly tells us that it was the function of the thralls "to toil incessantly, in order that by their labour the karls may obtain sufficient produce from the earth to enable the nobles to live with becoming splendour." This makes clear that the thralls were the labourers of society. From the *Rigsmal* picture it is also clear that the majority of them were not household slaves but had their own houses and possibly their own swine and goats. They were serfs. The karl was obviously a farmer for whom the thrall worked, as well as an artisan. It is equally obvious that he paid in kind to his aristocratic overlord from the produce of the land. The freedman appears to have been a manumitted thrall who obtained personal freedom either by purchase or in exchange for work or by bravery. When anyone manumitted a thrall he was bound by law to allot to him a piece of land to maintain himself and a family. The land granted was not freehold and certain services were required by the grantor. On the death of the grantee without children it reverted to the overlord. Incidentally we may notice that in Iceland no one was allowed to marry unless he had sufficient property to maintain a family; an amount fixed at six score legal ounces, that is equal to the value of 720 ells, of wadmel, besides clothes and other necessaries—an excellent principle that we should do well to copy. On becoming a freedman the thrall passed into the class of the karl, who enjoyed personal freedom but had no political rights, that is to say was not a thingsman. He was, however, entitled to bear arms and most of the wealthier landowners, the allodial lords, had a number of them in their service as armed retainers.

## THE KARLS AND THE RUNRIG SYSTEM

Mr Storer Clouston, in the introduction to his *Records of the Earldom of Orkney* remarks:

Indeed there seems to be evidence of a link with an even more remote past that was swept away by the swords of the first Vikings long before Harfager made Sigurd his Earl over the islands, the past of brochs and flint arrow-heads. This link, if it is one, is to be seen in those "townships" or "towns" as they were originally called [and still are in Foula] which may be said to have formed the unit of property for an odal family of good position at the period of these early records.

A typical township as it was in the year 1818 is thus described by Peterkin in his *Notes on Orkney*.

A town, then, is a portion of ground, partly arable and partly pasture, separated generally from *the hill*, or common moor, by a massy turf dyke round the whole (unless when bounded on any side by the sea), and containing a greater or less number of *houses*, acoording to the extent of the town; each *house* being occupied by a different udaller or tenant and each having attached to it various proportions of the arable lands—originally and still generally, in run-ridge— with patches of grass land, and sometimes detached and separate pieces of ground near the houses called Tumails or little enclosures called Quays.

This description exactly coincides with Foula at the present day. Peterkin, however, misses one of the main points, which still survives at Sefster on the Mainland, namely that the houses are all together in a group. This was so until recently in Foula. The runrig system is remembered in the isle and the remains are clearly seen. Under this system the arable ground was divided into strips or plots of approximately the same size. These "rigs" were apportioned periodically between the respective dwellers within the tun. The Hametoun was permanently divided by lot in 1842, and grouped into crofts. Some time before 1800 the Tun o' Eam was permanently divided, but the plots belonging to the various tenants are still scattered here and there throughout the tun, and not grouped beside the crofter's dwelling.

The runrig system seems to me to have been an ingenious devise to prevent any claim to absolute ownership. The suggestion that the constant shifting round was fairer to the farmer is absurd. A suitable permanent division that would give the farmer the benefit of his own husbandry is obviously preferable. Whatever its object the runrig system was not udal tenure, and therefore it appears to me to show a settlement of the unfree. Whether these were the karls or the thralls is the only problem, and I incline to think that there is little room for doubt that these were the karls. The thrall may have had a scrap of ground and kept pigs, but there is no evidence that he had agricultural land. In short the modern cottar is the descendent of the thrall and the crofter of the karl. The attitude of the jarl to those two classes survives in our words "thralldom," meaning bondage, and "churlish"—rude and uncivilised.

# 6

# THE REIGN OF THE SCOTTS

Ten years after the terrible storm in which Hakon Magnusson was carried away, the castle of Scalloway was built by the infamous Earl Patrick. The work was begun about 1600. A tax was laid upon every parish to provide funds and it is said that the mortar was mixed with the whites of thousands of eggs provided by the Shetlanders. It was soon completed and on the visit of Mr Pitcairn, minister of the parish of Northmavine, the earl asked him to compose a verse for the front of his castle. But the minister took the opportunity to reprove him for the wicked extortion and oppression through which it had been built. The earl at first threatened to imprison the minister, but after a time he calmed down and Mr Pitcairn said, "Well, if you must have a verse, I shall give you one from Holy Scripture. You will find that 'the wise man built his house upon a rock: and the rain descended and the floods came and the winds blew, and beat upon that house, and it fell not. But the foolish man built his house upon the sand: and the rain descended and the floods came and the winds blew, and beat upon that house, and it fell, and great was the fall of it.' What think you then of this inscription—'*Cujus fundamen saxum est, domus illa manebit: Labidis e contra, si sit arena, perit*'?" The earl pretended not to see the implication and, with the ready effrontery of habitual guilt, remarked that it explained why he had abandoned his other house on the sandy shores of Sumburgh and built this. "My father's house was built upon the sand; its foundations are already giving way, and it will fall; but Scalloway Castle is constructed upon a rock and will stand."

There were three brothers, Umphra or Umphray (an old Shetland name not to be confused with the southern Humphrey), whose names were, I believe, Andrew, James and John. They seem to have been Foula men, and held land in the isle. Apparently they went over to the Mainland and also took up land there. James Umphray worked on Scalloway Castle, and may even have planned it. Andrew worked a sloop and brought materials for the castle. When the building was nearing completion, the earl inspected it and, complaining that one of the lintels was slightly crooked, hanged James summarily from the top of the castle. Andrew at once went off with the sloop to the south and reported this act of injustice, which seems to have been the culminating incident in the misdoings of the earl; though the incorporation of the royal arms was made the ostensible reason for his execution. A government vessel was sent and they searched the castle in vain for the earl. It has been thought that the reason for hanging James was that he shared with Earl Patrick the knowledge of the position of a secret chamber. As they afterwards sat smoking [sic] on the green, they fancied they saw something moving within; and it seems that the earl had come out of a secret door, so they went back and captured him and took him to Edinburgh, where he was brought to trial.

He was held in such terror that one of the witnesses refused to give evidence until he had been solemnly assured that the earl would never be allowed to return to Orkney. He was accused of high treason and part of the evidence was the inscription on another castle of his at Birsay in Orkney, where he had put up his father's name and descent thus—"*Robert Steuartus, Filius Jacobi Quinti, Rex Scotorum, hoc Ædificium Instruxit, Sic fuit, est, et erit.*" [Robert Stuart, son of James V, King of the Scots, erected this building.] As it stands it reads "Robert, King of the Scots." The nominative instead of the genitive was probably a mere grammatical slip. The earl was beheaded, which was rather a severe penalty for false Latin. However, let the uncultured take warning.

This story may be coupled with that of a recent trial of a tramp in South Africa for the murder of a fellow tramp. The accused in reply to the judge happened to mention that he was reading Homer in the original Greek. This resulted in a more thorough enquiry, and the real murderer was found, and the tramp, who had been a schoolmaster, was acquitted. Thus we see that, though bad Latin may be a considerable danger, good Greek may be a considerable assistance.

In spite of its massive construction, the castle of Scalloway was never occupied after the earl's execution.

Towards the close of this century, or early in the following, Foula was swept by a terrible epidemic of smallpox which carried off almost the entire population so that out of about two hundred people only five, or according to some seven, were left alive. It was spoken of as "the muckle fever" and it is only surmised that it was smallpox. The islanders still speak of it with horror, and describe how the dead were laid outside the doors, as in the great plague, and the survivors used to come round at intervals to bury them. At last only one man remained who had sufficient strength to perform this office. The islander who acted as bailie and lived in Ham, and who possessed the only gun, threatened to shoot anyone who came from the south end. From this remnant what we may call the original blood of the island is all descended, and in investigating the pedigrees of those now inhabiting the island the descent is in the great majority of cases traced to some immigrant who came into Foula at this time. The historians give the date of "the mortal pox" in Shetland as 1720, but Foula tradition, taken in conjunction with the dates on the tombstones of those who were brought in to repopulate the isle after the epidemic, points to an earlier period.

About this time the island, as well as the estate of Melby, Vaila and other lands, was owned by James Mitchell of Girlesta and his daughter and co-heir Grizel, who married John Scott of Gibbleston, grandson of Sir John Scott of Scotstarvet (an author who had a seat in the Privy Council in 1617 and was Lord of Session in 1649) and Anne, daughter of Sir John Drummond of Hawthorn Den. Through Grizel the property was settled on her son John Scott (of whom there were nine in succession, which is apt to confuse even the most accurate memory), and it was he who is known in Foula as Old Melby; and many are the tales that are told of this scheming, violent-tempered, but not altogether unkindly old tyrant.

The Scotts settled in the island of Vaila, where they built what is known as the Old Ha', and as Vaila lies just opposite Ham Voe they changed their landing-place and abandoned the south landing, which the Danes had always used. Thus the Hametoun in the south end, which was the original Hame or home of the people with its Ha', school, temple-site, and later its Established kirk, ceased to be so to speak, the capital of the isle as it had been in the days of the Danish rulers. It is still the centre of the population, with its seventeen crofts surrounded by a stone dyke, but Ham (meaning harbour in Norse), has been the capital and seat of government since the Scott dynasty was established. The Hametoun is the Glasgow or New York, but the Tun o' Eam, although it has only ten crofts, is the Edinburgh or Washington of the isle. Here is the laird's house, the school, the post office and the shop—the centre of news and discussion. This, too, is the headquarters of the fleet—the fishing boats, the mail-boat and the Udaller's yacht! Although they did not live in the island, the extreme likelihood of their being storm-bound for long periods made it necessary for the Scotts to have some place in which to stay, so they built what is now spoken of as the Old Ha' on the ayre, or beach, of Ham—a most extraordinary position. To build the house and repopulate the isle they sent in a number of craftsmen, including a mason, a blacksmith to make nails and clogs, and a webster. This required a little scheming. Laurence Umphray, the webster, had land at Elviston and John Scott called on the wife when her husband was out and asked to see the title-deeds. He professed to discover some fault in them and, under pretext of having this corrected, took the deeds away and thus got hold of the land. Umphray was sent to Foula to act as webster, where he died in 1724. His son resolved to go south and try to recover his land. When he landed in Vaila Old Melby came to meet the boat and enquired where he was going. "To Edinburgh to get back my land," was the reply. "Well, you may get it or you may not get it, but if you go and fail to get it you shall never more cut land of mine. If you do not go but return to Foula, I will make you my factor and you can have your choice of any croft in the isle." Umphray agreed and chose the croft of Gravins in the Tun o' Ham. This necessitated turning out the occupants, about whom the following tale is told.

## THE STORY OF THE IRISHMAN'S GRAVE

One day a vessel appeared off the Voe and sent ashore a boat containing the body of a young man, Robert Daughters, the son of a wealthy Irish squire who was sending out a cargo of potatoes from his estates. The youth had wished for the experience of a sea voyage, and as he was in a delicate state of health it was hoped that the trip would prove beneficial. That at least was the ostensible reason for his presence on the ship, but some suspected that he had been sent to keep an eye on the cargo as there had been extensive pilfering and shady dealing. The sailors said that he had been unable to stand the fatigue of the voyage and that they had made for the nearest land, but that he had died before they could reach the island. The islanders, however, thought that he had died from neglect or ill treatment resulting from his attempt to check the dishonest transactions. The crew asked permission to bury him in the kirkyard but the brother of the Ranselman would not permit it as it was considered to be unlucky to bury strangers there. Later, when his own three sons were drowned, it was thought that this was a judgment for his hardness of heart. Daughters, therefore, was buried just outside the Ham dyke, but even there he was not allowed to rest. During the night the occupier of Gravins and his wife rose and dug up the body and stripped it of its fine clothes, returning it to the grave wrapped in some old rags of their own. His fine black cloth coat with silver buttons the old man used to wear to the kirk, to the great scandalization of the folk; while out of his beautiful linen sark they made a christening robe. Two of the bairns who wore it grew up deformed and went on all fours all their days. Not long afterwards the couple were turned out of their croft to make room for the Umphrays and were given a croft in the north end which, although it has the most beautiful scenery, is exposed and less convenient in every way. This so preyed upon the old man's mind that he went mad and used to come down to Ham every day to gaze regretfully at his lost croft. He lost two of his four sons. One killed himself wrestling with a heavy piece of driftwood, and the other by going to the hills in the early morning, fasting and with bare feet. The remaining sons took a young man from the Hametoun to help them to work the croft. This was the father of John Manson, the cragsman mentioned in Chapter 1, the present occupier of Blobersburn.

Old Melby insisted that when he arrived in Foula every able-bodied islander should go down to the Voe to greet him. One day his boat suddenly appeared out of the mist when Thomas Isbister's great-uncle was performing his Saturday's shave. Not daring to delay a moment he hurried to meet his laird with one side of his face still unshaved. The same man, however, could stand up to the laird if necessary. When Old Melby remarked that all the Foula people were thieves and rogues he doubled his fist in his face and invited him to repeat his statement. "Oh, not you, not you," said the old laird soothingly, "everyone knows you are as honest as the day."

It was the custom in those days to carry in mould or earth from the moor to enrich the crofts. The "mouldie heaps" were covered with feals or sods. This practice of "scalping" the ground was strictly forbidden but was continued with some obstinacy until one day the entire Hametoun received notices to quit from the exasperated laird. Naturally the consternation was great, and it was decided to send out a deputation to beg for mercy. A crew was hastily gathered, and when the boat arrived at Vaila the laird, whose wrath had somewhat cooled by this time, came down to meet it, as was his custom, and exclaimed, "What are you doing here on a fine day like this?" On hearing their errand he said, "Away back to Foula and get on with your voar" (spring digging), and that was the last they heard of the eviction.

The Ha' (hall—signifying a house with a stair) stood on the ayre for the best part of a hundred years. Several Foula lassies— mere children of twelve years old—went into service with the Scotts both in Foula and Vaila. One girl who had served them for nine years without breaking anything, had the misfortune to smash a dish. Her mistress deducted six pence from her wages in order to teach her to be more careful. In those days Foula had to supply a certain number of men for the wars, and it was Melby's duty, as laird, to select them. Scott Henry, the great-great-grandfather of the present tenant of Niggards, was skipper of a sixern used for the fishing, and Melby invited him and his crew to the Ha' for "a dram." He detained two of the hands in order to send them to join the forces. Scott Henry was so annoyed that he kicked the heels of his sea-boots through the Ha' stairs as he descended.

A story is told of two Highland deserters who escaped to
Shetland where they stole a boat and sailed to Foula. They stayed
in South Harrier at the north end—"nice, gentlemanly buddies."
A Foula man on going to the Mainland found that a hue and cry
had been raised on account of the missing boat. Feeling sorry for
the owner's anxiety he dropped a hint to the effect that he need
not worry as he would get his boat back. The authorities, hearing
of this, put two and two together and sent to Foula to make
enquiries. The officers were arrested and imprisoned in the Ha'.
The folk were very angry with the man who had let the cat out of
the bag as the gentlemen were like to hang for it. However,
owing to an amnesty in connection with a coronation or some
such event, the deserters were pardoned.

The Old Ha' as it is now called had a dramatic end. One
day, just before Christmas, Old Melby with his wife and children
were sitting at supper when a great sea came into the Voe. The
servant girl opened the front door and peeped out. She saw a
man sitting on the roof of the byre holding a line which was
attached to his boat. He shouted to her to shut the door, and a
moment afterwards the sea came down the lum extinguishing
the fires and broke through the house carrying with it the stair
which had given its proud name to the building. The occupants
escaped unhurt although the house was demolished. The present
Ha' was built immediately afterwards and stands on a steep rise
nearly two hundred yards back from the sea; yet in our own time
the sea has darkened the windows and entered the doors.

In Vaila Melby kept a muckle dog to frighten the folk who
came to complain of ill-treatment. He said he was "tired of
people speering at his lug," so built a great wall with two high
gates between the house and the kitchen which, as was the
custom in those days, was a separate building. Someone who had
the welfare of the people at heart warned him that he could shut
out the voice of man but not the voice of conscience. When a
critic remarked that the wind would blow down the gates, he

replied that he defied all the powers in hell to take down his yetts. One night a mysterious inscription appeared on the banks below his house. It was in foreign characters—Greek or Hebrew—so he sent to Lerwick for an interpreter. The translation ran, YOU ARE ALL IN POMP AND GRANDEUR NOW BUT MARK THE LATTER END. That night, although it was calm and still, the walls and gates fell down with a mighty roar like thunder. Many saw therein the hand of Providence, but there were others who stated that a strange ship had been seen sailing below the house, and they suspected that a charge of gunpowder had something to do with it.

Old Melby built the lighthouse which is still to be seen on Vaila, and one day when his son, who went everywhere on horseback, was riding out to look at it both he and his pony fell over the cliffs and were lost. He left a little boy, an infant in his mother's arms. About the same year Old Melby lost his third wife. She was said to be a very cruel woman as she used to order her servant to kill the hens by plunging them in boiling water, and when the indignant little maid refused she would do it herself. Another account says that she used to pluck and singe the hens while they were alive—a barbarous practice which I regret to say I have met with in other parts of the world. By this time the estate was heavily encumbered and the family was comparatively poor, but in spite of this the mistress always wore black silk. One day she was skimming the chicken broth and carelessly allowing the fat to drip down the front of her dress when it caught fire. The foolish woman rushed screaming from the house, in flames, and was burnt to death. This was regarded as a fitting judgment. That evening, when some friends came to condole with the old husband he remarked: "The de'il! she'll be having a hot time tonight." The following year he himself died, leaving the burden of the heavily mortgaged estate on the shoulders of the little four-year-old grandson. His guardians thought of selling the property but he was such a pretty child that they resolved to hold on and give him the chance to redeem it. Every now and again a summons would come for his father's and grandfather's debt, and they would solemnly place the missive in the little boy's hands. Nor did he disappoint them, for when he grew up he bought fish and sent it to Spain and made sufficient money to clear the estate. He died without issue.

It must, I think, have been one of the later Scotts who, when a youth of nineteen, jumped on the back of a cow, in a fit of exuberance of animal spirits. The terrified cow rushed over the cliffs and the rider saved himself only just in time. His father was so angry that he shipped him off to foreign lands. When he returned he was, like many another sojourner in hot climates, afflicted with an unquenchable thirst, and he used to walk about the island with a small keg of whisky slung over his back in the manner that one carries a camera or field glasses. He offered this refreshment to anyone he chanced to meet on his way. His end was what might have been expected, but the account is perhaps a little highly coloured, for it is said that the spirits ignited inside him and the flames appeared in his throat. Eventually the family was involved in a law suit and being unable to meet the solicitor's fees surrendered their estate, or at any rate part of it, including the island of Foula, in lieu of payment.

The excellent stories in which Foula abounds, giving interesting glimpses of old times and customs, furnish the real history of the island. The following is one of the earliest known incidents in connection with the newer landing place at Ham Voe.

## THE STORY OF THE IRON BOLT

In the old days it was customary in Shetland and Orkney to pay rent in kind, and as it was found difficult to keep check on the amount of the crops, the lairds made a strict rule that all corn should be sent to the laird's mill to be ground, and a certain proportion of it was retained as rent. By grinding as much as was possible or safe in a hand mill the people managed to cheat the laird of their rent thus fixed each year by the yield of the ground. These hand mill stones were contraband and there grew up a brisk smuggling trade in them, particularly from Shetland to Orkney.

One day a sixern with a Shetland crew arrived in Foula. They wanted to engage an extra hand as they were a man short and also to do a little quiet smuggling. John Henry, great-great-grandfather of David Henry, the last tenant of Guttern, agreed to go with them. They were away a week, and while in Orkney they found a ship that had gone ashore and they rummaged round the wreck and found two iron bolts, and made off with them. Iron in those days was a very scarce and valuable commodity, and a piece of iron that could be made into something was a prize indeed. When they returned they came to Foula to put John Henry ashore, and paid him for his week's strenuous service the magnificent sum of one shilling. He ventured to expostulate and say that he was rather underpaid for a voyage which had taken longer than he had expected. The skipper said that they would consider the matter, and the crew drew apart into a little group and discussed it, while John watched and wondered about his financial prospects. Finally, the skipper came to him and said that they had duly weighed the question, but John had agreed to one shilling and one shilling it must be. "Weel then," said John, "dinna ye think ye micht gie me ane o' they bolts, they'd be fine for making a crook, and I served ye weel." The skipper retired again and another consultation took place and again John watched them anxiously. This time they hesitated for a long while; but once more the skipper returned and said, "Ye said ye wad come for a shilling and a shilling it maun be." "Ah weel," said John, "it canna be haupit," and he went away home.

Now, as we have seen, Foula is a place where the

opportunity of tide and weather must be seized at the moment or one may be detained for weeks. The weather was doubtful and the tide was wrong; so the crew spent their time in a sort of sentry-go on the ayre, walking to and fro from their boat and keeping an eye on it. After he had been home John came down from his house and kept an eye on them. He slipped round by Mogil and down to the tun o' Ham, watched till they had looked at the boat and turned back for the next beat, came back, glanced into the boat and turned again. Then he slipped under the forehead, took one of the bolts and up the burn as before and home. The men were suspicious; perhaps they saw him in the distance; but they discovered the loss and sent some men in hot haste to Biggins. John had been and gone. They saw his wife and began to talk to her and tell her what a handy lad he was, and what a fine seaman, and how useful he had been, and then one of them casually remarked, "I suppose he didna show ye the fine bolt that he brocht back frae Orkney?" "Aye, that he did," she said. "It was a gey braw bolt, it must hae been sae lang and wad make a fine crook." "Man, it was langer or that," said another. "May be," said the first, "but I'd like fine tae see it again." "It's under the resting-chair where ye're sitting." So the bolt was got out and when they had it in their hands they explained that it was theirs and took it away. Not long after John came home and was wrath and told his wife she was "nae muckle gude tae lave in charge o' things," and off again he went to the ayre. He didna daur tae hide i' the boat this time, but slippit doun the burn and nabbit the bolt and awa' back hame afore the crew kenned what had happened. The manoeuvre was instantly discovered; but at that moment the tide was right and the weather was none too good and it was not safe to wait. So they had to leave the isle and the bolt too. Thomas Isbister's grandfather, Manse Georgeson, the island's most accomplished blacksmith was called upon for his skill and he made a crook that was no ordinary affair but with a fine twisted shank which was the admiration of all.

For many a year the muckle pots o' Biggins hung upon that hook and cooked the family dinner, and then for many more years it hung over the fire in Grisigarth, and when the occupier died his wife went to live in Dykes' taking the hook with her, and eventually it was given to the laird, and there, after about 175 years, it hangs in the Ha', this time with a lamp depending from it instead of a pot.

## JEAN JACK AND THE BLUIDY HEID

One of the immigrants to the island was a certain William Georgeson from the Mainland. His grandfather of the same name was born in the island of Papa Stour in the days of Earl Patrick, and, as not infrequently happened in those times, he was believed to have sold his soul to the devil. In return he learned a number of useful tricks. For example, when he went away to the market on the Mainland he used to stick his spade in the ground and hang his coat over it, and the spade would continue the delving of its own accord, working side by side along with Willie's wife. He always contrived to dispose of his cattle to his own advantage, and became more prosperous than his neighbours, who nick-named him Satan. In short he became rather unpopular.

His grandson, Willie, was a man of considerable force of character, though not exactly a favourite. He was a remarkably "ill-fard" man, and he may have been employed as a sort of public executioner. On one occasion, at any rate, he was travelling along the road carrying on his back a kishie containing the head of Barsey Reid, a murderer suspected of witchcraft. Barsey was walking one night, carrying a spade when he met his enemy, Gibbie Law, coming from Lerwick and walking against the moon. He killed Gibbie with the spade and buried him beside the road. After his execution in Scalloway Barsey Reid's head was entrusted to Willie Georgeson with instructions to take it to Sandness and expose it on a pike. It was a wearisome road, the sun was hot and Willie was thirsty. He came to a house at Hesten-Setter and after depositing the kishie on the ground against the dyke he knocked at the door and asked for a drink of water. His request was answered by a maiden of surpassing beauty, Jean Jack (or possibly more correctly Jeanne Jacques) who, being as kind as she was fair, invited him to sit down while she went to draw the water from the well. On the way (Oh, fatal curiosity of woman!) she must needs peep into the basket. A blood-stained human head is no fitting sight for gentle maidens even of those days. Small wonder that "the look that came over her face never left it more."

The intrepid but unprepossessing William fell in love with Jean but she refused him. He continued his courtship with great perseverance in spite of receiving no encouragement from the beautiful girl. One day to her astonishment she heard the banns of herself and William cried in the kirk. She then gave in saying that it was no use resisting as he was the kind of man who would get her even if she were dead. The hideous man and the lovely woman made a strange pair, and it is said that to this day their descendents are remarkable for either good looks or plainness. The couple could not find a house on the Mainland so went to Foula where John Henry in Mogil (said to be the great-grandfather of David Henry in Guttern) gave them shelter in a cellar or small house adjoining their own. Jean Jack and Willie remained at Mogil when the Henries flitted to the Biggins. Some time afterwards John Henry's wife lost her milking cow and was in great distress because she had a young baby who was starving. Jean Jack, mindful of past hospitality, used to drive one of her cows daily to the Biggins so that the children might have the benefit of the milk.

Jean Jack's tombstone bearing her initials is still to be seen in the Kirkyard, J. J. 178—; the fourth figure is illegible. Andrew, one of her children, married Kirsty Twatt on the Mainland, and it is said that they were the prettiest pair that ever came before a minister. "You've got a pretty woman," said a Foula man on his return. "Oh, she is a comely dame," answered Andrew. Their descendants have been nearly all good looking to this day. Andrew (or possibly one of his brothers) became a thief and was drowned.

Jean Jack's son or grandson, yet another William, fell foul of the minister as he did not pay his tiends (or, according to another account, was a thief) and the minister told him if he did not bring the tiends he would be read out of the kirk "the morn." Willie muttered, "The morn's no come yet." That night the minister was seized by paralysis and the next day was carried to a boat and taken to Walls, where he died, as the result, it was said, of Willie's witchcraft. The money was never paid.

Another of her descendants was much in demand as a cow doctor. If a cow fell ill it was thought that the trows had smitten her, although it as not wise to say so—the recognised phrase being that she had "gotten an ill air." The healer would then feel the cow all over to find the places where the arrows of the trows had entered and would rub tar on the spots. Then he would bring sunna—a certain kind of coarse grass—from the Kame, and when it was dried would whip it up with salt and soot and light it under the cow's nose, meantime telling the trows to go away to the horses of Vaila and not trouble the Foula cows. This kind of mild witchcraft was of course not peculiar to Shetland.

One of Jean Jack's sons lived in Mogil and used to steal the corn from the mill above. One night he set a sack of corn on the dyke and attempted to raise it on his shoulders, but the trows held it down. According to another version he was carrying a bundle of his own hay but it was held down by the spirit of a dead girl whom he had wronged. He struggled violently and injured himself seriously. The islanders diagnosed his injury as leprosy, and he was banished to a fealie-house (i.e. house built of sods) outside the Mogil dyke. His friends used to place food for him every day on the top of the dyke. When he died, instead of burying him the people tumbled the house on top of him. Many years afterwards, Sands excavated the place and found the skeleton, of which the bones were black, of a man minus a foot. This he found at some distance from the skeleton, enclosed in a leather bag. He took it to the schoolhouse where he was lodging, and as soon as he fell asleep the room seemed to rock and sway like a ship on the ocean, and was filled with the most unearthly noises, knockings and mutterings. He made repeated attempts to get to sleep, but each time the same thing happened. Eventually in the early morning he got up and replaced the foot, and afterwards was able to sleep soundly.

One of Jean Jack's grandsons was a splendid singer, and used to go round the houses and live eight or ten days in each. Another grandson sailed to Orkney, where an old woman kindly offered him a bowl of milk. Smallpox was raging in Orkney at the time, and the man, it is alleged, "saw the poxes floating in the milk," but rather than hurt the old woman's feelings, he drank the milk and caught the smallpox and gave it to his father. Both of them died.

The last chapter in the story happened a few years ago. The principal descendants of Satan Willie in Foula were a family of the name of Peterson. The habit of changing the names so that a son took the Christian name of his father and added "son" was still common. In this case Satan Willie was Willie Georgeson, and his son would be surnamed Williamson. An unpleasant story was told of old Robbie Peterson, whom I remember as a man of over eighty years, bent double with rheumatism. He and his brother James quarrelled over a woman. They went fowling together to the cliffs. Robbie let his brother down by means of a rope, and when he had landed on a ledge hundreds of feet below Robbie threw the rope down on top of him. Afterwards he boasted of what he had done but nobody dared to report him for fear that he would cast his evil eye upon them and bewitch them.

His brother, Scottie, was a well-spoken, pleasant, but untrustworthy old rogue, and Betty, whom I knew as a fine stately woman still a beauty in spite of her sixty years, was a true descendant of Jean Jack the fair. But she was the terror of the neighbours and when one came near the Hametoun one would often hear her voice in the far distance cursing and swearing. But the sins of the Petersons would fill a volume. The younger brother and sister treated the elder brother abominably and if rumour may be trusted, they left him to lie naked in the ashes by the fireside till he died, as he had done with his own mother. They were the filthiest people that I ever saw and it needed great courage to enter the house. On one occasion a calf died in the byre, which was really part of the house, and they left it to rot without removing the body. Truly they were a terrible family, and the Devil's curse had not failed. Not very long after Robert, Scottie died also and there were not wanting those to say that it was a judgment for the treatment of his brother, who in his turn had allowed his mother to died of neglect.

So Betty was left alone and Betty refused to pay any rent. But Betty prospered. Betty had twelve kye, the best kye in the isle and more than anybody else. How Betty fed her kye in the winter nobody knew. Perhaps it was the Devil, but whether he brought their food himself or sent Betty for it to her neighbours' houses in the night, nobody knew. Betty hocked away the green, and Betty swore and Betty drove away the neighbours' sheep and Betty cursed and Betty prospered. I could see no reason why Betty should pay no rent as she was better off than her neighbours, but Betty always said she had no money. I suggested one of the kye but Betty was obdurate. I am a long-suffering person but after several years I said to Betty, "Give me a cow for the rent or I will sell the lot." Betty first said she would, and then said she wouldn't, and finally, *pour encourager les autres*, I called in the law to my aid. When you call the law twenty miles across the sea in a special boat and thirty miles from the county town, it costs many years' rent and is not a profitable proceeding, but it may be worth while in the long run. So the law was invoked and Betty's cows were sold and paid the law-bill. It did not make any difference to me because now she could not pay rent, and it made no difference to Betty because she had made no use of her kye. The only people that benefited were the neighbours, and even they only partially, as Betty's swearing got worse and her voice louder. This went on for many years and then the poor old thing was taken seriously ill while I was in America. No one dared go near her as they were all terrified of her and of the awful house. I am glad to say that towards the end someone summoned up courage and was able to do a little for her during the last few days of her life. If I remember rightly, she was taken out of the house first. But even when she was buried no one could be persuaded to enter the horrible house, and so finally one night it was set on fire, and with the flames rising into the darkness the Devil's curse on Satan Willie and his descendants came to an end.

## JEAN JACK

### Part One—Satan

In Papa Stour ayont the Sound
    There dwelt a carl [country-man] lang syne
And he met a stranger at the grind [gate],
    When driving hame the kine.

"Oh, are ye come frae Scalloway,
    Or cam ye owre the sea?
Oh, are ye come frae Norroway,
    Or whatna mon be ye?"

"I dinna come frae Scalloway,
      Nor yet frae owre the sea;
But I come frae a place ye need na spier [enquire]
      And that's a far countree."

The stranger's face was lean and dark
      And he was tall and thin.
"What wad ye, Willie Georgeson, gie,
      Gin [if] riches ye suld win?"

"Oh I wad gie ye a' the kye [cows]
      Whilk I am driving in,
And I wad gie ma muckle [great] strength,
      Gin siller [money] I micht win."

"It's you may keep your kye, Willie,
      And you may keep your strength,
It's you may keep a' things ye hae [have]
      For a' your life's hale [whole] length.

"But gin ye sell your saule [soul], Willie,
      And gie your hand forbye [as well],
Ye'll live as easy as the Laird";
      And Willie answered:—"Aye."

Sae Willie rase upo' the morn,
      And tak his spade i' hand;
And o' the tap he hung his coat,
      And set it i' the land.

"Noo, Wife, I'm faring owre the Sound,
      And ye maun del' [delve] your lane;
And when I've sold oor bonnie quirks [heifers],
      Ye'll see me hame again."

At the first step that Willie tak
    The spade began tae lift,
At the neist [next] step that Willie tak
    The soil began tae shift.

He hadna gaen a league, a league,
    A league, but barely three,
When the spade had del'd the langest rig [ridge]
    As fairly as micht be.

And wife and spade together del'd,
    And Willie wandered wide;
And the Deil's luck and the Deil's aid
    Were ever at his side.

The quirks they made gude money
    And Willie sune cam hame:
Nae mair they ca'd him Willie,
    But "Satan" was his name.

They cursed him and his bairnies;
    But Willie gied na heed;
And the folks' curse and the Deil's weird [fate]
    Were waiting when he deid.

The Deil kept his bargain;
    For the Deil well may bide.
But the weird his bairnies' bairns maun dree [endure]
    Can ne'er be satisfied.

## PART TWO—THE BLUIDY HEID

Geordie was Satan Willie's son,
    And Geordie's son was Will;
And the curse fell on young Willie
    Tae work him muckle ill

The curse it fell on Willie;
    And an ill-faured [ugly] mon was he;
    And he left the Isle o' Papa,
A wanderer tae be.

He left the Isle o' Papa
    And on the mainland dwelled;
He left the Isle o' Papa,
    And cam tae bide at Skeld.
It fell upon a Lammas-tide,
    And a gey [very] hot day 'twas then,
When Willie wi' a kishie [basket carried on the back]
    Was ganging by hissen.

He cam til Hesten Setter,
    And saw a maiden fair,
Wi' eyes as true as they were blue
    And bonnie flaxen hair.

Jean Jack was tall and stately
    And a comely maid was she;
And a man micht gang a thousand mile
    A comelier lass tae see.

And Willie, he was wearie
    And the maiden she looked kind;
And Willie, he was thirsty
    And the maiden tae his mind.

Then oot and spak young Willie,
    And fair and saft spak he,
"Gin ye've ony bricht well-water,
    Hae ye ony drink for me?"

"Oh, I hae bricht well-water;
    And I will tak ye ben [inside the house];
And it's I will dra' the water
    And bring it ye masen [myself]."

He set his kishie by the door,
    And sat him doun inside;
And Jean, she brocht the water hame
    And the kishie there espied.

She keekit [peeped] i' the kishie
    And I wat she keek't wi' dreid [dread];
For, streakit owre wi' gouts o' blude,
    She saw a deid man's heid.

She keekit i' the kishie,
    And, oh, she trembled sair;
And the luke that then cam owre her face,
    It never left it mair.

She's taen a step ayont the door,
    And like a queen she stands,
Wi' the licht upo' her pale, pale face,
    And the water i' her hands.

"O be ye some rank reiver [thief]
    That's slain a man i' strife;
Or is it some foul warlock's [sorcerer] heid
    Tae charm awa' my life?"

"I am na a base reiver,
    That's slain a man i' strife,
And gin it be a warlock's heid,
    It's na tae take your life.

It's Barsey Reid's, the murderer
    And a warlock eik [to add to] belike,
That I maun tak frae Scalloway
    Tae set upo' a pike.

For Barsey Reid went oot ae nicht
    And I wat a spade had he;
And on the way tae Lerwick
    He found his enemy.

Agin the mune gaed Gibbie Law,
    And Gibbie walked his lane [alone],
But never yet by sun or mune
    Was Gibbie seen again.

A spade's a gruesome weapon
    That serves a double end;
And when the dying shrieks are owre
    The spade's a canny friend.

But ye're a bonnie lassie,
    As ever tak ma eyne,
And ye're the bonnie lassie
    That I wad hae for mine.

But Jean she was gey frichted,
    And begged him gang his gait;
And I trow—tae wed a mon like yon
    Wad be nae lichtsome fate.

Sae Willie drank the water,
    And Willie tak the road;
And Willie aye turned back tae luke
    Where bonnie Jean abode.

And aft he cam and spiered her,
    And aft she said him Nay;
And aft he cam, but when he cam
    He had na lang tae stay.

But Willie lo'ed the lassie,
    And Willie was na blate [shy],
And thocht him of a plan; and Jean
    She had na lang tae wait.

For Jean i' kirk was sitting
    A-folding her white hands,
And heard the parish minister
    A-reading o' the banns.

The first names that the gude man read
    Were names that she kenned well,
The second names the gude man read
    Were Willie and hersel.

She blushed a bonnie crimson
    As richest roses reid;
And I wat she was the bonniest flooer
    Frae Unst tse Fitful Heid.

And when the folk cam oot o' kirk
    They ane and a' did say
It was a maist wanchancie [unlucky] thing
    For ony mon tae dae.

"There is na use i' fechting [fighting],
    There is na use or need;
For sic a mon as Willie
    Wad get me were I deid."

Sae Jean and Willie married
    An unco [strange] pair tae see;
For his face was foul as hers was fair,
    But he lo'ed her loyally.

There was na hoose tae gang til,
    And nane wad gie them hame;
Sae they fled awa til Fughley
    Across the angry faem.

PART THREE—THE BRUNT HOUSE (*Unfinished*)

Jean Jack, she had the fairest face
    Of a' in Foula's Isle.
Jean Jack, she had the bonniest face
    That micht a man beguile.

O cherry, cherry were her lips
    And her eyne were pools o' blue;
But a haunted look was in her gaze
    And sadness in her mou [mouth].

She stepped sae lichtly doun the brae,
    And drave her milking coo;
And the lads, tae see the bonnie wife,
    Cam keekin roond the kru [stone enclosure].

Tae Biggins wi' the coo she cam,
    And a richt gude coo was she;
And there she found the Biggins wife,
    A-greetin [weeping] waefully.

"Ma croodlin doo [cooing dove], ma moutie wean [tiny child],
    I hae na milk tae gie;
And toom [empty] will be the weary warld
    Gin ye should flee frae me.

Gin ye should flee frae me, ma hairt,
    Tae the kirk abune [above] the wave,
Twad nae be lang or I should be
    Beside your peerie [little] grave."

Jean Jack, she spak the Biggins wife:
    "Noo dinna greet sae sair;
For I hae brocht a milkin coo,
    That ye may want nae mair.

'Twas ye that gave me hairth and hame,
    When we fled owre the sea,
And o' the mnir [moor], where nae mon cared,
    Were like enough tae dee.

'Twas ye that gave us hairth and hame,
    When we oorsels had nane:
'Tis I will gie ye what I can,
    Noo that we hae oor ain."

The bairnie o' the Biggins wife,
　　It sune grew well and strong;
And Jean, wha gave it a' she had
　　Will be remembered lang.

And Jean Jack hersel had weans;
　　And they were braw and fine;
But they maun drain the De'il's cup
　　That Willie filled lang syne.

O Jean Jack, O Jean Jack,
　　For a' your bonnie face,
The curse can only work its weird
　　And follow a' your race.

O Jean Jack, O Jean Jack,
　　For a' your lovin' hairt,
The curse can only work its weird,
　　Or ever it depairt.

O Jean Jack, O Jean Jack,
　　Your grave is bleak and cauld;
The curse could only work its weird
　　Until the tale was tauld.

## ELLEN WALTERSON, THE WITCH

This romantic and weirdly beautiful island with its stupendous cliffs dropping sheer into the wild North Atlantic might have been created as a background for strange legends and uncanny tales; and the awful incidents of death by treacherous sea and perilous crag seem almost inevitably to be coloured by a supernatural atmosphere.

The Sneck o' the Smallie—that gloomy chasm some two hundred feet deep, always with some dead creature lying in it—is a particularly eerie spot "full of mutterings." The ballad of Ellen Walterson is nothing but a bare record of facts, often in the actual words handed down—a point in which the islanders are meticulously particular. Ellen's callous phrase, for instance, of over a hundred years ago, when she married her second husband, "to cast him in the jaws of the old debt" is probably verbatim. The only slight departure from the facts is that the nine cows did not all perish in the Smallie but died in various ways.

It may be noted that there were no surnames in the island until quite recently. Thomas Manson, therefore, means Thomas son of Magnus. Magnus was the son of Andrew, hence he was Magnus Anderson. This, as may be imagined, complicates the task of the pedigree-hunter. The same form is used for the daughter. Bessie Manson was daughter of Magnus.

Ellen Walterson was a witch and was proud of it. She came from Dale on the Mainland to marry Peter Jamieson, and they lived in Breckins, which lies between Quinister and Broadfoot. Her husband died leaving her with five small children to feed. There was then little or no money in the place and the staple diet was fish, fresh or salt, including the cod-livers. There was usually plenty of milk, and potatoes for part of the year. Meal was apt to be very scarce. Fish was bartered to the curers in exchange for goods, frequently maize meal and not much of that. One man told me that when he was a boy he and his brothers were given each morning a little cake weighing perhaps two or three ounces which had to last them the day, and there was always the question whether to "eat your cake or keep it." In spite of this (or was it because of it?) the family grew up exceptionally big and strong.

A household without at least one man at the fishing was very hard hit indeed, and to save her five children from starvation Ellen killed her best cow and set it in the cellar to be salted. During the night someone came and stole the whole of it. Such a peculiarly heartless theft is so foreign to the spirit of the Foula folk that I find myself wondering whether it might not have been the trows (rats there are none)! The needs of the poorer members of the little community were felt to be the responsibility of all, and everyone contributed according to his ability to a common "screw" of corn for fodder, from which anyone in dire distress might help himself after, but not until, the bonxies had returned to the isle for it was in the early summer that the pinch was felt and the cattle grew weak for want of food. There was a belief that at Christmas the well would run wine for anyone who had done good to his neighbours by stealth so that even the recipient did not know of the kindly deed.

Poor Ellen cursed the thief and hoped that "the hand that did it would bear trouble," for she was "a bad-praying, tainted sorceress." She suspected James Christie, so she cast the evil eye on him, and his wife Bessie fell ill with white swelling in her knee. They took her to Papa Stour to try and find a cure, but it could not be bettered so they brought her home again, and she grew unruly and used to abuse her husband as the cause of her trouble.

Now Bessie had a brother Thomas in Broadfoot, the next croft to Breckins, and Ellen said to his wife, "You need not be so proud of your fine croft for within two years my sons will be in it." Soon afterwards their son Magnus was putting out the kye when one of the beasts started like mad and in spite of all efforts to stop her tore along the valley of the Daal and rushed clean over into the Sneck of the Smallie. Later another did the same, and that year every one of their nine cows died from one cause or another, so that they had to give up their croft, and within the two years Ellen's sons moved in. Next the curse passed from the cows to the sons.

About Lammas the Foula boys were in the habit of going to the cliffs to kill puffins for food. They used to cover up their clothes with sheepskins so as to be able to creep up to the birds and knock them down with a stick. Three of the sons of Thomas were fawling above the Smallie when the youngest, who had skins over his knees, slipped on the hillside and slid down into the Sneck and was killed. Not long after the other two boys went to look for driftwood and never returned. It was thought that the sea took them, but some weeks later a piece of an old wreck drifted ashore on the Mainland and on it were the bodies of the two boys. The son Magnus, grew to manhood and went to the Greenland whaling. An English frigate came and pressed him for the navy. He went off and dressed himself in his best clothes and walked on board the man o' war without uttering a word to anybody. He became a petty officer and was stationed in the West Indies, where he died of fever.

When Ellen was an old woman her little three-year-old grandchild died. Ellen took the body on her lap and rocked it and wept over it saying: "Alas, she's gaen where I can never be."


## ELLEN WALTERSON

### A Ballad

Are ye sleeping i' the kirkyard, Ellen Walterson,
    Are ye sleeping by the shore?
Are the flans [whirlwinds] a'howling round ye, Ellen
  Walterson?
    Dae ye hear the great tides roar?

It is nigh upo' the day twa hunder year agane [ago]
    When ye were born, I ken [know],
And ye cam fra' Dale tae marry Peter Jamieson;
    And a douce [sober] lass were ye then.

And wi' Peter ye were living by the burnieside,
 I' the Breckins, a' folk say,
And the Breckins tae the So'th'ard marched wi' [was bounded
by] Quinister,
 And tae Nor'ard Braidfoot lay.

But a witch it was, they thocht ye, Ellen Walterson,
 And ye thocht the like yoursel;
And it cou'dna be but sorrow's dool [grief] and travailing
 On the lang mirk [dark] road tae hell.

They ca'ed ye a bad-praying tainted sorceress;
 Yet I doubt they had na need;
But, alas, your puir mon died and left ye penniless
 Wi' five young weans [small children] tae feed.

Syne [Then] the winter cam a skirling doun by Helliberg
 And ye hadna food tae eat;
And ye killed the best o' a' your kye [cows] and saltit it
 For a muckle tub o' meat.

And a body i' the necht he reived [robbed] the hale [whole o'
it];
 And ye were angered sair [sore];
Sae ye cursed the hand that carried it away frae ye,
 That tribble [trouble] it suld [should] bear.

Jamie Christie was the mon wham ye jaloused [guessed it was]
 Bessie Hanson was his bride;
And her brither, Thomas, son o' Magnus Anderson,
 At the Braidfoot used tae bide.

Nor was it lang ere Bessie kenned the curse that fell
 Wi' "white swelling" i' her knee;

And they took her owre til Papa Stour tae better it;
    But it cou'dna bettered be.

And Bessie grew unruly and abused her mon [man, husband];
    And I wat he was sair tried;
But they rowed the fey [doomed to death] wife hame again til
    Fughley Isle
And she cam til [til = to, generally of motion] her deith and died.

Maun [must] ye never gie forgiveness, Ellen Walterson,
    Cou'dna your vengeance cease?
Did the ghaist [ghost] o' Bessie Christie never visit ye,
    Cou'd your ain saule [soul] rest in peace?

O fie upo' ye ever, Ellen Walterson,
    For the neist [next] ill curse ye laid;
When ye envied Bessie's brither his prosperity
    And the braw fine [brave splendid farm] he made.

What gar'd ye tell his wife she need na pride hersel
    O' the Braidfoot's bonnie land,
For there wad na be a second year afore it cam
    Into ane o' your sons' hands.

It fell upo' a day, that Walter, Thomas' son,
    Was a-putting oot the kye,
And that ane o' them went mad, nor could he quiet her
    Howsoever he micht try.

And she ran as though the devil were pursuing her
    Til the Smallie by the Sneck;
And they found her lying fa'en frae the craigs abune [crags
above]
    As a mangled lifeless wreck.

Syne anither and anither followed after her,
    And they gaed the selfsame gait [went the same road]
And still ye had na pity, Ellen Walterson,
    When the ninth had dreed [endured] its fate.

O, the Smallie, it is in the Wick o' Mucklaberg,
    Where the great cliffs touch the sky;
And the chasm o' the Sneck is full o' mutterings
    When the trows [ghosts, evil spirits] gae riding by.

And the chasm o' the Sneck was full o' mutterings
    When Tam's peerie [little] lad was killed;
For he tumblit frae the Smallie into naithingness
    As your evil thochts had willed.

And the wailing o' his spirit micht hae chastened ye,
    As ye couched aside the fire;
But your son was into Braidfoot after Martinmas,
    And ye had your hairt's desire.

Did ye wonder what had happened, Ellen Walterson?
    O I trow ye did na spier [ask],
When the laddies oot at Ruscar cam na hame again
    And poir Tam was crazed wi' fear.

They had gaen away for driftwood over Sukkimires;
    And the wearie weeks gaed past
Til they found the bairnies' bodies thirty mile awa,
    And they brocht them hame at last.

And Thomas had ae son ca'ed Magnus left tae him,
    Wha was on the Greenland sea;
But they pressed him for the navy, Ellen Walterson,
    And he died in a far countree.

What said ye, when ye married Andrew Jamieson,
     In the words remembered yet?—
That ye'd tak him and wad cast him, Ellen Walterson,
     I' the jaws o' the auld debt.

When the shadow o' the end was drawing nigh tae ye,
     And yoursel were auld and grey,
Ye were greeting [weeping] at the death o' the wee lassockie,
     Wha had gaen afore her day.

As ye held your peerie grandchild and ye rockit her
     Wha had reached the heavens hie [hie is pronounced
hee],
"Alas," ye wept, "She's gaen" (Puir Ellen Walterson!)
     "Where I can never be."

O, the Smallie, it is in the Wick o' Mucklaberg,
     And the curse o' death is nigh,
And the chasm o' the Sneck is full o' mutterings
     When the trows gae riding by.

Are ye sleeping i' the kirkyard, Ellen Walterson,
     Are ye sleeping evermore?
Is the lang necht a' around ye, Ellen Walterson,
     Do ye hear the black roost [tide race] roar?

# 7
# THE GRAYS' SAGA

[It was the intention of Professor Holbourn to write a history of every family in the isle. That the Grays are the only ones treated in any detail is not because they were any more interesting than say, the Ratters or Mansons, but because John Gray was the keeper of the shop, which adjoins the Ha', and on many a wet afternoon, if there were no customens in the shop, the laird would slip in with book and pen, while, instead of meal and sugar, old-time yarns were passed across the counter.]

MCSH

The family of Gray, or Grey, is said to be descended from Earl Grey, brother of Lady Jane. He came to Shetland with Patrick Stewart and was his partner in the building of Scalloway Castle, escaping to Denmark when Patrick was captured. There were three brothers of the same family from whom all the Grays in Shetland are descended. They settled in Burrafjord, Bressay and Scalloway respectively. There is said to be £2 million in chancery belonging to the family.

John Gray in Burns used to work in Scalloway. "I was lodging with my sister Betty," he said to the writer, "who was married with John Manson. I came in for my dinner one day and a gentleman was sitting on a chair in the house and Betty turned round to me and said, 'John, here is a gentleman from London asking about the Grays, for there is money lying in London in chancery for them.' Lady Jane Grey was crowned queen and the earl was a brother of hers. The Greys came across from Normandy with William the Conqueror—they were in his army. The earl escaped to Denmark in a vessel, 'and,' said the gentleman, 'we have a lineage straight from them to you here. But what became of the earl? That is where the link is broken. We cannot trace him for he assumed a different name' (and the man from London had a big book on his knee the same as you do)."

The Grays were renowned for their strength. There are two stories of a Thomas Gray, who lived on the mainland. On one occasion he met a biting pig and tore its jaws asunder with his hands. He had six sons. There was a great stone in Setter, where they lived, and the sons could not lift it so the old man Thomas, who was on his death-bed, got up and said, "Boys, flit awa'," and he lifted the stone and laid it upon the yard dyke, remarking, "Well, boys, is this what ye have been working at and could mak' naething o'?" Laurence Gray, one of the six sons, was put into Foula by the laird father of Old Scott of Melby, to be a blacksmith and to make clogs and also nails for the Ha' which was to be built on the ayre of Ham.

The following was taken down from John Gray in Burns, told to him by an old man whose grandfather witnessed the incident.

There was a man in Scalloway of the name of John Gray who went to the whale fishing when Scalloway was still the capital of Shetland. There were two ships came into Scalloway to engage hands, one of whom was this John Gray, who was noted for his strength. The captains of the two ships were ashore in a public house and they were a good bit acquainted with each other. Each man began to brag of his crew. John's captain said that he had a man on board who could take on the whole crew of the other ship. The other captain replied that he had a trained fighter on board who would be a match for anyone. A wager was struck and a boat was sent to the ship to tell John Gray to come ashore and speak to his captain; when he came ashore the captain told him that he wanted him to fight the man who was in the other ship, because he had made a bet with the captain that John would beat him. Gray was very much against it. He, said he had no ill will to the man and did not want to fight him. However, they both stripped. The other man was an Englishman. He offered to shake hands with Gray as a pledge that no unfair advantage should be taken on either side. They fought in the road and at the first engagement the Englishman struck Gray on the head with the heel of his boot and knocked him insensible. His side tried to restore him and he recovered and sat in the road. "Well," said he, "you have taken advantage of our agreement. I am down but I am not done. I want another round with you." As they prepared to strike, Gray shouted, "Look out for yourself!" and drove his fist through the man's side, and took out his bowels on the street. They buried him in Upper Scalloway. Gray was so strong that he lifted the anchor of the ship and put it on the quarter-deck, and it took twelve men to carry it forward.

Laurence Gray, the blacksmith, who lived in Ljorabeck, had a son John who married Lily Henry in Guttern, granddaughter of Jean Jack. The wedding was held in Guttern on a fine summer evening, and during the festivities while the fiddler was playing his bridge kept falling down. He set it up three times and then refused to play any more as he regarded this as an ill omen. Just at that time two lads were fishing at the eila at the back of the

Noup when their boat overturned and they were drowned.

As a young man John Gray acted as Congregational minister. When over seventy a new baby, James Gray, was brought to see him. He was drinking a cup of tea preparatory to setting out for the Meeting House, but died before finishing the cup. Until recently there was a chair in Dykes with the date 1744, thought to be the date of John's birth or possibly that of his wife, Janet Umphrey. I bought the chair, which was washed and put outside to dry, but unfortunately a gale came and broke it to pieces.

John Gray had six sons, one of whom, Walter, was a skipper of a schooner that fished for "Old Melby," and another, Henry, a captain, who eventually was drowned. Three of the other sons, John, Laurence and James, remained in Foula. The first assisted his father to break out the Stoel Croft and the family has lived there ever since; James broke out the Springs and was succeeded by his son John, a fine old man who was in the mail-boat when the writer was a young man. He was a very fine singer and to him we are indebted for some fragments of songs, especially the New Year song. His son Andrew is the biggest man in the island. Laurence broke out the Loch tun, draining the loch, which was the largest in the island, by cutting the channel at the north end which his son Laurence blasted with powder and gradually deepened.

Laurence Gray, who broke out the Loch tun, came to a tragic end, as has so often been the case in Foula families where men followed the perilous occupations of the sea and fowling on the cliffs. Accounts of the disaster differ, but I give the tale as it was told me by a member of the family. There was at the Loch a party of kamers (i.e. women engaged in combing the wool preparatory to spinning). The men went cut to fish for sillocks from the banks. James, the eldest son, put his poke (net) into the water and brought up three sillocks. He shook the poke and said, "Father, let us gang awa' hame to the kamers for we're daeing naething here." His father said, "Put thy poke back into the sea, boy. Three sillocks this time and it may be three score neist." "Oh, if you say that, well be it done." He put down the poke again and there came a great mountain of sea. He was slightly built and was not strong enough to hold the poke and allowed himself to be dragged down with it into the sea. His father leant over and hooked his fingers in those of the boy and slipped in and disappeared. Another brother was standing high up on the skerry and he ran down the slope and jumped in where the others had disappeared and never came up at all. Yet another brother was standing clad in oilskins, which he proceeded to tear off preparatory to jumping in, when a friend restrained him with the words—"Three gone and wilt thou make a fourth?" So the brother and his friend had to go home and break the news to the mother that "her man and two sons were in another world."

"Now they speak about ghosts and things like that," continued the narrator. "There was an aunt who lived in another house on the other side of the road, and there came a great back rattling at the door. She rose and ran forth and looked and said to her husband, 'Johnny, the men have been no time at the fishing. I hear them coming down to the house, and they seem to be disputing about something for I hear Laurie's voice speaking very high.'" Two other people saw the men walking over the green towards their house after they had been drowned. One of the observers followed them towards the house and saw a figure lean a poke against the door, then pass round the gable end, but on coming round the gable end himself he found there was nobody there.

The disaster took place at Yuletide. The Grays had been in the habit of going round the island guising, dressed in coats of straw and one with a headdress representing a horse, who carried a bag in which to collect victuals. They sang the New Year song (to be quoted later), but after this disaster the custom was discontinued.

On another occasion a somewhat similar apparition was seen by Thomas Gray in Stoel, whom I remember as a gentle old man. He had been at the fishing for three summers with a certain John Leslie on the mainland. The latter used to take with him an orphan child whom they called Moutie (tiny). When the fishing was over Thomas Gray came back to the island, and one night he was coming home in the moonlight and there came on a "caavie shoor" (driving snow) and he saw two people walking in front of him, and nearly overtook them. He recognised the old man and the boy with whom he had been fishing during the summer. They went down the road before him to his house but instead of entering went round the gable end. He followed round the corner but found no person there and there were no footsteps in the snow. That same night the man and the boy were out fishing and got lost in the snowstorm. Their boat came ashore just below their house. When found both were dead. The boy had jumped ashore and killed himself on the rocks. The old man was sitting under a cairn with his knees drawn up as though waiting for rescue. They were very poor and the child was thinly clad with bare legs and feet and bare head. Moutie had a brother who was adopted by another old man and was afterwards heard of in America.

The eldest son of Laurence Gray of the Loch, who was drowned, had a romantic history. As a young man he and a chum were persuaded to go south to work on the Granton pier which was then being built. His father did not approve but at last consented and gave the boy thirty shillings for his expenses. The two lads went together to Lerwick, but while they were moving about in the crowd John's money disappeared. His friends advised him to go back to Foula, but he declared that he would never do that. The navy was recruiting in Lerwick at the time and by giving his age as three years older than he was Gray was able to enlist. Two years later a certain ship was becalmed off the isle on the North shoals, and the crew asked some of the Foula men who were out fishing if they could supply them with green vegetables. As the Foula men returned after fetching the vegetables and approached the ship they noticed a man leaning over the side and gazing at them very intently. Jamie Gray in Dykes looked up and exclaimed, "Good Father! It's Johnnie o' the Loch." (The Roman Catholic expression "Good Father" still survives in Foula). The man hastily drew back and disappeared. As they drew away from the ship after delivering the vegetables a man on the jibboom waved his hat to them three times and they all recognised him. When this story was told to me there was a silence and then one of John's nieces remarked in a shocked voice, "My! You was an awfu' thing t' dae." "What was?" I enquired. "To speak to the poor boy like that. If they had spoken with him civilly—"My! It was awfu'." "But the man was so surprised to see him," I ventured, "He did not stop to think what he was saying. "But the girl shook her head with a gesture which implied that there could be no extenuating circumstances in a case of such shocking breach of manners.

The Foula people never saw John Gray again but it was heard that he was in America and had married an American. Not long ago his brother, Laurence Gray, who succeeded Magnus Manson as skipper of the mail-boat, spoke to a man who had returned to Walls after many years in business in Edinburgh, who told him that he was "well acquent" with a Foula man who had lived in Portobello and died when well over ninety. It proved to be the same John Gray. This discovery affected his friend deeply. "Let me shake hands with you again, man," he said, "for you are the brother of the best friend I ever had."

This Laurence Gray, the skipper, who was six years old at the time when his father was drowned, was a most kindly, delightful man, an example of the absolute straightness of the typical Foula man, always a courteous and pleasant host, and many is the happy hour I have spent in his house at the Loch.

He died at a very old age sailing the mail-boat up to the end. He is one of the men I count it an honour to have known.

The second son of Laurence Gray the blacksmith moved with his family to Dykes. This was the school-teacher's house, built in 1841, and at that time the best in the island. The little school itself, which superseded the school at Northerhouse where Norse was taught when the Danes owned the island, is now one of the outbuildings of the Dykes. Magnus had a son, Thomas, who intended to go to Greenland to the whale fishing, and set out along with another Foula man for that purpose. In Walls they met that formidable but not altogether heartless tyrant, Old Melby. He asked them "Whither bound?", and on being told their intention replied with, no doubt, an eye to the profits of the cod fishing on the Foula shaalds, "If you go you shall never more delve my ground." "I think he did nae geng," my informant dryly concluded. Possibly Thomas' decision was unwise for he died as an old man in debt, which was inherited by his son, John in the Burns, who paid off seven pounds of it. No young man was allowed to leave the island without the laird's permission.

Thomas Gray and Laurence Ratter were the first Congregationalists in the isle and they went together to Lerwick to sign the documents relating to the gift of the Baxter Chapel.

In view of the £2 million in chancery, it is a pathetic fact that part at any rate of the Gray family have experienced great hardship and poverty in days gone by, though probably not more so than many another Foula family. John Gray, for example, who broke out the Stoel Croft, was a very hard worker as well as a strong man, but they were greatly kept down. It was in the days before the Truck Acts were passed and great hardship was experienced through unfairness in this method of barter. The Grays would land a "great power of fish" upon the ayre (i.e. beach) and would go away. The man in the shop would then weigh it and mark it down, and they never knew if it was right or wrong. Then they would come to buy things from the shop, and he would mark them down also. At the end of the year he would read over the account to them but they were unable to understand his figures, and it never appeared that there was any money due to them. If they appeared to be owing for anything the merchant would refuse to give them any goods except half a lispund of meal a week, and so they had a very bad time for they seemed to be always in debt. When they sold cattle what they got in return was "just nonsense." They had to take what they were given, and there was no appeal. What they sold was always cheap, and what they bought was always dear. Sands, the archaeologist, championed the cause of the islanders. He used to go into the shop and when asked if he wanted anything he would reply politely, "No, no, I am in no hurry. Serve the others first." No one suspected that all the time he was keeping an eye open and noting down the various transactions. He found that he was charged less for goods than the islanders were. He worked to procure a boat-load of goods for the islanders, but the minister, who one regrets to record was hand in glove with the merchant and fishcurer, said he would "put a pin before his nose" to stop him. Sands wrote to the papers and composed "most horrid" verses about them. When the merchant received a stack of these papers someone asked why he did not stop them. "Because we cannot deny a single word," he replied. "Yes," said Sands, "I sail close but I never strike."

The following verses by Mr Sands are still quoted by the Foula people and show the extent to which he had their cause at heart.

> In Vaila Isle* I now reside,
>     A pleasant dwelling place to me,
> And far across the azure tide,

---

*An island in the Sound of Walls.

The peaks o' Foula I can see,
Which seem to say whene'er I look
"Perform the task you undertook."

In all our houses you have been,
    You ate our bread, you shared our cup,
Our joys and sorrows you have seen,
    You know the wounds we cover up.
Oh! speak for us; we dare not speak
    Lest those in power their vengeance wreak.

Put not your trust in parliament;
    Many may suffer e'er it save;
But shout until the heavens are rent
    That Foula sits a fettered slave
Chained to the oar and kept in tears,
While " Truck," the pirate, domineers.

Agitation grew so strong that a commission was set up to
investigate matters. Even then many of the islanders were too
frightened to speak plainly. One man declared that he owed
everything to the fishcurer, for if it had not been for the latter he
would not have been alive. The commissioner, with double
meaning, called him a "poor indebted slave" and this encouraged
the man to reveal facts without realising that he was doing so.
Eventually the "Truck" Acts were passed, prohibiting the
bartering of goods.

8

# THE HEALING WATER OF THE SNEUG
(By MCSH. Reprinted by kind permission of
*The Edinburgh Evening Dispatch*)

In the remote island of Foula, just below the summit of the highest hill—the Sneug—hidden away beneath a projecting shelf of rock, lies a small basin, hollowed in stone by water slowly dripping from the rock above. It is a feeble little trickle, dry in hot weather, yet it has restored to health many whose condition had been regarded as hopeless. A century ago its existence was unknown and unsuspected; it was a secret held by the brooding, sphink-like Sneug, to be revealed by the dream of an island youth living in one of the little group of crofts still to be seen far down in the valley below.

About the year 1836 a boat set out from the island of Foula for the mainland of Shetland, twenty miles distant. A gale sprang up, both wind and tide were adverse, and the strength of the rowers was taxed to the utmost. One man, rowing on the weather side, was constantly drenched by the spray. When land was reached at last, he was so exhausted by hard rowing and exposure to wind and wet that he fell ill and developed the dreaded complaint known as the king's evil, called locally "the cruels," a scrofulous disease which may attack any part of the body in the form of suppurating sores.

The man was brought back to the island and carried to his

home. The waist, in this case, was the seat of the trouble, and it became tremendously swollen. No less than forty-two ulcers appeared at one time, and, when they broke, the discharge soaked a pair of blankets. So wasted was the sufferer that, although he had been an exceptionally big man, his wife could lift him in his bed like an infant. It must have been a sad time for the little family, from the eldest, a girl of twelve, to the baby boy just "creeping upon the floor," to say nothing of the poor mother, whose husband, her sole support, lay helpless, beyond all hope, at the early age of thirty-six.

In a neighbouring house lived one whom the writer remembers as an old man, then "a muckle boy." One day this youth came in and announced that he had had a strange dream. A vision of the sufferer's dead mother had appeared to him and said that, if he would stand at the door of his cottage and look to the top of the Sneug, he could, by taking certain "medes," or landmarks, see the position of a spring whose waters would heal his unfortunate neighbour.

The boy was received with laughter. In an island where every boulder and rock is known and every change noted, how could there be an undiscovered well; or how could pure water heal such a dreadful ailment? He went away abashed, but next night the dream was repeated, and he became so troubled that he was unable to sleep. The third night the vision again returned, but this time in a threatening mood. If he would not do as he was bidden "it would be the worse for him." The youth resolved to obey, and immediately peace returned to him and he fell asleep.

Next morning he set out for the Sneug, accompanied by the twelve-year-old daughter of the sick man. Following the directions given in the dream, they found the well without difficulty, although it is by no means easy to discover. One can imagine the joy with which the children filled their vessel with the precious fluid that was to restore health and hope to one who had suffered so sorely and so long. The grateful man washed his sores, and drank freely of the water. Soon his condition showed signs of improvement, and before long he was restored to his former vigorous health. He died at the age of eighty-five, leaving a numerous and healthy family.

Since then scarcely a year passes without some cure being effected by the healing water—often to the surprise of the medical attendants, for (as one of these significantly remarked to me last year), "We have been accustomed to regard this disease as incurable."

There is a tradition that the water will lose its efficacy if sold or put to commercial uses, yet there is never any lack of willing volunteers who will climb the Sneug in any weather, to bring aid to those whose only claim is helpless suffering.

Years ago, the duke of Edinburgh visited the isle, and was greatly interested in the story. Finding a spring on one of the cliffs, he declared it to be "pure sulphur," and said that if it were in the south "money would not buy it." He took out a small flask and invited his island attendant to dispose of the contents in order to make room for the water of Foula.

There are some who are anxious to analyse the Sneug water, but those of us who have climbed the rocky heights, where only the muffled roar of distant Atlantic rollers breaks the vast silence of the hills, and have looked far down the valley upon the little group of crofts, where nearly a century ago a youth dreamed dreams of one whose mother-love survived the grave, know that there are forces in the universe which never can be analysed.

# 9

## OUR OWN TIMES

Although I have it on the very best authority that in 1816 Foula was owned by a somewhat mysterious Mr Nicholson, whom I have never heard mentioned in the island, yet it was undoubtedly in the hands of the Scotts at the end of the century. In 1891 a letter appeared in the *Times* on the subject of wild bird preservation, by a firm of Solicitors acting for "Mr Scott, the Proprietor of Foula ... living on the Mainland of Shetland where his main property lies." An extract from the letter reads: "At present although the island pays Police Rates it has no policeman, although it pays tithes or stipend it is but rarely visited by the clergyman, and although it pays Road Rates there are no properly constructed roads on it." It might have added that although it paid rents it was seldom visited by the laird.

Not long after this the isle was purchased by Mr W. Ewing Gilmour, from whom I bought it in the first year of this century. The entire population turned out to welcome me, and I still cherish the address, wrapped in its original biscuit bag, which was presented to me by the Congregational minister on behalf of the islanders. It was a stirring occasion, perhaps for both sides, for it was, as the address states "long since any proprietor of Foula has lifted the light of his countenance on its population.

Such an event may be within the remembrance of the oldest inhabitant, but to the younger members of the community it is a far-off event of which they have only heard or dreamed."

Some fifteen years earlier a road had been made along the centre of the island. The fishing had been a failure that year, and the people had been reduced to a state bordering on destitution. An appeal was made in the south and a considerable sum of money collected. Instead of distributing it in the form of relief the minister of that day called out all the islanders (men, women, and children) to assist in making a road. The idea was a good one, and would have been even better if the route of the road had taken some account of hills and valleys. Hitherto all the peat and even the building stone had been carried on the back in kishies, or large baskets, but now the wheelbarrow came into use although it was still regarded as "a won-chancy machine" given to over-turning on the rough hillside. Remains of the old fealie-houses, with even their "restin' chairs" built of sods, were still in occasional use as byres, but for human habitation they had been superseded by houses of round or roughly squared stone. About this time, however, a regular little spate of building activity set in. There were heated discussions as to who could build the finest, by which is generally meant the "tightest," house—and to keep out the Foula wind and rain is no child's play. The laird started a grand new porch to the Ha', but alas, the war came before it was finished and the laird was left hopelessly behind in the race. Nevertheless the fashion of finely dressed stone was quickly copied and some good building appeared in the isle, particularly in the war memorial, which has been described as "the best in Shetland."

Except in three or four cases the central hearth has now disappeared, although it was almost universal when I first came. This older type of house was usually approached through the byre, and one would be warned against cracking one's skull on the lintel of the low doorway. In the centre of the stamped earth floor was the hearth stone on which a peat fire burned continuously, "smoored" with ash at night and always alight in the morning. The glowing peats were gathered in the middle and in a circle around these the black ones stood on end. A cauldron hung on a chain above the fire and usually there were tempting oatcakes browning on a brandering iron on the hearth. The smoke wandered about the room and eventually found its way out of the two holes in the thatched roof, curing in the course of its passage the strings of fish hung up to dry in preparation for the short days of winter. Ranged around the walls were several box-beds—strange looking erections into which the various members of the household shut themselves for the night. A kist (chest) containing the family treasures, a resting chair or bench, perhaps a small table, a chair and a stool or two completed the furniture, except of course for the spinning wheel by means of which the sacks of wool stored on the roof of the box-beds would be converted into yarn for knitting lace-like shawls to adorn the dainty shoulders of some society lady. In the further wall would be a door leading to the "ben end," where only the most intimate friend could gain admission.

It must not be imagined that these houses were either unpleasant or unhealthy. I know nothing more delightful than to sit in a circle round the glowing peats and watch the smoke wreathing upward, twisting and twining amongst the soot-festooned rafters and lines of drying fish. This ever-rising smoke forms an excellent disinfectant and in the days of the "muckle fever" a patient lay sick of this deadly disease beside the hearth while the rest of the family living on the other side of the fire did not catch the infection. Tudor says that he met no peasantry in the whole of Shetland to equal that of Foula especially as contrasted with the "savage apathy" of the people of Fair Isle!

A wealthy landowner who came to see our hills noticed a little house and wanted to see who lived in it; but Nannie, "a contented old body," was afraid the gentleman could not put up with the reek. "If she can put up with it I can put up with it," he replied. After a long chat he gave her one pound and came away remarking: "That old woman in her little cottage is more contented than I am with all my lands."

A large proportion of the population reach an advanced age. A Foula man living in Scalloway applied for the old-age pension but had forgotten the exact date of his birth. "Never mind," he said, "I will send to Foula and ask my mother, she is sure to remember." And the old soul, busily hoeing her tatties though well over ninety, supplied the desired information. Whether the health and longevity of the islanders has actually deteriorated or not it would be hard to prove, but it has certainly not improved, although it has not suffered through the activities of the sanitary authorities as severely as have other rural districts where the inhabitants of outlying cottages have been, and unfortunately still are being, removed to low-lying crowded villages in order to secure baths and sanitation, with results which the sanitary inspectors themselves regard with astonishment and dismay. Thus progress in its passion for destruction sweeps away not merely the homes of the hill folk but the hardy race itself.

It was my great privilege on one or two occasions to share a meal in one of these old houses, and the grace and dignity with which the simple repast was eaten impressed me very much. A large cod was placed on the little table and there was a cauldron of potatoes in their skins (which, as we all know, is the best way to cook potatoes). The family helped themselves and skinned and boned the fish and skinned the potatoes very neatly and daintily with their fingers. After the meal the mother swept up the remains on the table while the daughter brought round to each in turn a little cauldron filled with warm water in which we dipped our fingers, and those who had beards wiped their mouths, and dried on a towel that was passed round. Afterwards pipes were filled and then came the yarns.

## WEIRD TALES

Did you ever hear tell of the man who was away on the Mainland for a day or two and when he came back to the house he found a lot of women baking? He asked what all the bread was for and they said it was for his daughter's funeral. She had died that day of some kind of fever which had made her go all black. That fever was a bad kind of affair. There were two lassies who died of it, and soon after a man also died. It was the custom then for a "corse-man," as he was called, to sit up with the corpse; for a dead body must never be left alone, or if it was you had to be sure to open a large Bible and lay it on the chest of the corpse. Well, the corse-man and another man were watching the body when the two lassies, or rather their fienis [wraith] came in and sat one on either side of the dead man. Then they smiled at each other and rose and went out . . . though why two women should leave the land of Glory to come and sit beside a corpse is more than I can say. Then there was the man whose wife was dead and streaked in the barn, and the husband went in to fetch a kollie, and the corpse of the wife spoke and said: "What are you seeking?" "I'm seeking the kollie," the man replied; but I think he did not wait to get it.

These tales are told in the most matter of fact manner without any air of mystery. Like the Aurora Borealis or the Will o' the Wisp these things just happen and no explanation is to be expected. The people are not at all fanciful or hysterical—they have no need artificially to inflame their imaginations. Whether what in the Highlands is called "second sight" is a faculty which thrives in lonely islands and hill countries, or whether it is racial I do not know. In Foula it certainly tends to run in families.

Our faithful factor, Lewis Umphray, was a grandson of the discoverer of the Sneug well and he, too, seems to have had this power of pre-vision. When he lay dying two neighbours used to take it in turns to sit up with him. One day, a week or two before his death, they both developed bad colds so stayed away for fear of carrying the infection. The next evening a friend asked Lewis if he had felt very lonely. "No," he said, "I was not lonely for I had plenty of company. The house was full of bairns, playing and running about. You may laugh—I suppose it was a dream, and yet I was wide awake and I saw them as plainly as I see you. There was a bed standing over in that corner and the bairns were playing upon it. They had found a long strip of dark sort of plaid stuff and were playing with this. There was a half grown lass with them and I said to her: "Could you not get a needle and sew the cloth down the centre to make a blanket?" Some months later his brother came to live in the house with a family of young children and a girl in her 'teens. One day a neighbour called in to see them, and when he returned home his old mother asked what the children had been doing. He replied that they had found a long strip of dark cloth and that the girl was sewing it together to make a blanket. A bed was standing exactly where Lewis had indicated.

Less happy is the story of a little boy who went to the school until he was eight years old. Then one day he went out and did not return and was never seen again. That evening his father was walking up and down the banks and was very sorrowful when a voice called from the sea, just once, "Da!" which is the old word for father. The sea was smooth and there was nothing to be seen. His brother, who told me added that "it was just a voice; it was not the child's speaking body."

Some fifty years ago a number of children were playing together near the old kirk. They were building a wee house and wanted a nice flat stone to make the roof. One of them who was a rather reckless boy found a suitable stone on a child's grave and wanted to use this. The others were very distressed and begged him not to touch it, but to tease them he persisted, saying:

"What good is it doing lying there anyway?" He would not listen to their objections but brought the stone and built the roof, leaving a hole to represent the lum. They all crept inside the little house and were playing together when the hand and arm of a little child came down the lum-hole and rested on the boy's shoulder. He was terribly scared and immediately replaced the stone on the child's grave.

The comparatively low ground in the middle of the island—the Manse, Hamnabreck, and Headley Cliff—is said to be haunted. A lassie told me that here she had seen a little old man in moleskins with a kishie on his back about the width of a house in front of her. She tried to overtake him but he kept the same distance from her no matter what she did, stopping when she stood still and hurrying when she ran. She was not at all frightened but thought it strange.

In the far-away past an old woman was murdered near the Manse, and sounds of children wailing have been heard at Headley Cliff not far off. A little distance north of the Manse a small rill passes under the road and on crossing this drain several people have heard a metallic "ping" immediately followed by cries from the direction of Headley Cliff. Before hearing this tale a member of the writer's family had this experience and investigated the contents of her purse to make sure that she had not dropped a shilling. She was startled by the sudden outburst of cries. The Manse itself is haunted by a black dog. On one occasion when the minister's wife was out of the island she left her baby in the care of two island women. They were sitting with the child on the lap of one of them when they saw a huge black dog as big as a calf standing in the room. When they got up to turn it out it vanished through the floor. Just north of the Hamnabreck dyke a black horse appeared to two children and followed them all the way to the Lierabeck gate where it vanished. The children were terrified.

Somewhere hereabouts an old man, now dead, was nearly

throttled by the trows. The men who were with him thought he had been seized with a fit of some kind and supported him, struggling and half-fainting, to the gate into the croft where he at once recovered. The same man rushed into a house and stood in front of the fire trembling and "all in a sweat." When asked what ailed him he said: "Man, they nearly got me that time!" He used to go to the kirkyard to talk to the trows, and one day he said he was bidden to go and speak with his departed cousins. He told the man who went with him to "stand away" so as to be out of ear-shot. His friend could hear the man speaking but heard no replies. He said that the first spirit he met was an old man whom he did not know. He described him and the islanders recognised the description as that of his grandfather. Whatever the explanation, there is no doubt that this man himself genuinely believed that he could communicate with departed spirits. He declared that a ship with a lot of Negroes on board had been wrecked at the foot of the great west cliffs and lost with all hands without the knowledge of the islanders. The drowning men had died cursing the land that had caused the disaster, and their malicious spirits haunted the place trying to work evil; but they were prevented by the fact that there were so many good people living on the island. (May these good people never be so reduced in number as to enable the powers of evil to gain the upper hand!)

Once, at least, this same man seems to have had tangible confirmation of his premonition. In 1833, before the days of the mail-boat, when the island used to be cut off from the Mainland for more than half the year, an island man went to the hills in the early morning and was horrified to see a stranger approaching him. No boat had come to the island and the intruder had appeared over the top of the Uffshins— a vertical cliff crowned by a grass-covered slope as steep as the roof of a house, and reckoned to be unclimbable. One foot was bare and the other clad, and his general appearance was sufficiently unprepossessing to suggest that he had sprung from the nether regions. "Art thou earthly or unearthly?" shouted the islander as soon as the stranger came within ear-shot. In very human language he replied that he was decidedly earthly, and explained that his ship had struck this confounded island and that he alone of all the crew had been able to save himself by climbing out to the end of the bowsprit and jumping ashore as the vessel struck the foot of these barbarous cliffs. The islander took him to his home, and it was then remembered that on the previous day there had been a standing peat in the fire, which indicates the approach of a visitor, and that one of the bairns in a mischievous moment had lifted it with the tongs and, instead of placing it in the heart of the fire to insure a warm welcome, had plunged it into a pail of water. The family, and indeed all the islanders compensated for this chilly welcome by entertaining the shipwrecked man in turn throughout the winter until a boat visited the isle in the spring.

When he heard of the wreck, our friend who talked to the spirits set out for the cliffs on the chance of seeing some remains of the vessel. There was a high wind and driving rain, and as he pressed forward up the steep hillside he was startled by a piercing scream right in his face. He stopped and looked about him but could see nothing. When he reached the summit of the hill which ends abruptly in a precipice the shriek was repeated. It was impossible for any sound to carry from the scene of the wreck hundreds of feet below, but knowing that his aid had been invoked he started to climb down the dangerous cliff. When half way down he paused and peered through the thick misty rain, and seeing nothing decided to turn back. As he did so there rose from the sea below such violent cries that he dared not disregard them. He completed the descent and found the headless body of a man lying in a pool just above the water's edge. "What," I exclaimed, with lamentable lack of imagination, "had the man died in that short time?" "Na," said the narrator, with a pitying glance, "He had been dead for hours. It was his spirit body that was crying out." However they carried him home and buried him, and there were no more screams. When he grew old this poor man was very much troubled by the trows. An old woman went to see him and asked him how he was. He complained that he couldna get sleeping because of the row they made, singing and laughing and shouting and carrying on. "Wheesht man!" said the old woman, "Dinna speak o' sie things. It is only the unholy nonsense of thy ain witless heid." "Ah weel, it's a' very weel for you to talk, but thy ain son is no' the best of them. He's sitting singing 'pon the top o' my bed e'en noo—sing a little louder, boy, so that the visitor can hear thee!"

The trows, by the way, seem fond of music, for a Foula man saw a man in front of him and followed him along the valley of the Daal to Grutfleck—a stony place north of the Sneck of the Smallie—where he disappeared under the ground and there were sounds of music and dancing coming up from below the earth.

The behaviour of peats in the fire was considered significant. If a burning red peat from the fire falls towards you good fortune is coming to you but a smouldering black one foretells disaster unless it is replaced by the person concerned. We have already mentioned that at the wedding of John Gray, the blacksmith's son, the bridge of the fiddle kept falling down, but that is not the whole of the story. There were several weddings in Guttrun that night for a travelling mumster was staying in the isle and a number of young couples seized an opportunity which seemed to promise unusual gaiety. An old man was lying by the fire when a black peat rolled right to his hand. The folk drew his attention to it but he only scoffed. There were two boys in the house, apparently brothers of Lily Henry, John's bride, and they suggested going to the evening fishing to try for a few piltocks. The old man said he would go too, but their father told them not to go. Unfortunately he did not wait to see that his orders were obeyed, as he was just setting out for

Walls. They fished at the back of the Noup and caught a great lot of piltocks. Their boat was very slender and the old man sitting in the stern was "stuffed heavy and broad." Whether his weight swamped the boat or whether they struck a skerry is not known, but a woman—Thomas Isbister's great-grandmother—walking along the banks saw their overturned boat and the three people clinging to the keel. She called to them to hold on while she went for help. They shouted to her to "hurry up, or it will be too late before you win." By the time help arrived there was no sign of the boat or its occupants.

# 10

## SUPERSTITIONS AND FAIRY TALES

Sailors and fishermen are superstitious all the world over, and Shetland, a great centre of the cod and herring fishings, is particularly rich in this respect. I do not know to what extent Foula superstitions differ—or shall we say differed?—from those of the Mainland. It is almost impossible for an outsider to discover much about them. After the religious revival of a generation ago it was considered wrong to repeat these "vaardies," especially to children. An islander who died some years ago told me that the basis of these superstitions, or at least some of them, is the fear of envy. "There is a saying that 'Envy biteth upon a stone wall'; still more will it bite upon you or your beast. For instance, perhaps you get a good fishing, and then some one says you've got a big lot of fish, and then maybe they begin to envy you a bit, and the next thing that happens is that your cow has turned ill or your ewe has gone over the banks . . . and if you do not believe me you have only to look at the people who take notice of these things—those who have the best fishings in the isle are those who pay most attention to luck and witchcraft and all that kind of thing." And this, I had to admit, was true.

The recognition of fundamental antagonisms seem to

underlie these superstitions. Fire and water cannot mix, and there must be no association of the one with the other. A fisherman will throw his cigarette-end on to the rocks, if possible, and never into the water. If a lighted brand is thrown into the sea it will frighten the fish away from that spot for all time. Some men at the South end thought they might attract the fish by throwing a flaming faggot into the water, with the result that the fish deserted that part for ever.

There are age-old antagonisms between the sea and the land, the ship and the hearth, the roving adventurous spirit of man and the stay-at-home seclusion of the woman. It follows that while at sea, no direct mention must be made of anything connected with the home. If these are to be spoken of at all it must be in such language as will deceive the listening spirits of the deep. A woman is spoken of as "hameult," that is—the one who goes about the home. A cat is "the one who goes softly," or "she who goes on four feet." A light is "luminar," while cock and hen are called "chanticleer and yonsis." The survival of the sub-conscious Pagan past is seen most clearly in the attitude to the Minister, or "Upstander." To have one on board is extremely unlucky; even to meet one on the way to the fishing meane bad luck, and many a day's fishing has been postponed through an accidental encounter with the Minister. The newer Christian religion is all very well for people who are safe ashore, but on the ocean all the elemental terrors possess the soul and it is well to propitiate the ancient heathen gods and the capricious spirits of air and water.

### THE BREGDIE

It has often been said that the ballad, except as a purely literary production founded on literary material, is now impossible; but an old folk tale that has never been written down, if put into ballad language, which, after all, is still the language of current speech in Scotland, surely can claim to be a true ballad. The following is founded on an old Shetland tale. The names are fictitious.

### THE BREGDIE [Monster]

It fell at the turn o' Lammas tide,
  I wat it was na eight year syne,
A boat frae Fughley was at the haef [deep sea fishing]
  And fishing wi' the lang ling-line.

There were Hakon and James o' Northerhouse
  And Magnus Umphray o' Soberlie,
And Wattie and Scott o' Leirabeck
  And the sixth was Tam Olsen o' Crugalee.

The sun had sunk o' the Fughley shoal
  And the Isle lay mirk [dark] i' the south-east sky;
But the moon was up and the stars were bricht
  And gied them a licht tae steer her by.

Hakon and James were fast asleep, [the stem,
  Straked [stretched] under a taft [thwart], jist aft
Wi' Wattie and Scott and Tam and a'
  But Miagnie he was na waukin' them.

She sailed close hauled and the airt [breeze] was saft
  And Magnie he sat at the helm and dreamed,
While he fancied the face o' a lichtsome lass
  I' the silvery swirl that past him streamed.

When suddenly, peerin' doon below,
  He cam tae himsel' and saw wi' a stairt
A strange broun shape o' the starboard side;
  And he gazed transfixed wi' a beating hairt.

As the boat moved on the shape moved tae,
    Broun and dull as a weedy clett [rock covered with
      seaweed]
He keekit tae port and he haud his breath,
    As the same dark thing his vision met.

He keekit fore and he keekit aft;
    It was braid and flat like a monstrous skate,
He slackened the sheet and let her run;
    But I wat the broun thing did na wait.

It raised a fin tae the gunwale's hecht
    And the slimy edge was curled inboard:
He drappit the helm and seized an oar
    And struck till the sweat frae aff him poured.

Hakon had leaned his head tae port
    And the cauld wet flipper touched his broo
Was never a mara waur [nightmare worse] than yon
    That gar'd him loup [leap] tae the starboard boo.

He shouted tae Wattie and Jamie and Scott,
    Fu' loud he bellowed, fu' loud he cried;
They screeched and hollered and shook wi' fear,
    For a fin was owre the ither side.

The boat was caught i' the saucer-shape
    That haud her fast as a closing mesh,
Sliding owre on every side,
    A living sucker o' creeping flesh.

They swung an axe and they plied a knife,
    And an iron hoop frae a keg they tore,
And hacket great lumps o' the bleeding flesh;
    Yet ever the fins cam more and more.

Yet lower she sank, and lower yet
  And shippit a sea wi' ilk jaw [dashing wave] that came.
They piled the foul flesh up tae the knee,
  But the Bregdie grippit aye the same.

The boat sank deep wi' the weight o' flesh
  When Magnie minded that he'd been told
When he was a bairn that the smallest piece
  Of copper would loosen the Bregdie's hold.

The clouds blew owre the mune, and loud
  Magnie cried i' the mirk, cried he—
"Hae ye nae copper aboard tae fling
  That we shoud be drookit [drowned] unchancily?"

They searched their pouches, the locker, the bilge,
  And turned the flesh and the ballast below,
But never a copper coin they found,
  Or a scrap of wire or a nail to throw.

The gunwale crackit, the end seemed near;
  When Wattie bethoucht himsel' and said—
"Ma shoe is tackit wi' copper sprigs";
  And he hurled his shoe at the Bregdie's head.

The boat gied a lurch, but the Bregdie sank
  And a cloud like reek [smoke] rase up frae the sea,
And they lookit at Wattie, but never spak,
  And Wattie, never a word spak he.

They sailed her in at the break o' day,
  Six strang men as white as a clout;
And they gibbered their tale as they passed me by
  On their hameward run, as I sailed out.

But a gale blew up and I canna say
    Whether they lost their wits wi' the shock;
For they never set foot o' the Foula Isle,
    For the boat gaed doun by the Logat rock.

There were Hakon and Jamie o' Northerhouse,
    And Magnie Umphray o' Soberlie,
And Wattie and Scott o' Leirabeck
    And the sixth was Tam frae Crugalee.

The following was used to charm away the mara or nightmare.

Arthur Knight, he rode all night
With drawn sword by candle light;
He sought the Mara and found the Mara,
He bound her with her own hair
He gar'd her swear with all her might
That she should never lodge a night
Wherever she heard tell of Arthur Knight.

The nygel or nigel is a terrifying monster probably the same as the grundleman. He is a spirit that appears near streams of running water and particularly round about watermills, where in the night he seizes and holds fast with his teeth the mill-wheel until driven away with brands of fire. He varies in size and colour but is always shaped like a quadruped, with glaring eyes like saucers, terrible teeth, and a fiery tail turned up over his back like the rim of an immense wheel. He once entered a house and drove out the people and it was not again inhabited for over thirty years. The more modern bogey-man, that terror of bad children, was said to live in an old wrecked herring boat which had been drawn up and converted into a sawing-mill. When a big sea came and swept it away a small boy watched it floating out in Ham Voe and remarked with satisfaction: "The bogey-man will be getting his feet wet!"

It is said that a giant who lived in Foula flew into a rage and threw from the island to the Mainland a large boulder which is still to be seen near the road between Walls and Lerwick, and is the only piece of stone of the kind in the district. Presumably this is the same giant whose grave is on the west side of the South Ness, marked by two cairns or circles of stones forty feet apart. This giant jumped from Foula to Walls Ness. He came from Orkney in three strides, and the mark of his seven-toed foot still remains. Apart from fairy tales, there was once a giant on Foula who was sent to the island by his friends in Orkney in order to escape persecution. He was very sensitive and unhappy and used to go about with his head hanging down in an endeavour to conceal his great height.

# 11
## SHIPS THAT PASS . . . OR STRIKE

A group of rugged rocks in the vast expanse of ocean, battered and pounded by thunderous waves that hurl their mighty weight upon the land and then draw back with a sucking sound leaving the seaweed hanging like long hair from the edge of the rocks, and swept by screaming hurricanes till the trembling stranger feels that the entire island must be carried away, has naturally been the scene of a number of wrecks. Yarn caps yarn; a long pull at the pipe . . . "I mind ae time . . ." Now we are fairly under weigh.

There was the *Teal Duck*, a wooden trawler. That was in the first week in March about 1900. It was a nasty night with snow showers; and the captain anchored a buoy with a light on it and kept steaming up to it and drifting back again. But it must have broken adrift, for he missed his way and brought up on the point of the South Ness. The boilers exploded and the ship split open like a kippered herring, although her deck remained entire. Some people in the Hametoun going to the well about midnight heard shouts. All hands were lost. It was about a week before this on a Sunday afternoon that a boy heard cries from the sea. He told his father and they went and searched in every geo, but there was nothing to be seen. The same evening a man came into his houee looking very white and shaken. When asked what ailed him he said that he had heard someone call from the sea: "Ahoy, ahoy, ahoy!" three times.

On the east side, three miles off the shore, lie the dreaded Hoevdi rocks, the graveyard of many a stout ship. The Hoevdi Gründ (Norse *hoevdi* meaning headland and *grind* = gate, road or gap) is the place where Wester Hoevdi is visible in the Daal gap between the hills. Speaking of these rocks Robert Cowie says:

> With low tides when they are about four feet under water the tang, which grows on them, is distinctly visible above the surface. In one or two deep depressions on the surface of one of the largest rocks of the Hoevdi Gründ are several large loose boulders, which seem to have lain there for ages. Whenever the sea is much agitated—and it is never still— the boulders are set in motion, and by their friction wear away the substance of the rocks and deepen the pools in which they lie. These boulders suggest two curious questions, the one for the geologist, the other for the hydrographer, viz. how came they there? and, why are they not washed out of these basins over the reef and allowed to sink in the deep water alongside?

Once the Hoevdi has claimed its victim, large or small, the angry waters, which even in calm weather boil and swirl over the rocks in a seething maelstrom and in a storm shoot their spouts of spray to the height of a ship's mast, pound and batter the unfortunate vessel to fragments. The *Flora*, an Aberdeen trawler, struck in fine weather, and the crew got ashore in their boat. The ship turned turtle and Magnus Manson, a youth at the time, went out to her, but he could make nothing of her and she drifted away.

Occasionally wreckage is seen on the Hoevdi that no one

knows anything about. Here side by side with many a humbler vessel lie the twisted remnants of the 17,000-ton armed auxiliary merchant cruiser *Oceanic*, once the pride of the White Star fleet. On 5 September 1914, the giant liner was seen approaching the isle. The islanders watched with some anxiety for she was making straight for the sunken rocks. Anxiety gave place to admiration when it was seen that the vessel was taking a narrow passage that lies between two rocks, and the islanders applauded such daring seamanship and intimate knowledge of the chart. Suddenly, however, the *Oceanic* discovered her danger and, instead of backing out in the same direction, turned broadside to a nine-knot tide and was swept to her doom with a crash that was heard all over the island. The tide is reported by the Admiralty as one knot. The launch of the *Lion*, a salvage boat which hurried to the scene, was capable of a speed of ten knots, yet she was unable to make any headway against the tide although she tried with full steam for fifteen minutes. Even then it was not the top of the tide, and the officer in charge reckoned that the full tide would be twelve knots. He confessed that he would not have believed it if he had been told. Before long every able-bodied islander was commandeered to assist in the work of salvage. Troops and guns were safely removed and an attempt was made to take off some of the more valuable furniture and books. The salvage boats and the trawlers made "a bonny sight" with their searchlights that lit up the hills. But before long a gale blew up and the great ship slipped below the waves. We often think longingly of the many tons of coal, blankets, linen, pianos, and all the furniture of the luxury liner lying just beyond our reach, so near and yet so far. Although the *Oceanic* has altered her position and now lies in deeper water she can still be seen beneath the waves.

Towards the end of the war Thomas Umphray woke up one morning when it was barely daylight and saw from his door at Gravins two figures above the banks at Ham Little. Then a third appeared and he thought they were Foula men seeking sheep. However he took the telescope and saw that they were wearing big overcoats, which was very strange, and the number increased to five or six. He walked down to the Voe and counted nineteen men, but as there was no sign of a boat he concluded that it was the crew of a German submarine come to work some mischief. He went back to his house and watched from a window. The strangers knocked at the house of the Brae but the lonely woman who lived there lay low, and they concluded that it was uninhabited. They fared no better at the next house and finally approached the Gravins, and Thomas went out to meet them. They had the appearance of foreigners, but they were dripping wet and cold and in a sore state, and our hospitable Tammie decided that even if they were Germans they must be treated kindly, so he went up to them and wished them "Good Morning," and they replied in the same tongue. "If you please will you come in?" continued Tammie; and very glad were they to accept the invitation. With the help of neighbours they were fed and given dry clothes. No one of course asked them whence they came or how they had arrived in this unexpected fashion, for, as everybody knows, it is rude to ask impertinent questions, especially of strangers. Fortunately, however, we are in a position to satisfy the reader's curiosity for the captain, who, like most of his crew, could speak English perfectly, volunteered the information that they were Norwegians and that their ship had struck a mine forty miles north-north-west of Foula. They lost one man. The remainder rowed through the darkness of a bad night, thick with snow, and reached the inhospitable cliffs on the west side of the island. Finding no landing there they rowed round the South Ness and eventually beached their boat in Ham Little and clambered up the banks. They thought the isle was uninhabited, in which case their plight would have been even more serious. The wartime cable was in operation then and they were able to wire for a boat to come and take them away. The skipper would not allow his crew to explore the island for fear that the boat would turn up unexpectedly. They were very nice men, and paid handsomely for their entertainment, and the islanders were sorry to say goodbye to their uninvited guests.

Very different was the visit of "the notorious brothers de Greave." This was in the summer of the year in which the road was made. John Gray of Burns was at work on the road. Thomas Umphray was at the banks looking for driftwood, and Andrew Manson was working on his croft at Veedale and saw all that happened. On the preceding day the *Tib-Doig*, which means the fast-runner or swift, had been observed three miles south of the isle lying close to a similar vessel—probably the *Merchant* or the *William Martin*—both fishing vessels and notorious smugglers, afterwards caught on the east coast of Shetland. A small boat was going between the two and the assumption is that the *Tib-Doig* was transferring her cargo to the other vessel, for reasons which will be apparent. On the morning in question she made a tack towards the Hoevdi Gründ, stayed, came about and stood in for the mid shooting geo on the Taing. Here she went to stay again when suddenly the mainsheet ran off, the boom snapped on the runner, and so she refused to stay. She ran ashore on the north side of the mid shooting geo, where the whole crew got off with ease by way of the bowsprit. The first men who landed swore that the mainsheet had been cut, but under the skipper's instructions they afterwards denied this. The vessel drifted down on to the Baa Head, where she struck and rapidly went to pieces. She was completely rotten and even the wreck-wood was not worth salving. The gear was divided amongst the islanders and Andrew Manson's father received the mainsheet, which showed a very decided cut. Just as the boat struck the first time the crew threw out a keg of spirits and some tobacco. The minister of that time came hobbling along, and an islander threw the little barrel into a patch of corn. The tobacco was secreted elsewhere, and the small quantity remaining on the boat was salved before she broke up. It was hawked through the isle—"poor stuff, the spirits were much better."

The captain and the mate were Lewis and Eugene de Greave, known in Leith as "the notorious brothers de Greave." The elder was six feet two inches, and the younger six feet four inches. Lewis had a swordcut on his hand, and both had scars on the face and body. They were the sons of a French nobleman and were well educated. The eldest particularly was a well-read man, an excellent linguist, and indeed a real scholar. They walked about with a four-ounce shot suspended up the sleeve by elastic for use as a life preserver. The JP of the island was requested to sign a paper saying that the boat had missed stays and that no-one was to blame for the wreck, but he stoutly refused. During their stay in the island Eugene went through a form of marriage with an island lass, pretending that he wanted to demonstrate the form of ceremony in use in Belgium. The girl's father wisely stopped the ceremony. Afterwards Eugene tried to persuade the girl to go away with him.

The brothers induced old Scott Henry of the Wilse, who had a large boat, probably a herring boat, to take them to the Mainland. This was a risky undertaking as it was not unlikely that the foreigners would seize the boat and sail for Belgium. However they reached the Mainland and, despite the fact that the police were hot on their trail, they sailed from Lerwick by the north of Scotland steamer. As soon as they landed in Shetland they pretended that they could not speak a word of English. At Aberdeen they managed to elude the police who had been warned by telegraph, and got away from the country.

The next news of them was an account in the Glasgow *Daily Mail* of the trial in Sydney of the brothers de Greave for manslaughter and piracy on the high seas. The story is as follows: A Mr Wilson, of Hull, owned a trading schooner in the South Seas. He put his son on her as super cargo and the brothers de Greave were acting, one as mats and the other as "serang." The skipper was a white man. A quarrel arose—

obviously a put-up job—and Lewis shot the super-cargo in the
head while Eugene shot the skipper, thus leaving the brothers as
the only white men on board. The natives bolted below and were
battened down, and were afterwards given the choice of either
coming up on deck to be shot or jumping overboard. All chose
the latter and were drowned or eaten by sharks, with the
exception of one boy who was retained to act as cook. The
brothers altered the ship's name, forged new ship's papers, and
put into some small and unfrequented port to report their crew
as "washed overboard in bad weather." For some time they ran
the schooner themselves and did very well with her. One day
they anchored in Sydney harbour to enable Lewis to go to a bank
in connection with some document. On finding that Eugene's
signature also was required he returned to the ship to fetch his
brother. The native boy who had been retained as cook seized the
opportunity to run to the nearest police station and give
information. The pirates were arrested and sent to Durban for
trial. They claimed French nationality and were handed over to
France and given a life sentence on Devil's Island. The elder is
said to have been eaten by sharks while trying to escape, but the
younger served his sentence and, posing as a reformed character,
published his confessions in *The Wide World Magazine*. How far
the reformation was genuine can only be surmised. In 1914 the
Foula postmaster, and also the registrar in Lerwick, received
letters from a wealthy French lady asking if there was any truth
in the story that Eugene de Greave had a wife in the Shetlands,
as he was proposing to marry her seventeen-year-old daughter,
who had a considerable fortune in her own right. The mail-boat
was delayed, and by the time it was possible to reply the
reformed character had eloped with the daughter plus fortune. It
is rumoured that he left her soon afterwards, minus the fortune;
but as the gentleman may still be living we will give him the
benefit of the doubt and assume that the aged pirate has settled
down to a life of domestic felicity where his learning and

polished manners are the delight of an admiring family.

Near the shore of the grand North Bay, are two lonely little graves known as "the Frenchmen's graves." The older one, which is to the south, is the body of a man who was washed ashore at Wurwick. The story of the other is that one Sunday forenoon about the year 1868 a French fishing smack anchored in the North Bay and the crew came ashore carrying a body sewed up in a hammock, and asked the way to the graveyard. They were told that it was at the south end but that there was a solitary grave at the north end, so they decided to bury their comrade beside the unknown seaman. A very touching service was held, in the course of which each man made the sign of the cross three times, and placed a clod in the grave. They erected a little wooden cross, which stood until it weathered away. The name was Boutel or Beautelle. Many years afterwards a sailor on a French trader asked a Foula man, "Is my friend that they buried on your island still there?"

At the back of the Noup is a cave high up in the cliff, called "The Thieves' Hole." Here, over a hundred years ago, two brothers from the Mainland lived for a considerable time unknown to the islanders. They came from the Nean of Brindister, where they had another brother, and also one at Fitful Head who was known as Black Eric. After sinking their boat they took up their abode in the cave, coming out at night to steal meal and blankets and to kill sheep. With the skins of the sheep they covered themselves so as to be able to creep up to the flocks unnoticed. The natural hole in the freestone rock where they placed a rod on which to hang a kettle may still be seen. Many months passed before they were discovered. Then they grew careless and forgot to cover their peat fire while they slept in the daytime, so that a boat at the fishing noticed smoke rising at the back of the Noup. The Hametoun people captured and bound them, but while they were away at the fishing the women used to loose them and compel them to thresh their corn. Eventually the unwanted visitors were taken back to the Mainland.

The dangerous, if understandable, temptation to relieve the tedium of a long voyage by drinking is responsible for many a wreck. The crew of a foreign vessel which struck the Hoevdi were too drunk to realize their peril. They succeeded in floating the ship off the rocks and anchored her about two miles from the island, while the crew came ashore, leaving the captain, mate and boatswain still aboard the wreck. They were all quite unconcerned, especially the cook who sat with a coffee-grinder on his knee and continued to grind regardless of wind and wave. A Foula sixern, skippered by Magnus Manson, pulled out to the ship and begged the officers to quit while there was yet time, but they would not even speak to the Foula men and "disdained them as if they were not there." Later on the ship's boat tried to return to the ship but could make no headway against the tide. Next day there came a flying gale from the south and the stranded men hoisted signals of distress. Once more Magnus Manson went through the isle calling for volunteers for what was now a very dangerous task—indeed it is said that but for Magnie's superb seamanship it would have been impossible. While they were rescuing the officers the ship's martingale crashed down on to the little boat and nearly laid her in pieces. But the return to land was the most difficult part of the business, for in order to reach the Voe it was necessary to cross the furious tide-race at the Strem Ness. It soon became apparent that this would be impossible, so Magnus steered for a tiny rock-bound cove north of the Strem, and they prepared to swim for the shore. The islanders, however, seeing their plight, rushed into the sea with planks and ropes and seized the boat as it came in on the crest of a wave and pulled her up over the rocks. Not one of the rescued men had the grace to say thank you. When the storm showed signs of abating they all set out once more for the ship in spite of the islanders' efforts to restrain them. They hoisted a canvas bag in place of a sail, but found themselves unable either

The Isle of Foula

The hills – Hamnafjeld, The Sneug and The Kame

Magnus Manson, former skipper of the mail-boat

Launching the mail-boat advance at Ham (Shetland Museum)

Magnie Manson and his wife, Grace, Hamnabeck. Magnie sits and carves outside while Grace churns butter. (Shetland Museum)

The Kame

Peat carriers

Woman carding wool

Lewis Umphray with kishie of peats

Three men outside a croft, Brekins. The first is Jeemie Isbister, the second is "Muckle Joannie" Henry, North Biggins. The first and third men carry kishies with peats on their backs. (Shetland Museum)

Ham Voe

Pounding grain in a kubbi (1902)

A hand-mill

John Gray, making a quern (1902)

Interior of a cottage

Inside the croft of Stjoal. Andrew Gray, Jeannie Gray, Nannie Gray, woman knitting (Shetland Museum)

Croft interior. Margaret Twatt sitting by an open fire. Dried fish and fishing nets/line (?) hanging from the ceiling. (Shetland Museum)

Gaada Stack

The Hill of Soberlie

A widow

Croft of Springs, with tekkit roof (Shetland Museum)

Wilse, rekkir roof and outhouses (Shetland Museum)

Croft of Bloburn, with tarred roof (Shetland Museum)

Croft of Ham, with rekkit roof (Shetland Museum)

Crofthouse, Daeks, with Gray family – Louisa, Tammie, Jeannie and James (Shetland Museum)

to reach the wreck or return to land. Marvellous to relate, the providence that is said to watch over drunken men did not fail them, and they were blown across to the Mainland in safety.

Ungrateful crews are unfortunately not exceptional. There was, for example, the Faroe smack which bumped along the rocks below North Veedale in a thick haze. The terrified sailors jumped ashore, with the exception of the captain. Andrew Manson, an islander, seeing that the vessel did not appear to be damaged, boarded her and assisted the captain to sail her into the Voe and anchor her there. The crew could not be persuaded to return to the ship, so Andrew and his brother had to sleep on board to keep the captain company. They received no payment or recognition of their services. Another smack went on to the Baa Head and was seriously holed. She lay on the rocks all night and next day the captain asked Andrew to bring his boat and assist in salving some of the gear. It was then low tide and the vessel lay on her side in shallow water. Andrew observed that the water inside the ship was above the level of the water outside and remarked that if she could keep water in she could still keep water out. Thomas Umphray, who is an expert carpenter, examined her and thought he could patch her up. The skipper exclaimed: "If you will save my ship there is nothing I would not give you!" She was pumped out and beached, and Tammie spent a week repairing her and making her thoroughly seaworthy; but exactly nothing was what they all received for their skill and labour! Both these ships were lost within the next year or two.

It speaks well for the seamanship of the islanders that the mail-boat, an open sixern, has been running for over sixty years without an accident of any kind. Indeed tradition records very few mishaps to Foula boats. The boys lost at the back of the Noup, and two men drowned while fishing in Dog Geo, are the only instances—unless one includes the story of Katrine Henry and the muckle pot. Katrine, the daughter of William Henry, a teacher in Foula, was, in the phrase of the narrator, "one of an unreasonably large family as I understand it." They had one very small pot for cooking—not nearly big enough for the ever increasing and growing family. Katrine planned that if ever she were old enough to earn money she would buy a pot large enough to satisfy all her hungry brothers and sisters. At the age of sixteen she went over to the Mainland and worked at the kelp industry. She was away for four months and at the end of the season had saved up enough money to buy a splendid pot to take back to the isle. There was no mail-boat in those days so she returned in a sixern owned by a Foula man who had gone over to the Mainland "for the news of the day." On the way home they passed the Foula boats at the fishing and stopped to have a talk. Perhaps the news was particularly exciting, tidings of Trafalgar or Waterloo maybe, for while they were speaking the boats drew too close to one another and Katrine's boat capsized—an accident that is very liable to happen in a heavy swell. Katrine clambered into a fishing boat and then leant over and grabbed the skipper of the overturned sixern by his long pigtail (the fashion of the time) and hauled him aboard. She lost her precious pot and all her belongings, but she took the matter very philosophically. "Well," said she, "I have lost my kettle but I have saved a man."

There is a pathetic story of an old half-witted woman from Dale on the Mainland who had longed all her life to visit Foula, whose cloud-capped hills of mystery she had often seen on the far horizon. She set out in a little boat with only one oar and actually succeeded in accomplishing the voyage. But her friends set out in pursuit and overtook her just as she reached the Voe. Although they themselves landed on the island they refused to allow her to do so, and thus the poor, plucky, old adventuress was foiled in her life-long ambition.

In most parts there is deep water right up to the cliffs and in fog a vessel will sometimes discover her danger barely in time to put about. From Mogil, which lies in a valley a quarter of a mile up the burn, in a sudden lifting of the mist, the top-masts of a large emigrant ship were seen above the cliffs of Durganess. The band could be heard playing a lively air as the great ship stayed just in the nick of time. How many of the passengers, one wonders, knew that they had been within inches of disaster. Even the mail-boat has missed the isle in a fog with a strong tide, so that the crew looked back and saw the mighty west cliffs frowning above them. Even when there is no question of danger it is an awe-inspiring experience to look up and see these towering precipices looming through the mist.

# 12

# THE DOMINION OF NATURE

Amongst our prehistoric visitors were the little brown seal-men who came singly in their boats of skin. Although in the distance they were actually mistaken for seals, the islanders would not be long in discovering that they were harmless and very courageous traders from the frozen North—Lapps or Finns. Selkie-geo is crowded with seals of all shades and sizes, and their uncanny and almost articulate cries mingling with the incessant chattering and muttering of the sea-fowl have a very human sound; yet we have no MacNamaras or MacCodrums to claim seal descent. There are, it is true, tales of a man with a seal-wife who found her skin under a hay-cole and burnt it to prevent her from visiting her people under the sea; or again the man who fought with a bull-seal and left his knife in the beast's shoulder, and found it again to his horror sticking above the bed of a sick friend; but these tales are told of "people on the Mainland" or "somewhere about Walls." The quietly observant Foula people with their intimate knowledge of nature would find such stories unconvincing. To be sure there is not much love lost between the islanders and the seal-folk, for the seals eat fish by the ton.

We crept up to a sleeping baby seal and grabbed him by the tail. He did not object to being carried over the rocks but when he found himself above green grass he went mad with fury and bit through a thick coat sleeve. Finding that he had, fortunately, no flesh between his teeth, he suddenly turned his attention to exposed knees, hands and face. We were not sorry to see him go lolloping and slithering in great haste back to the sea. Just before he dived into the water he turned and gave us over his shoulder an indescribably human look of sulky hatred: "I'll tell my Ma! I'll report you to headquarters! I'll be even with you yet, you great big human bullies!" It is said that seals' heads were used by men as a disguise, for what purpose I do not know.

A more serious enemy of the fisherman are the sharks which infest these waters, damaging the fish and attempting to overturn the small boats. Often cod caught on the line are half eaten, and on one occasion a shark, gripping fast with his teeth a hooked cod, was hauled to the level of the gunwale and the fisherman had to push him off with his foot. The basking shark, often thirty feet in length, as we can tell by comparison with a boat of the same length anchored in the Voe, is comparatively harmless. He may slash at a floating object with his powerful tail but he is not a flesh-eater. The so-called sea serpent was often met at the Haaf and in the distance resembles the sails of a full-rigged schooner. This is the dreaded "bregdie," although the same name is applied to an enormous flatfish like a giant skate or ray. The thresher whale is also occasionally seen and looks like the mast of a fourern. It appears to proceed "head over heels," alternately standing up and lying flat on the water.

The land animals—cows, horses and sheep—are diminutive and shaggy but very hardy. The sheeps' wool is extremely soft and fine and, besides the ordinary white, the fleeces are of many colours and shades, varying from dark brown to pale fawn, or "moorat," and from black to a bluish grey. The wool is not sheared, but is plucked, or "rooed" from the back of the sheep. This is not a painful process, as the old fleece naturally separates itself from the new, and will fall off of its own accord if left too long. Natural dyes are made from the lichens on the rocks, and little "bannocks" of these used to be sent to Lerwick to be sold. Rats, fortunately, there are none, and a pair of rabbits was introduced "for a fancy" within living memory by one who has had ample cause to regret his unfortunate experiment. The mouse, however, is a very distinguished little animal, for we are the proud possessors of a species of our own.

### MOUSE THULENSIS

The Foula hill mouse is a sub-species of the Fair Isle hill mouse, and should be called *Apodemus fridariensis thuleo*. We have here a species in the making. It is distinctly smaller than its Fair Isle ancestor. It has dark flanks, a bluish white under surface, and a long dark tail, white below. Its hind feet, white on their dorsal surface, are exceptionally large, with small sole pads.

A pathetic story of a Foula mouse was told me some years ago. This little animal had a nest of young ones in the Sneck of the Smallie. There had been deep snow on the ground for a long period, and eventually poor mousie had run out of provisions. She set out for the nearest croft, the Stoel, three-quarters of a mile distant, and procured an ear of corn which she attempted to carry home to her starving young ones. When almost within sight of her home she was overcome with exhaustion and her dead body, still grasping the ear of corn, was found by an islander who had noted the tracks and was thus able to reconstruct the little tragedy.

The bird life of this "paradise of the ornithologist" is one of its most interesting features. The Little Kame, a projecting cliff of 400 feet, 820 feet below the summit of the Great Kame, was the last breeding place in the British Isles of the sea eagle. On one or two occasions when one of the birds died the survivor brought a new mate. They used to live principally on fish, but when this became scarce they took to killing lambs. Exasperated by their ravages, a man climbed down to the Little Kame and destroyed both nest and eggs, and thus exterminated this rare bird. He found that the nest was composed of literally cart-loads of twigs and small branches, which must have been brought from the mainland of Scotland. The prince of the gulls is the great skua, a majestic bird who lives by piracy, never fishing for himself, but beating the unfortunate kittiwakes until they render up their catch. Any animal, even man, approaching his breeding place is fiercely attacked. Thomas Umphray was so severely beaten that he was forced to crawl away on his hands and knees, with a bleeding head and minus his cap. At the end of the last century Unst and Foula were the sole breeding places of this bird and in Foula they were reduced to three pairs. In consequence of determined protection they have now become plentiful and have established colonies in other parts of Shetland. They are very useful to the shepherd as they drive away the raven and the crow and thus protect the young lambs. The bonxie, to give him his local name, inhabits the hilltops, while the Allen Richardson skua takes possession of the low land. These smaller birds are even fiercer than their lordlier cousins.

The first time that I experienced the ferocity of this bird I was walking over the rough moor which in winter amply justifies its suggestive name of "Sucky Mires," but which in summer is dry, except for a few swampy patches which are crossed by means of miniature turf bridges. My enjoyment of the peaceful beauty surrounding me was suddenly interrupted by a smart blow on the back of my head. In angry surprise I looked round to discover what islander dared to insult me in such a manner, but there was no-one in sight, and the silence was broken only by the distant roar of the waves and the plaintive cat-like cries of the Allen Richardson skuas. Several of these graceful birds circled round me suggesting to my mind giant swallows. As I stood watching them I discovered the author of the attack on my innocent head, for as a bird swooped past me I felt the alarming swish of his wings against my face. He was swiftly followed by his mate, and the pair of them smacked me mercilessly till they had driven me to a safe distance from their nesting place, where they left me, marvelling at the moral courage which enabled a slender little bird to defeat an animal fifty times its own size. Even the sheep recognise the Allen's undisputed right to their breeding ground, and if they venture to trespass they are chivvied away to a place where they can feed without endangering the lives of the little Allens. In time curiosity revived my courage, and I approached the breeding ground in the hope of seeing the eggs of this interesting bird. To my surprise I saw a bird in evident distress, crying piteously and flopping about hopelessly trailing a disabled wing. It made no effort to escape until I stooped to catch it, when it ran for a few feeble steps, and I followed, each time just failing to capture the wounded creature. It increased its pace and I increased my efforts, till suddenly it spread its wings and, circling elegantly round, came and derisively hit me on the head, while I realized that I had been tricked by this extraordinary bird. Setting my teeth, I walked back to the breeding ground. This time my courage was rewarded for, in spite of much shamming of broken wings and furious hitting on the part of the parents, I discovered a young bird trying to hide itself behind a tuft of grass while watching me with one wide-open eye. When I attempted to stroke the little brown speckled ball of fluff it showed itself a true son of its parents by standing up and pecking me with all its might.

The kittiwakes are severely punished by the Allens as well as by the bonxies. The Mill Loch is a favourite freshwater resort of the kittiwakes. Flocks of these birds gather on the loch and constantly travel to and from the Voe. As soon as one flock reaches the Voe another rises and makes way for the newcomers. All day long the detachments pass and re-pass crossing in incessant relays from Voe to Mill Loch and back again. But Allen land is to be passed en route and many are the fierce attacks that the poor screaming kittiwakes have to endure. Perhaps the prettiest bird is the eider duck or dunter. She makes her downy nest on the moor, and great circumspection is required before she can pilot her little family safely to the sea— for both ravens and bonxies are watching to gobble up these dainty morsels. The perilous journey is made at night. The mother and chicks creep cautiously to the nearest burn, and the remainder of the journey is made by water. If they are fortunate in eluding their enemies you will see them next morning swimming a few yards from the shore, the proud mother-bird swimming straight ahead with an air of importance, while the chicks dart joyfully hither and thither, like a cruiser surrounded by her destroyers. Tammy Umphray, who seems to know every nest in the district, will be watching from the banks. "Ah," he beams, "the pretty creature. She has gotten her family safely to the sea for another year."

It was he who told me the following story of a jackdaw which had been tamed by the family of a former teacher. They used to torment the bird and one day went so far as to put tar on its feet. The sagacious bird alighted on the dyke and watched the good wife hanging out her washing to dry. Then he flew to the clothes line and paraded up and down, deliberately wiping his feet on the white linen!

The many flocks of migrants in spring and summer find the island a convenient resting place; indeed it is one of nature's sanctuaries. An exceedingly rare straggler alighted there some years ago and was found dead in a yard, wedged between some sacks of corn. It was a miniature owl, so small that it could easily lie in the palm of the hand. The plumage was grey with brown bars, while the ears were tufted and the legs feather-puttied. The Royal Scottish Museum identified it as a Scop's owl, the only Scottish specimen that had reached them, although some ten individuals had been observed. The bird inhabits mid and southern Europe, whence it migrates to Africa in winter, which explains its extreme rarity in Scotland.

Until comparatively recently sea-birds and their eggs formed a large part of the food of the islanders, and no doubt many a man has lost his life in quest of them. In the childhood of the present generation children used to tease each other by saying: "My father died like a man at the cliffs; yours died in his bed." Another saying is attributed to the men of Foula, who despised a "straw death"—"My gutcher (grandfather) gied afore, my fader gied afore, and I maun gang ower da' Sneug tae." The Sneug is not a sea cliff, but as the word is Norse for snow hill the proverb may merely mean "lost on the hills." The last accident of the kind took place less than a hundred years ago. The man was newly married, and the first baby was expected, and, as they were very poor, he went to the Mainland to look for work. He was unsuccessful, and returned home late at night to find that there was no food in the house. It was dark and wet, but he took his ropes and went to the cliffs to look for eggs. He never returned, and the people took ropes and went to look for him, but they never found him living or dead. "But folk held their lives cheap in those days." A short stake, or even a knife, was driven into the ground, and three ropes were used—two round the waist and one in the hand. The climber tied the birds round his waist before ascending. Walter Isbister, for example, at the age of fourteen, would climb down a thousand feet and return with four-score of puffins round his waist and two dozen eggs in his blue bonnet held in his teeth. The ropes were often very rotten, which caused many of the accidents. The cliffs were apportioned out and each house had its corresponding portion of the cliffs, usually named after the croft. Widows inherited their husband's portions and, as some of the women can still climb, it is possible that they too took part in this dangerous enterprise. The name of one of these cliff allotments is "the Sigefer Tage o' Guttorm." This was the most dangerous of the crags. To reach it the cragsman climbed or was lowered to a projecting point some five or six hundred feet above the sea, and then, after untying his rope he walked along a ledge only a few inches wide to the mouth of a cave tenanted by thousands of looms. A native has suggested that Guttorm chose to end his life here instead of following the ancient custom of setting out on his last voyage in a boat in which a slow fire had been lit. As the word *tage* is Norse for end, to end one's life, this is a possible explanation.

The Foula climbers were famous throughout Shetland. In *Old Lore Miscellany*, October 1931, the following description of the Isle of Noss appears:

> Here, as in Foulah, the lower ledges of this magnificent precipice are tenanted by the shags, razor bills and guillemots, while the puffins, herring gulls and lesser blackbacked gulls occupy the upper portion of the cliff. The entire height is estimated at 484 feet above the level of the sea, which, though lower by 1,000 feet than the cliffs of Foulah, presents from its great perpendicularity a most imposing effect.

Speaking of the Holm of Noss, the writer says:

> Everyone has heard of the cradle of Noss and of the circumstances under which it was first slung across the gulf. A Foulah man induced by the tempting offer of a cow, first accomplished the perilous undertaking. He climbed up the North side of the Holm, carrying along with him two large stakes to fix in the ground at the summit, and from the moment he set foot thereon the undivided empire of the gulls was at an end. But they enjoyed a terrible revenge. The daring rockman refused to return by the rational mode of the basket, but insisted upon descending by the way that he came, and in the attempt, as might have been expected, he fell and was dashed to atoms.

So far we have been unable to trace the Foula man which, if the story be true, is very surprising.

## BIRDS THAT BREED IN FOULA

The following does not profess to be a complete list of the birds of the island; but it may form a basis for a fuller record. The island names are given in italics.

Blackbird, *Black Starrie* or *Brown Starrie*
Cormorant
Crow—Black Crow
      Grey Crow, *Cra'*
Eagle—White-tailed Eagle or Sea Eagle or Erne
Eider Duck, *Dunter*
Falcon Peregrine
Guillemot—Black Guillemot, *Tystie*
        White Guillemot, *Loom*
        Ring-eyed Guillemot
Gull—Black-headed Gull
    Common Gull, *Maa*
    Herring Gull
    Greater Black-backed Gull
    Lesser Black-backed Gull
Kittiwake
Lapwing
Lark—Skylark
    Ground Lark
Merlin
Oyster-Catcher, *Shalder*
Petrel—Fulmar Petrel, *Maallie*
    Stormy Petrel
Pigeon—Rock Pigeon
Pippit—Rock Pippit, *Banks Sparrow*

/

Meadow Pippit, probably *Hill Sparrow*
Plover—Ringed Plover, *Sandy Loo*
Puffin, *Tammie Norie*
Raven, *Corbie*
Razor Bill, *Wulkie*
Skua—Great Skua, *Bonxie*
     Little or Arctic Skua, *Allen Richardson* or *Scootie Allen* or
          *Allen*
Sandpiper—Purple Sandpiper
Shag, *Scarf*
Sheerwater—Manx Sheerwater, *Leerie* or *Lyrie*
Sparrow Hawk
Stone-Chat
Tern—Common Tern, *Tirrock* or *Pterick*
     Arctic Tern
     Little Tern
Turnstone, *Ebb-Fowl* or *Ebb-Pickie*
Waglail—Water Wagtail
Wheatear
Wren

REGULAR VISITORS AND BIRDS SEEN IN FOULA

Auk—Little Auk, *Rochie*
Corncrake or Land Rail
Cuckoo
Curlew—*Whaup*
Diver—Great Northern Diver
     Red-throated Diver—*Rain Goose*
Dunlin
Duck—Common Duck
     Runner Duck
Firetail
Flycatcher

Gannet or Solan Goose
Goose—Barnacle Goose
Goshawk
Gull—Glaucous Gull
　　　Ivory Gull
　　　Iceland Gull
Heron
Kingfisher
Lark—Norway Lark
Linnet
Merganser
Redshank
Robin
Rook
Sandpiper—Common Sandpiper
Snipe, *Snipoch*
Sparrow—*Kirk Sparrow*
Swan
Swift
Thrush, *Ground Thrush*
Tick-bird
Tit
Twite
Warbler
Whimbrel
Woodpecker—Great Northern Woodpecker
　　　　　　Lesser Spotted Woodpecker
Wryneck
Wheatear—Desert and Black-throated
Wren—Gold-crested
　　　Fire-crested

Foula is one of the stormiest places in the world. The Shetland seas are the roughest in the northern hemisphere, and Foula is by far the most tempestuous of the isles. Those who have lived in the Fair Isle and come to Foula say that there is no comparison, yet even in the Fair Isle the official records at the North Station do not show a single calm day in seven years. So heavy are the wind and seas that the spray carries right over Foula's cliffs of over a thousand feet. The North Ness, some hundred feet high, is strewn with stones, many of them larger than a man's head, thrown there by wind and sea. The stranger is apt to be sceptical. A man was warned by one of the islanders not to go outside during a winter gale. "What, you do not mean to say you are afraid of the wind?" he scornfully asked. The islander replied that he would see for himself. One day during the following winter, when he went out in a gale to take in some clothes off the line, he was thrown down with such force that his arm was broken. One of the nurses, who was similarly scornful, was lifted from her feet and sustained a broken ankle. Naturally the islanders cannot stay indoors whenever a gale is raging, but they learn to listen for an approaching squall, and lie flat on the ground while it passes. On one occasion the wind lifted a small shed full of heavy paraffin casks, made extra secure by chains to the ground, and carried it for twenty feet. The corrugated iron roof of a porch was hurled a quarter of a mile through the air.

But the best example of these tremendous "flans" is the story of the late Mrs Traill's house. This lady used to introduce herself as "the best known and best hated woman in Shetland." She was, as a matter of fact, a remarkably clever and capable woman who had acted as factor for a former laird. She boasted Stuart descent, and had inherited much of the uncompromising determination of those absolute monarchs. But in a small community of people who tend to adhere to the customs of their ancestors, and where in these degenerate days the powers of even the laird himself are sadly restricted, the possession of a decided gift for management without sufficient scope for the exercise of that talent, is apt to lead to friction. On account of her masculine appearance and dress, and her not inconsiderable knowledge of navigation, she was known behind her back as "Captain Traill." There was only one man, however, who, when specially enraged, ventured with characteristic subtlety to raise his hat and solemnly address her as "Sir," which, he declared, made her so mad that she would not speak to him for months afterwards. We sometimes went so far as to discuss the advisability of terminating her lease, and wondering how far such a proceeding would be justified. At last I received word that "Providence had intervened and settled the question."

Mrs Traill lived in a substantially built wooden house embedded in a concrete base, in the centre of the island. One day a squall of wind came and lifted the house bodily into the air so that the inhabitants of a croft on a much higher level on the other side of the burn had a clear view of the distant sea under the house as it hung in mid air. It sailed over a fence, paused for a moment, dropped its floor, and then poured down upon the earth an avalanche of furniture, stoves, books, papers, bedding, bags of wool, china, provisions, cooking utensils, clothing, and all the rest of it. Then, having emptied itself of all its contents, the house alighted upon the ground and splintered into matchwood, and the wind came and playfully caught up every scrap of house and gear, whirled them round, and deposited them in the sea half a mile away, so that within a few minutes not a vestige remained to show that there had ever been a house on the site. Close beside the house had stood a little out-house and two empty packing cases. These the wind did not touch. No wonder that some of the islanders said that "there was more than wind in yon." But what was the additional power?—that was the question. Mrs Traill herself supplied the solution. She had actually been on her way to the island when she was recalled on business; otherwise she would have been in the house when it was carried away. Obviously the hand of Providence had intervened on her behalf.

The tide-ranks also are notorious. At Fraserburgh an islander was conversing with a group of shipmates and was asked where he came from. When he replied: "From the island of Foula," a sceptical sailor said he did not know there was such a place. "But I do," put in a companion. "I have good reason to know the Foula rank, for it broke my arm!" Truly, when the powers of air and water are at their wildest there is nothing to equal their ferocity, unless it be a raging fire.

Awe-inspiring in a different way is the Aurora Borealis— the merry dancers, or the weird sisters, who predict bad weather. Sometimes it moves in vertical streaks of light, sometimes in horizontal waves, and occasionally is a red glow—redder than a sunset. The spectral figure of the Brochan adds to the terrors of the mist. One feels sorry for the "peerie boy" who met this apparition on the steep hill-side of Soberlie and ran away in a great fright from the "big man" who pursued him. But the Will o' the Wisp is a jolly little fellow. If you put your foot into his lantern the light will glow all over your shoe. "Fire balls" are sometimes seen in the air on sultry nights.

According to Tudor, Foula is interesting geologically, preserving as it does a fragment of the old red sandstone formation of Shetland.

Isolated though it be [he says], it conveys to the geologist a vivid impression of the extent and vast thickness of the strata of this age in Shetland. The magnificent precipice on the West . . . consists throughout of red and grey sandstone and shales. From the top of this cliff the observer may descry, far to the east, the irregular outline of the Mainland of Shetland, and as he dwells on the history of the Old Red Sandstone as told by the relics of the period, he cannot fail to be impressed with the immense denudation they have undergone. The strata of this age in Foula are brought into conjunction with the crystalline rocks by a North and

South fault, which is admirably seen in the bay near Ware
Wick and the North coast and in Schoble Geo to the South
of Ham. They cover the whole of the island to the West of
this fault. The general dip is to the south-south-west, at an
average angle of 30 degrees, but close to the fault they are
tilted to an angle of about 60 degrees. The lowest beds
exposed consist of coarse gritty sandstones, which are
succeeded by fine-grained sandstones, flags and shales, in
alternating bands. We detected plant remains in the shales
in the North part of the island similar to those met with on
the Mainland.

He mentions that there are throughout the islands abundant
traces of glacial action and argues that there were two periods of
glaciation, as the markings on some parts of the Mainland and
isles trend west-south-west and in some parts south-south-west
while in Papa Stour and Foula the striae veer round to north-
north-west.

In 1929 Mr John Gladstone made the first botanical survey
of the island and collected 150 varieties of plants. Most of the
common meadow plants are found on the low ground, while the
hill plants include the rare *Cornus suecica Linn*. Many of the local
names of plants are of Norse origin.

# 13

# SOME LITERARY FRAGMENTS

For more than a quarter of a century the writer has suspected that there were old songs and ballads of an early date that had found a lodgement here when the Norse language began to give way to English about one hundred and fifty years ago. But puritan ministers taught that the ballads were wicked, and they were sternly repressed partly on religious and partly on moral grounds. Secular songs were considered a waste of time, and Moody and Sankey hymns took the place of the old love ballads—"the height of nonsense," as they were called. Manners, too, changed; and coarse expressions which were in everyday use in Elizabethan times appeared shocking to the more refined Victorians. Recently, however, the writer heard a couple of lines quoted by accident; and, once the ice was broken, he was able to discover remnants of some score of ballads and songs, in a few cases obviously of pre-Reformation date. Early in the eighteenth century a Foula child was named after the ballad of "Fair Rosanna." "It was not a very good song," said an old woman to me, and added after an embarrassed pause, "She had a lover."

Rosanna was the fairest flower
That ever blomed in all Yorkshere,

A gentleman a-courting came
Still begging her to be his dear.

Eventually he put an end to her, and she prayed that a rose might grow on her grave. When folk picked the rose it grew again until at last the guilty man came and plucked it, and then it grew no more. They hanged him for it, and he confessed the crime.

Many years ago we visited a bed-ridden old woman of ninety-four, whose mind was remarkably clear although her memory for recent events was failing. After a discourse on the subject of Balaam, she suddenly began to sing, and glided from song to song in a voice which, though weak, was very true and sweet. The peculiar haunting cadences echoed in our memories for many a year. I jotted down such words as I could as she was singing.

Doun in the Lowlands a poor boy did wander,
Doun in the Lowlands a poor boy did roam,
By his friends he was neglected, he lookit so dejected
That poor little fisherman's boy so far away from home.

In the course of his wanderings he passes beneath a lady's window, and the lady takes pity on him. "I will relieve you; I will receive you." The song ends happily, but the next moment we were in a graveyard where a young girl is seeking for her lover amongst the victims of a flood. She recognized him by a mark on his arm.

She kissed him, she blessed him . . .

Meanwhile the aged singer's daughter is quietly wiping the tears from her eyes—a tribute which many a prima donna might envy. Sad to say, before our next visit to the isle, the old woman was dead.

The tunes were in some ways easier to secure as they did not have to be gathered piecemeal, but the fact that they were largely in unfamiliar modes, such as the Dorian or Hypolydian, presented difficulties. To ears accustomed to our modern major and minor modes and the tempered scale, the avoidance of a sharpened seventh in the minor scale gives a curious effect. There is a tendency, too, to end a tune on the supertonic, which gives an unfinished feeling. Each singer or fiddler adds his own grace notes, with the result that different versions of the same tune in course of time become almost unrecognizable.* A large proportion of the songs were gathered from the Gray family. One afternoon we were sitting round the central fire in a house of the old type, blinking sleepily at the glowing peat—for we were tired after a long walk on the hills or watching the smoke twining amongst the rafters. The only chairs were occupied by the visitors, while our white-bearded host sat on the resting chair, and his daughter seated herself on a stool beside her spinning wheel. The graceful measured movement of her arms, as she alternately drew out the yarn and returned it to the pirm, was accompanied by the rhythmic tapping of the treadle and the low hum of the wheel. Softly, perhaps unconsciously, she began to sing. The melody somewhat resembled the refrain of "Green Grow the Rushes, O" and the words also have a little of the flavour of Robert Burns.

---

*Mrs Stoughton Holbourn's collection of some of these old airs, arranged for violin and piano, is published by Messrs E. Kohler & Son, 6 Blenheim Place, Edinburgh, 7.

## MY NANCY, O

My Nancy, O; my Nancy, O;
My kind and winsome Nancy, O.
She holds my heart in love's dear bands,
Which nane can dae but Nancy, O.

At preaching time she gars me stand,
She's gentle and she's bonny, O,
I canna get a glimpse o' Grace
For thinking o' my Nancy, O.

My Nancy, O; my Nancy, O;
My kind and gentle Nancy, O.
If heaven and earth should meet in storm
I'd go to see my Nancy, O.

"That's all well enough," remarked her father; "but what I like
are the *old* songs."

"What do you mean by the old songs?"

"Well, the old, old songs."

When pressed he said he meant a song that everybody
knew—such as "The New Year Song."

We had the utmost difficulty in convincing him that we did
not know this particular song, and still more in persuading him
to sing it. This, possibly, was because, as we afterwards
discovered, it had not been sung since the disastrous night on
which his father and two brothers were drowned. Until then it
had been the custom at Yuletide for a party of young men to
dress up and go round from house to house. One of their number
was garbed in a coat and hood of straw, supposed to represent a
horse, and it was his business to carry home the victuals that they
collected. At the conclusion of the song they ran round and
round the fire and then out of the door. If they were not satisfied

with their entertainment they would kick out the fire and scatter the ashes over the room.

There seems little room for doubt that this song is, like the Papa Stour sword dance, a survival of a mediaeval festival play, in which one or more of the characters wore a mask representing an animal—frequently a horse—or even the head and hide of the animal itself. This in turn was a survival of animal sacrifices. Innumerable versions of these plays exist all over Britain, and indeed all over Europe, and it appears to be almost impossible to disentangle the various characters, or to trace with any certainty sources and origins which are buried in remote antiquity. It seems probable, however, that both the Papa Stour sword dance and the Foula masquerade formed part of the mummers' play of Saint George. This was in three parts—the presentation, the drama, and the *quête*. The first part introduces the characters, the second consists of a fight, and the third part is a quest for alms. We have in Papa Stour a version of the first and second parts while in Foula only the *quête* remains—which may account for the fact that it was never a very popular entertainment. Although very little of a song may be recalled, the number of stanzas is generally known, probably in order to assist the memory of the singer. This one contained sixteen stanzas, all of which were eventually with some difficulty recovered. One or two are slightly indecent and have been omitted.

## THE NEW YEAR SONG

Good Year E'en and Guid Year Night,
    Saint Mary's men are we;
We are come here to claim a right,
    Afore Our Ladye.

We're not come here for any good cheer,
    Saint Mary's men are we,
But for the honour of our New Year,
    Afore Our Ladye.

Here hae we a carrying horse—
    Saint Mary's men are we—
The De'il sit upon his corse,
    Afore Our Ladye.

For he can eat nothin' but bread and beef—
    Saint Mary's men are we
For hai and strae stick in his teeth—
    Afore Our Ladye.

Guid wife gang til thy butter kit—
    Saint Mary's men are we,
And gi'es a spune or twa o' hit,
    Afore Our Ladye.

Guid man gang til thy beef barrel—
    Saint Mary's men are we,
And gites a piece aneist the sparrel,
    Afore Our Ladye.

Guid man gang til thy mutton reist—
    Saint Mary's men are we,
And gites a piece neist the breiet,
    Afore Our Ladye.

Cut wide and cut roun'—
    Saint Mary's men are we,
And watch thou cuts na thysel i' the t'umb,
    Afore Our Ladye.

Gie us the lass wi' the yellow hair—
    Saint Mary's men are we,
Gi'e her to us and we'll ask nae mair,
    Afore Our Ladye.

It's up, let's up my jolly trip—
    Saint Mary's men are we
And run about the fire and skip
    Afore Our Ladye.

The first line of the second stanza bears a resemblance to a west of England version of the Christmas play of Saint George, "I'm not come here for to laugh or to jeer."

The custom of kicking out the fire is probably a survival of the custom of starting new fire for the New Year. In some of the mediaeval plays there is a character who sweeps up the hearth.

In spite of the English words, Sir Walter Scott thought that the Papa Stour sword dance was of Scandinavian origin, but this theory has been rejected by later writers. Olaus Magnus describes a Scandinavian sword dance in which a *quarata rosa* of swords is placed on the head of each performer. This figure occurs in the Papa Stour dance and also in a variety of Yorkshire dances. It is interesting to notice that in Yorkshire the sword dancers carried the image of a white horse, and in Cheshire the horse's head and skin. In Scandinavian festivals, although various animals were used, the horse—and especially a white horse— was the favourite cult animal. It represented the corn spirit and was sacrificed in mid-winter to restore fertility. The horse is a principal character in very many mediaeval plays and it is interesting to find that Shakespeare's statement (itself a quotation from an older ballad) that "the hobby-horse is forgot" does not apply to the remote Isle of Foula.

Even more primitive in construction is a carol "The Seven Sights." This is a variant of "Joys Seven," of which there are many different versions. The whole is built up by refrains and repetitions and the very favourite device of an inevitable sequence—in this case the numbers one to seven—to which it probably owes its survival. It is surprising what a dramatic effect can be obtained by such comparatively slender means, yet the effect is almost powerful.

## THE SEVEN SIGHTS OF OUR LADY

The first sight Our Lady saw
    It was the sight o' one;
It was the sight o' Jesus Christ
    When first he was her son.

The second sight Our Lady saw
    It was the sight o' twa;
It was the sight o' a puling babe
    A-prattling i' the straw.

The third sight Our Lady saw
    It was the sight o' three;
It was the sight o' her little young son
    A-standing at her knee.

The fourth sight Our Lady saw
    It was the sight o' four;
It was the sight o' a clever young son
    A-reading the Apostles o'er.

The fifth sight Our Lady saw
    It was the sight o' five;
It was the sight o' a pretty young son
    A-growing up to thrive.

The sixth sight Our Lady saw
　　It was the sight o' six;
It was the sight o' a fine young son
　　A-bearing a crucifix.

The seventh sight Our Lady saw
　　It was the sight o' seven;
It was the sight o' her fair young son
　　A ruling king in Heaven.

In Foula this was combined with the refrain of "The Holly and the Ivy."

The rising of the sun, the sun;
The running o' the deer [or her dear],
And playing on the merrier green
The song that Mary sware.
　　[or The Herald o' the year]

Cecil Sharp gives the version—

The playing of the merry organ
Sweet singing in the choir.

The following is another song gathered from the Grays in Stoel. I may mention in passing that Laurence, the skipper of the mail-boat, spelt his name Grey while his brothers preferred Gray. The song was described as "A good song that you could sing Sunday or any day." All the clan were good singers. "We were very poor, there were a great many of us and not much to give them; our mother had a very hard time, and it was just singing which kept us going; sometimes when things seemed just almost impossible, she would gather us round the fire and start us all singing." Sweet indeed are "the uses of adversity."

## THE FREEMASONS' SONG

Come all ye Freemasons that dweell around the globe,
Who wear the badge of innocence abin the royal robe,
Which Noah he did wear in the ark wherein he stood
When the world was destroyed by the deluging flood.

Noah was a man well beloved of the Lord
He was found to be faithful over Jehovah's word
He built up the ark and he planted the first vine
And his soul unto Heaven like an angel doth shine.

The fifteenth day arose the ark, let's join hand in hand
As the Lord spake to Moses by water and by land
Near by a pleasant river through which Eden ran
When Eve tempted Adam through that serpent of sin.

Abraham was a man well beloved of the Lord

. . . . . . .

He stretched forth his hand with a knife to slay his son
When an angel appeared and said: "The Lord's will be
done.

Abraham, Abraham, lay not thy hand upon the lad
For I sent him unto thee to make thy heart glad.
Thy seed it shall increase like the stars around the skies
And thy soul unto Heaven like Gabriel shall rise.

I saw twelve knights of dazing lights, which did me
    surprise;
I listened awhile and I heard a great noise;
The serpent appeared and they fell to the ground,
With peace, joy and comfort the secret was found.

The secret was lost and likewise was found
By our blessed Saviour as is very well renowned;
In the Garden of Gethsemane where He sweat the bloody
   sweat
Saying, "Repent ye, my brethren, before it is too late."

For once I was blind and I could not see aright;
It's then unto Jerusalem I soon took my flight.
They led me like a pilgrim through the wilderness of care,
As you see by the sign on the badge that I wear.

Now when I think on Moses it makes me to blush;
Upon the Mount of Horeb I saw a burning bush;
My staff I threw down and my shoes I hove away;
Now I'll wander like a pilgrim until my dying day.

It's now against the Turk and the Infidel I fight;
Let all the warring world see that I am in the right;
For in Heaven there's a lodging, Saint Peter keeps the door,
And none can enter in but such as are pure.

The ancestors of the late Scott Henry in the Wilse were said to
have come from England. He, too, was a great singer and reciter
of ballads. His favourite was the old Border ballad "The Dowey
Dens o' Yarrow," but the words differ considerably from any
version that I have seen.

## THE DOWEY DENS O' YARROW

"Oh Father dear, I dreamed a dream—
   I fear me 'twill prove sorrow—
I dreamt me plucking the heather green
   On the Dowey Dens o' Yarrow."

"Oh daughter dear, I read your dream,
    I fear me 'twill prove sorrow—
Your lover John lies dead and gone
    And his body lies in Yarrow.

As he gaed doun yon dowey den
    His heart was struck with sorrow
For there he spied nine gentlemen
    On the Dowey Dens o' Yarrow.

'Oh, I hae lo'ed your sister dear
    And she shall be my marrow [wife],
Come unto me, come three by three
    And I'll lay you low in Yarrow.'

Then three withdrew, and three he slew,
    Wi' muckle doul and sorrow;
Her brother John came up behind
    And stabbed him to the marrow.

'Go home, go home, thou false young man,
    And tell thy sister's sorrow,
Her true love John lies dead and gone
    And his body lies in Yarrow.' "

Her hair it was three quarters long,
    The colour it was yellow;
She wound it round his middle strong
    And dragged him home from Yarrow.

This woman being big with child
    It brought on all her sorrow
She threw her arms round her father's neck
    And she was dead the morrow.

For a singing version it is suggested that the following might be substituted for the last stanza:

> She laid him doun upon the groun'
> Wi' muckle doul and sorrow;
> Her babe was born before the morn
> And she was dead the morrow.

Rosanna Umphray, who was named after the heroine of the ballad, taught her daughters the following song, which deals with the vexed question of the equality of the sexes from a Scriptural standpoint.

## OLD ADAM

> Old Adam was cast into slumber
> When he lost a share of his side;
> And when he awakened with wonder
> He beheld a most beautiful bride.

> With transport he gazed upon her,
> His happiness then was complete.
> He thankit his bountiful banner [donor?]
> Who thus had bestowed a helpmeet.

> She's not ta'en out of his head, sir,
> To rule and triumph o'er man;
> Nor is she ta'en out of his foot, sir,
> By man to be trampled upon.

> But she's ta'en out of his side, sir,
> His equal and partner to be,
> And they're both united in one, sir,
> And that is the top o' the tree!

The following is another version of a song which Robert Burns adapted. The first two lines appear to be from another song as they are of a different metre and do not fit the tune of "Atween the kitchen and the Ha."

## TAK' ME IN THIS AE NIGHT

Atween the kitchen and the Ha'
The wind blew the bony lady's plaid awa',
Sae tak' me in this ae necht,
I'll never come again O!

I wis' the wind wud turn again
And I could get my plaidie alane;
Sae tak' me in this ae necht,
I'll never come again O!

The wind it is baith cauld and weet,
Ma shoes are frozen tae ma feet,
O tak' me in this ae necht,
I'll never come again O!

The necht it is baith wind and weet,
The morn it will be snaw and sleet,
Sae tak' me in this ae necht,
I'll never come again O!

Tak' me in this ae necht,
This ae necht, this ae necht;
Tak' me in this ae necht,
I'll never come again O!

In the old days the islanders had a great love for songs and ballads. During the long winter nights when the sun only peeps above the horizon for an hour or two and in some crofts is not seen at all for six weeks in mid-winter, the hours of darkness, and enforced idleness for the men, were enlivened by singing and dancing, reciting and story telling—to the accompaniment of the whirring wheel and the scraping kames and cards. The island had its own minstrels who went from house to house and were gladly entertained for several days in each in return for their music. Occasionally a wandering mumster would visit the isle, and pedlers sometimes carried the much prized broadsheets— the predecessor of the modern newspaper. Thomas Isbister remembered these and thought that there might still be some in the island.

Goldsmith, in the *Vicar of Wakefield* mentions "that cheerful ballad 'Death and the Fair Lady'." This was a favourite in Foula. It was in the form of question and answer. Death calls on a wealthy and worldly woman who has made no preparation for his unwelcome visit. She offers him money, and pleads for even one more hour of life.

| | |
|---|---|
| *Death:* | And whether thou be prepared or no |
| | This very night with me must go. |
| *Lady:* | And wilt thou cut me down so soon |
| | And I a flower just in my bloom? |

Ballads of the sea or of naval engagements were naturally popular, and the following is an example.

## THE TURKISH MEN O' WAR

We set our course right east-nor'-east,
    Just as the wind did us allow;
And onward we sailéd merrily—
    For England we were bound.

We hadn't gone a league from land
    No not a league but one,
Till we spied ten sail of the Turkish men o' war
    Just close by as we did stand.

"Streak, streak your sails, ye English dogs,"
    The men o' war did cry;
"Streak, streak your sails, ye English dogs,
    For our bond slaves ye sure must be."

Then up and spake our captain brave,
    A man of courage he;
"Before we streak our sails to you
    We'll fight your king and your countrie."

So we fought on like men of war
    Like champions brave, when we did meet;
And the next morning before the sun arose
    We spied but one of the Turkish fleet.

Three we burnt, and three we sunk,
    And three for fear did flee away,
And one we carried home to old England,
    To show that we had gained the day.

A few fragments which were supposed by the reciters to be Norse were quoted to me, and I give them, without comment, on the chance that they may prove of interest to some "snapper-up of unconsidered trifles."

"Brims goen and brims goar," said to mean "The sea comes over the green grass."
"See he comes blata bruna (white on the brow).
"Oh, hear him come rearna tuna" (rearing and snorting).
This refers to the white horses of the sea.

The following is part of a ballad about an eagle which was attacking a sheep and the man set a dog on to it.

A dog and a foula
A scrieg and a houla
The mothera hearda Antew
At the Norder yellina.

Antew is Andrew—Anty is the deminutive. The meaning is:

A dog and a fowl (or bird)
Crying and holding
The mother heard Andrew
Yelling at the North.

The following from a different source may or may not be part of the same. It has rather an "Abracadabra" flavour.

Anty padua sitten skua
Padua cut and grua
Anty gear skrika rola
Sita rola feeska
Inchina mura pedla
Seti kyorla mesa mura.

The next is a remarkably fine ballad which may, perhaps, be as early in origin as the fifteenth century. Other fragmentary variants of it are known but this is an exceedingly good version and nearly complete. The refrain, which is not in any other version that I have seen, is magnificent—one of the very best. I heard it from Gideon Alanson, who was an interesting character. He was probably the last person in the kingdom to decide upon his own surname. He was the son of James, and grandson of Magnus, and great-grandson of Robert. Consequently his father was called James Manson, while his grandfather was Magnus Robertson. Following the custom of "turning the names," Gideon should have called himself Jameson, but he decided instead to adopt his father's name, Manson, as his permanent surname. Though many boast an ancient name, few can claim a surname that has been established for one generation only. Gideon was unmarried and lived in a tiny house on the hillside called Muckle-Grind (big gate). He was a fisherman, but the coming of the steam trawler robbed him and many another of their only means of livelihood—for he had no croft to form a second string to his bow. For many years he could not pay his rent of ten shillings per annum, but when the old-age pension raised him to comparative opulence he proudly paid up all the arrears of rent. His pastime was composing poetry. All the chief events of the life of the island were recorded in verse, sometimes of a biting and satirical nature, and he used to say that after his death he would be recognized as a second Robbie Burns. Yet he had the greatest objection to reciting his own poems, and it was only by bribing him with tobacco when his pouch was growing lean that he could be prevailed upon to do so.

## THE CRUEL MOTHER

She used to live by the bonny babbis tree
    Along by the greenwood side ay;
And there she bore her sweet babes three,
    All low and alane ay.

She's ta'en out her little penknife
    Along by the greenwood side ay,
And twined the three of their sweet life,
    All low and alane ay.

She buried them under a marble stane,
    Along by the greenwood side ay,
And thought to walk her leal-maid hame,
    All low and alane ay.

She hadna gane a mile or twa,
    Along by the greenwood side ay,
When she saw three bonny boys playing at the ba',
    All low and alane ay.

"Oh, bonny boys, if you were mine,
    Along by the greenwood side ay,
I'd clad ye in the silk sae fine,
    All low and alane ay.

"I'd feed ye or the fallow cow's milk,
    Along by the greenwood side ay,
And ye suld wear the finest silk,
    All low and alane ay."

"Oh Mother, dear, once we were thine,
    Along by the greenwood side ay,
And you would not give us the coarsest twine,
    All low and alane ay.

"We have been at our Lord's knee,
    Along by the greenwood side ay,
Begging mercy for us and thee,
    All low and alane ay.

"Begging mercy for us and thee
    Along by the greenwood side ay—
There's mercy for us but nane for thee,
    All low and alane ay.

"Oh Mother, hell is wide and deep,
    Along by the greenwood side ay;
There are but twa steps to thy feet,
    All low and alane ay."

# 14

# THE CHURCH IN FOULA

The older generation refused to talk to the younger ones about the days of the Danes. The reason is fairly obvious, and has its origin in a remoter antiquity. The struggle between Christianity and paganism had been a very real one and perhaps there were still some who hankered after the gods of their fathers. Be that as it may, it was unwise to initiate the young into the fierce glamour of the old customs—the relentless blood feuds, the spirit-worship, the sacrificial rites, and finally the last grim voyage of the worn-out body in the ship of flame to the halls of Valhalla with their endless feasting and re-enactment of deeds of valour and where the Christian virtues of temperance, meekness and mercy would be of little account, fit only for slaves. Moreover the heathen gods, though dethroned, were by no means dead, and were, like the old superstitions, amongst "those things that must not be mentioned."

Little trace remains of the Roman Catholic days. The "three friars," whoever they were, are now nothing but a name. One or two carols are pre-Reformation, but they were probably brought in by the Grays. There is a cross incised in the under side of the door lintel at the old Ha' of Quinister. The Rev. Peter Brown, a former Congregationalist minister, possessed an old

map in which the Norse place-names of the island were changed
for those of the saints—Saint Mary's Bay, Saint Peter's Point,
and so on. But for many generations the Foula people have been
strong Protestants. The Established church stands in the
Hametoun and is very old. It probably dates back to the
Reformation at the least. About 1870 it was widened and re-
roofed, but except for funerals it has not been in use for many
years.

Writing in 1733 Gifford says that "Foully which did
formerly belong to the parish of Walls" had recently been
"erected" into the new parish of Fair Isle, Foully and Skerries.
There is a little church at Fair Isle, one at Foully and one in
Skerry; the minister thereof resides at Fair Isle and visits Foully
and Skerry once a year, staying in each of them a week or two
and then returns to his common residence. He has his stipend
paid him by the general assembly of the Church of Scotland out
of the fund allowed by the King for defraying the charge of the
assembly: his stipend is only 400 merks Scots a year, which is
little enough considering his travel and dangerous passage."

Foula is roughly forty miles from Fair Isle, and the Skerries
nearly seventy; one lies on the West and the other on the east
side of Shetland. A decidedly awkward parish to work, especially
in an open fishing boat. We are not surprised to read that the
religious life of the islands was at a low ebb. James Alexander
Haldane, the Congregational preacher who toured Scotland
in defiance of the General Assembly's fulminations against
"vagrant teachers," found the Shetlands in 1797 in a state of
"great spiritual destitution." When Low visited the island in
1774 at the earnest request of the islanders he preached to the
entire population. "These honest creatures, in the simplicity of
their hearts are not shy to express their approbation of a public
discourse, even in words, and that aloud." This was a red letter
day for the islanders, and I have no doubt that Mr Low's
discourse was remembered and discussed for many a long year.

Formerly it had been the custom after the service to gather in the churchyard and hold a competition in trials of strength—"who should throw to the greatest distance a large stone, named a *putting stone*—the old men standing by to tell what feats they and their ancestors had done, and to lament the feeble powers of a newer and degenerate race." But by this time they had given up this frivolity and had become strict Sabbath keepers which indeed they still are.

The Disruption of 1843 had its echoes in Foula and James Manson in Sloag conducted services for a little gathering of staunch Free churchmen. Outstanding amongst these was Manse Georgeson, who used to hold a Sunday school at Guttern. He was a son of the bailie who lived at Ham at the time of the muckle fever and was the first to live at Goster or Gossameadow and may have broken out the croft for himself. He went to Sandness on the Mainland to learn to be a black-smith and then returned to the isle. On account, no doubt of his very good smithing as well as his fine character he was highly esteemed, and he was always called "Manse" instead of the less respectful "Mansie." In those days children had to address their elders by their "true" names, such as Magnus or Andrew, while the diminutives, Magnie and Antie, were used amongst equals. How vividly a few simple phrases stored in the memories of the islanders brings to the mind's eye a picture of bygone days. Manse and his wife used to go to the kirk arm in arm and their children walked behind them, step for step. They had four daughters all dressed alike in white gowns with red haps (shawls). They were a snappy kind of folk but real good and true. They would not even look at the sea on the Sabbath for fear they should see drift wood.

This commodity is not only valuable in itself in this treeless place but it provides a very exciting pastime, which is entered into with sporting zest. The first man to sight the piece of wreckage starts the race. If the object is far out from the land, crews are rushed out and the boats hauled down. Then comes a pulling race and the struggle to secure the floating log, or barrel, or whatever it may be. If, however, it is near the shore there is a scramble down the cliffs and a competition for the best position from which to seize the drift wood as soon as the waves bring it within reach, or to throw over it a rope with a weight attached, by means of which it may be coaxed ashore. It becomes the property of the first man to haul in the prize and land it; but that does not end the game. If he requires help to carry it up the cliffs he must share the booty with those who assist him, and his companions watch his struggles with keen interest and assist him with gibes and applause. No wonder Manse thought it best not to look seaward on the Sabbath!

Early in the last century there was a small group of Methodists, or "Ranters," as they were called, but there were never more than about half a dozen of them and they had no regular meeting place. Haldane's movement led to the founding of a Congregational church in the island in 1817. The building which was afterwards occupied by James Henry and which had previously been a dwelling house and then a school, was probably their first place of meeting. The names of the preachers who visited the island were Kerr and Alexander. Among those whom they influenced was an islander, Laurence Christie, who became the first Congregationalist minister. A little chapel was built on the ayre of Ham and the congregation continued to grow. One evening a girl was going home from the peat stack in the twilight when she saw the little meeting house surrounded by a halo of light and heard sounds of singing all around her. Soon afterwards the island was swept by a religious revival and a still larger chapel was built. This is the Baxter chapel, built in memory of an ardent Congregationalist, Dr Wm Baxter, by his sister. After a long record of good work this denomination has now withdrawn and left the field clear for the Church of Scotland.

A sidelight on the discipline of the Church may be seen in the fact that there are people who still remember the time when a girl who had "gone wrong" had to go to church and sit with a hap wrapped round her as a mark of disgrace.

Only nine tunes were known but were varied by the addition of grace notes as it pleased the singer. Yet another denomination, the Plymouth Brethren, found a footing in Foula, and there are still a few left. But although Churches may come and go the people remain much the same. As one comes out of the dim quietness of the little chapel and the congregation divides, some to go north, some south, one stands for a moment to admire the dazzle of the sun on the wide ocean, where the distant outline of the Mainland stretches like a crumpled ribbon on the horizon. Our neighbour the Fair Isle is a misty speck, and here and there a tiny feather of smoke shows that a trawler is at work. Kittiwakes calling and splashing in the Mill Loch, sheep bleating on the hills, make the only sounds. Here as the seasons, with their various tasks and problems, succeed each other year by year, and the struggle is not so much for mastery over nature as a refusal to be enslaved by her, one feels that there must lie in the quiet heart of the islanders some sure anchor against the vast forces of the universe and the infinitesimal nothingness of human individuality.

### AN ISLAND FUNERAL

There is a fascinating old world simplicity about the isle that, once experienced, will never be forgotten. The stranger feels in visiting the "Old Rock" that he has been admitted to the intimacies of a home, the friendliness and warmth of a large family, and it will be an abiding recollection. At no time is this more felt than when we bury our dead, for a death in the isle is a personal loss to all.

Despite their sadness, there is a beauty in these memories.

Some typical Foula veteran, well on in the nineties, has been called away and it seems like the removal of an immemorial landmark, but sad rather than poignant. Or it is some young lad, and the poignancy is shared by all, for to each he was "My boy." We may not believe in ritual, but we have our simple observances and ceremonies, and they seem to help us. The rest of the world is giving up the wearing of mourning and they may be right: we suppose that the theory is that our beloved have gone away to happiness and therefore that we should rejoice. It may be so, but when we send our child away on a long holiday to friends in the south and the boat has become a speck on the horizon, as we turn back into the house we hardly feel it an occasion for festivity. There are two sides to everything and if love means anything, parting must be pain and our pain is the measure of our love. If we get a little melancholy relief out of our black are we to be blamed?

There is a lad lying dead and as the news reaches a young girl standing at her door, she exclaims, "Dear me, I must run and take off my white apron." He was an exceptionally bright boy and full of promise. Herein lies the darkest mystery of death. We could understand a definite close at the completion of a rounded task but this defies our probing. The isle is subdued, and faces the strange enigma of existence. A few hours later two men are seen walking slowly with bowed heads down the little roadway, which is only a glorified path, toward the Voe. We do not require to be told things in the isle—we know—and John o' the shop remarks casually, "They will be coming to buy the wood." Unfortunately the supply has been exhausted and this causes something like consternation; but "maybe the master will have some," says John, and the men move on to the Ha'. The laird comes to the door himself; he has a saw in his hand and the sawdust is sprinkled over the faded tartan of his kilt. Joinery is one of his hobbies and, with the clever assistance of men who have no special training but can turn their hands to anything, he has remodelled and panelled the little old hall that has stood just above the sea for some 150 years. Yes, the laird can oblige and the wood that was to have made the store cupboard for the dainties of the festal board changes its destiny for the grave. We do not employ undertakers; we make the coffins for our dead ourselves and in the afternoon as the laird returns from his visit of condolence, he drops in to talk with the friends who are making the coffin. "The sky is rather weety looking," they remark, as he takes his leave, and the night closes in with a howling sou'wester, and the old hall rocks to its base.

The following day a near neighbour of the bereaved family makes his way round the island in spite of the wind and rain "bidding" to the funeral. At the Ha' there is hammering in the passage when a smart rap sounds on the door. Again we do not require to be told. The men lay down their tools and stand up and one opens the door. A figure in black stands outside. "Is himself at hame?" he asks, and the laird steps forward. Then without the usual elaborate preliminaries of a Foula conversation: "Sir, I have come to ask you to attend the funeral tomorrow at twelve o'clock." "Thank you, I will come," replies the laird. Nothing more is said and the messenger departs on his mournful errand to every house in the island.

The next day is Thursday but it seems like Sunday. No boat puts to sea and no one works in the new-mown hay. The shop and even the post office are closed. About midday the black-clad figures are seen drawing towards the chapel from all points of the island. The ceremonial is not fixed and is influenced to some extent by geographical conditions. The kirk and the kirkyard are at the south end, but the chapel is more central and, therefore, more convenient if the house of mourning is in the south end. In old days the service was generally held in the house but this has become less usual. The minister or catechist officiates unless prevented by illness or absence, in which case another, frequently the laird, will take his place. During a recent epidemic of

influenza, when more than half the island were laid up by a
serious form of this illness, James Ratter, brother of the engineer
of the mailboat, had to rise from his bed of sickness to bury his
own mother.

On this occasion the ceremony takes place in the chapel and
every male in the island not too old or too young is on his way;
no women are to be seen. It does not always rain in the island
and some of the loveliest sunlight effects in the world are frequently seen, but it nearly always blows. The Admiralty records
one calm day in the year in this area. Those who have not felt it
blow in Foula do not know what wind is. Today we gather
outside the chapel on the lee side and huddle closely against the
wall to get what shelter we can from the lashing rain. After some
fifteen minutes, the laird ventures to ask the cause of delay and is
told that some of the folk have not arrived from the north end—
a more or less foreign region, seldom visited by dwellers in the
south end but beautiful beyond belief with sea and crag and
sweeping bay. Another ten minutes passes as the rain is driven
absolutely horizontally in a manner known only to Foula, and at
length the laird hazards the suggestion to his neighbour: "Could
we not wait inside?" "Well, I suppose we could indeed," says
Magnus, wiping the rain from his face. There is another pause
before Magnus ventures to put the unconventional proposal to
the company—"Boys, I'm thinking we should be warmer and
drier inside." The men guess its origin and glance sidelong at the
laird, while custom strives with politeness. Premonitions of
rheumatism to come are strong additional advocates and the
sense of the meeting inclines to declare Magnus' suggestion to be
sound. "Well, that is true indeed," observes an elder, and the
obedient company files in.

A southerner appearing amongst us would notice with
surprise that along the bookrests are rows of large ships' biscuits,
with cups and saucers at intervals and in each pew a large plate of
butter and a knife. The weather-beaten gathering enters the

pews and sits down, and a long period of silence ensues. We are in the presence of death and if the funeral had come from the north end the coffin would be waiting outside. The wind rages and howls round the building and the rain drives against the windows, but it is far away and the unseen presence is very near. After a long pause the minister asks a blessing, not a short form but a long heartfelt prayer that would be strange and unmeaning to the busy modern city where "we never once possess our souls before we die." Meanwhile, in the small vestry at the back two lassies are stirring and tasting the contents of two giant teapots, into which they have put milk and a plentiful supply of sugar, in addition to the strong tea. After another protracted period of waiting, a couple of men emerge carrying the teapots as it would not be seemly for the lassies to appear in the monastic gathering. The silence is unbroken save for the occasional chink of crockery as the cups and even the saucers are filled to overflowing. After a few sips the men pour the contents of the saucers into the cups. The laird is seen to appropriate a spare saucer, but in his case such fastidiousness is overlooked. They may do these things in the south and the laird has travelled over most of the globe. The biscuits take a long time to consume, particularly by those whose teeth have seen service for over three score years and ten. Yet the laird, whose teeth are without reproach, only consumes one while his neighbour disposes of five. At last the silence is again broken as the minister says "Let us return thanks for what we have had," which he does in another lengthy prayer. This he follows by appropriate readings from the Scripture and a simple homily delivered with an easy eloquence that would surprise the sophisticated visitor who has previously imagined that these things are better done in great cities. A hymn is sung and another prayer concludes the ceremony and the congregation rises and proceeds to the home of the deceased about a mile away. There is a momentary lull in the rain and the mournful cry of the Allens is heard across the bleak moor, a veritable picture of desolation, owing to the wanton scalping, and dotted with the ugly little mouldie heaps. Here too is death where once all was green and fair.

When the house is reached the men stand round the door in a half ring and wait for the principal mourners to appear, bearing the lad's remains in the white deal coffin. This is placed on the little stools from the hearthside, often known as coffin stools because of this occasional usage. A shawl, knitted from the blackest of the island fleeces, is then laid over the coffin and corded on, and then the whole is skilfully tied to three masts from the smaller boats, one across the centre and one across each end so that twelve men may carry, two at each end of each mast, for we carry our dead by hand all the way to their last resting place. It may be as much as three miles over hill and dale, rock and moss, and the coffin has to be lifted over the dykes, as it cannot pass through the narrow grinds or gates. Every man takes his share of the burden in turn. At length the kirkyard is reached where stands the disused kirk, whose place is now taken by the more centrally situate chapel. The grave is shallow, and a heap of skulls and bones of the once-loved but now forgotten dead add to the sombre sadness of the scene. The laird is given the "south cord to the west" and the coffin is lowered into the grave. The wind still wails and screams and the rain patters on the thin boards: below thunders the surf, booming ever and anon, with thunder in the caves beneath, and the minister's voice is heard with difficulty above the tempest—"Ashes to ashes and dust to dust." The brief ceremony closes with a touching but harrowing ritual as each man comes forward and lies down beside the shallow grave, so made that he can just reach to the coffin, and laying his hand above the heart he bids his last goodbye. Even then the spirit of quiet resignation is hardly broken and only one turns aside for a moment to the kirk wall to hide the sobs he cannot restrain.

In our crowded cities our neighbours die and it is a passing interest for a few weeks. But in Foula our dead live on in the hearts of all. This promising youth will not be forgotten; come back to the isle in fifty or even a hundred years and his name and something about him will still be remembered. The life of the city is by no means all gain. There is a tenderness of humanity, a kindly human interest, that cannot flourish there, and those who are not too eager in their hunt for money and amusement may find much to be learned in Ultima Thule, in the very heart of the sea and the sky, and remote from the strident clamour of progress.

## OUTWARD BOUND

Some day when all the work is done I shall hie me down to
    the shore
And bend my sail in my little white boat and never return
    any more;
Away and away with a following breeze I shall sail away to
    the west
In my little white boat on a lazy tide to find me a lonely
    rest.
I shall never return any more to the things that I leave so far
    behind;
They shall keep a long look-out for me, when the great all
    knowing wind
Whispers its welcome song in my ear; and I shall laugh at
    length
As I have not laughed in the slow mean years, to the sound
    of its growing strength.
Oh, the grand grey seas will bring me to rest on the wide
    uncharted ways,
And I shall laugh and never return to the foolish round of
    days—

The loves that never my love might reach and the achings
    that never were passed,
For I shall never return—ah no!—when they gulf me down
    at the last.

## 15

## THE WAR IN FOULA
From a diary by MCSH

*August 10th, 1914.* The weekly mail-boat had been delayed by a storm so we had heard nothing from the outside world for nine days. We were delighted to see a small black speck which gradually grew into a sail, and when the sound of her engine was actually heard everybody hurried to greet the mail-boat. We were longing for our weekly supply of fresh bread, for our last mouldy crust had been toasted and eaten the previous day, and we eagerly seized the parcel of new bread—new, that is to say, only ten days old. But more exciting still was the advent of a jubilee nurse. Hitherto the island had been entirely without medical attention of any kind, the doctor not unnaturally showing extreme reluctance to desert the ninety-and-nine Mainlanders for the sake of one Foula lamb! His fee was five pounds, and it was said that Foula folk lived to great ages because they could not afford to die! As I was hastening to welcome the nurse, Mr Greenaway, husband of the schoolmistress, stopped me by thrusting a *Scotsman* before my eyes and exclaiming, "There is war!" I scanned the headlines: GERMANY DECLARES WAR ON RUSSIA . . . BRITAIN MOBILISES . . . RESERVES CALLED OUT. It was so totally unexpected that it seemed incredible. I sat down on the grass dazed and stupified, and watched the islanders quietly unloading sacks of flour and meal, and talking calmly about things in general.

"It seems strange," I said, "to see them working as if nothing had happened."

"They may well take care of the provisions," said Mr Greenaway meaningly, "They will be the last we shall see here for some time."

Meantime the laird and the minister were holding a consultation and decided to call a meeting of the islanders to discuss what steps, if any, should be taken to secure provisions. One difficulty was that the banks were closed and it would be necessary to pay cash. The laird, who had been "taking up the rents," had nearly twenty pounds in the house and he offered to lend this for the purpose. "And I have two pounds," added the minister. The pier was in process of construction and it was obvious that the contractor would have plenty of money in hand. He was accordingly invited to the meeting but replied that it was out of the question as it was low tide and he intended to do some blasting.

When the islanders gathered at the meeting I was struck by their serene faces—with the exception of the shop-keeper, who was visibly perturbed, as well he might be for upon him rested the responsibility of provisioning the island. It was agreed that although we did not definitely know that Britain was involved we should face that possibility, and that while it might be considered selfish to think of our own provisions, and while we should certainly avoid panic supply, yet it was the duty of the islanders to insure themselves against hardship as far as was reasonably possible. So the laird and his little sailing yacht were dispatched in search of flour and meal, and arrived in Walls just in time to secure Foula's supply of meal, which the Mainlanders had thought of appropriating. Meantime our three little boys came running in to dinner enquiring why they had not had their usual lessons. I replied that I had been too upset and that in after years they might remember that on the day of the outbreak of the European War they had been given a holiday because their mother was too miserable to teach them. They had no idea what it was all about, but when five-year-old Alasdair clamoured for more jam on his pudding his father delivered a little homily on the magnitude of the disaster that had befallen us and the sacrifices which even children might be called upon to make. After dinner Alasdair took an account out of the waste paper basket and, tearing off the blank part, stored it away saying that we might run short of note-paper and be glad of every scrap. (Two years later we were glad to buy "economy labels" by means of which old envelopes could be used over and over again). When the yacht returned with confirmation of our fears that Britain had entered the war the people took the news very calmly. Few, if any, of us realised the horror ahead, except perhaps one "witless" old woman who spent the night wandering up and down the banks and cliffs weeping and wringing her hands and bewailing with prophetic foreboding the sorrows that were to come upon the earth

Under this date I find the following entry:

The reluctant northern sun has sunk at last and darkness creeps over the sea. The forms of the little boats passing up and down at the eila grow dimmer and dimmer till they are merged in the blackness of the water. At last the grating of the keels on the shingle and the quiet voices of the men show that the evening fishing is at an end. The sound of slow footsteps of men heavily burdened with their kishies of piltocks, followed by the shutting of a house door, carries across the Voe on the clear night air. The red glow from a window shows that there is a fire waiting to cook the newly caught supper. Perhaps a flaring kollie will be lit in order to afford another glance at the newspaper which has brought the strange tidings of a world at war. Then the light goes out; the peats have been smoored, for only a faint dull glow shows the outline of the window, and clouds have long since obscured the wreaths of blue smoke which rise from the thatched roof in never-ceasing incense. All is peace; even the sea-birds have for a little hushed their crying. Only along the cliffs above the fretful waves an aged Cassandra wanders wringing her hands in an agony of prevision, and wailing "Oh! for the woe that is coming to the earth; woe for the bitter punishment that is to fall upon the world because of the sins of man!" A sudden shivering seizes me and with chattering teeth I turn within.

When a week had passed without further news of the situation a sail was sighted and a motor-boat approached the isle flying a flag which, after some discussion, was pronounced to be the Blue Ensign. We were relieved to hear that our visitors appeared to be friends, although some suggested that it might be a press gang. The laird took a boat out to meet them and returned with the news that some naval reserve-men were to be stationed on the island. We gathered to watch the landing of the troops. These turned out to be two middle-aged men, one a native of Foula, and neither of them very imposing, although one wore a naval cap which gave him a warlike appearance. They carried no weapons except for a telescope with which they were instructed to watch from the hilltops for the approach of the enemy. Within a week, however, the boat returned and removed our representatives of the British navy, and we felt quite deserted. Now and again we heard the rumble of guns; once our windows rattled alarmingly and a few men-o'-war were sighted round about the island. In reply to all our questions we were told that there was "no news"— except for the casual mention of one item, namely that there had been a naval engagement in the Firth of Forth when seven German ships had been sunk. Some weeks later these seven vessels resolved themselves into seven interned trawlers.

It was prophesied that the war might last five weeks, and we looked dubiously at our provisions. By August 19th we had thrown off our gloom sufficiently to make merry at our annual school treat, when we were called to look at a large man-o'-war in the act of anchoring off our shore. "Can this be the Germans at last?" "No, it is the British flag." "But the Germans would fly the British flag fast enough if it suited them." "*I'm* not afraid of the Germans," said a small boy bravely, though with trembling lips. A boat was lowered to put ashore an officer and signalman and we recognised with joy a strong Cockney accent. The officer purchased a catch of cod, which had just been landed, for five shillings; two shillings less than the very moderate price asked, not realising that in Foula it is customary to pay more rather than less than the price named. We invited the visitors to the house. The officer went in while the signalman, a beardless youth, kept watch outside. I asked how long it was since he had set foot on land and he replied "Oh, a very long time, quite two months." I asked if he wanted to see active service and he said he would like to see a little of it, with a decided emphasis on the "little." The officer, whose name was Mallet, of the *Forward*, explained that he was on the look out for aircraft, as it was thought that enemy aeroplanes might have a secret landing place on the west side. He said he was going to walk to the "next village" and that the ship was to pick him up on the other side. We asked if he knew that the lowest ground on the other side was a thousand feet. He espressed the opinion that the Germans had "bit off more than they could chew" and wished they would come out and "let us have a smack at them." I asked admiringly if he was not afraid. "Oh no," he said, "we are as brave as lions now. At first I don't mind admitting that we were terrified. We were in Ireland dealing with the gun-running business when we heard that war was declared and that Germany was waiting to mop up any vessel she came across." He said that this was the first time he had been ashore for a month and told us of his wife and baby living in the south of England. "How I should love to settle down in a little place like this," he added with a sigh. "You will have a nice long holiday when this is finished," I said. "Yes," he answered grimly, "perhaps a nice long holiday beneath fifty fathoms of water or six feet of earth"—a prophesy all too soon fulfilled, for the *Forward* was lost with all hands.

In course of time the island contributed its toll of victims, who are commemorated by an impressive memorial perched on a conspicuous headland, designed by the laird and built by island labour. The five men whose names are inscribed thereon represent a very high percentage out of a total population of 135.

John Henry, RNR. Killed when the *Bulwark* was blown up
    in Sheerness Harbour.
Robert Henry, RNR. Died of fever in Portsmouth.
John William Henry, Gordon Highlanders. Died of
    pneumonia. Buried at Corstorphine.
George Ross Robertson. Died of wounds in France.
Cedric Robertson. Joined the army shortly before the
    Armistice; was drafted to India where he died of
    fever.

The two last were the sons of our last Congregational minister, and fine handsome boys they were. Perhaps the most pathetic case was that of John William Henry, who was the only son of a crippled father and was actually under military age when he was conscripted. The Mainland Tribunals had heard that Foula was full and overflowing with lusty manhood, so they determined to make a raid on these slackers. Investigation showed, however, that these Foula stalwarts were nearer eighty than eighteen, for the island had already given all her available manhood. But rather than return empty-handed they fastened upon this boy of seventeen. He pleaded that the harvest was ready for cutting and would rot if he were to leave the island. "Let it rot!" was the reply.

He never saw active service but died in hospital, within a few weeks, of pneumonia, aggravated no doubt by homesickness and heartbreak. The islanders showed no bitterness. "It was hard luck, but war is like that." Were it not for the fear of re-opening old wounds, tales could be told of apparitions of our war victims, but I like to think that the spirits of those whose bodies had suffered in strange lands returned at last to rest in their dearly-loved isle of Foula—and is there any place in the world more likely to draw homeward the disembodied spirit?

# MEMOIR

# MEMOIR

The late author of the notes from which this booklet is compiled, left unpublished manuscripts on many subjects, extending literally to thousands of pages. Perhaps it is not unfitting that the first of these posthumous works to be presented to the public should be the chronicles of the isle which he owned and passionately loved for thirty-five years. "Foula has its worries," he wrote to one of his sons, "but on the whole we have been happier there than anywhere else."

Many, too, will feel that no account of the island would be complete without some picture of the familiar kilted figure—of medium height, exceptionally well-built, vigorous, keenly alive, intensely vital—which might be seen striding rapidly over the hills on almost any afternoon in summer. His clear voice, with its remarkable range of pitch, would be heard by the travellers on the lower ground, who would smile and say, "The laird is away to the hills."

Or maybe "Himself is at hame" in the little sitting room of the Ha' with its low, coffered ceiling and half-panelled walls, and he will be found in the deep window-seat that overlooks the sea—made in the thickness of a four-foot wall—drawing-board on knee and pen in hand, dreaming a poem or wrestling with some problem of philosophy. As he clambers down to shake hands, the visitor is aware of a mobile face, strong yet gentle, a broad brow, deep-set penetrating eyes, a well-formed sensitive mouth, and a smile that reveals strong regular teeth. (Unconsciously I have slipped into the present tense and it shall remain uncorrected). "The most remarkable thing about him was his *personality*," more than one friend has remarked. I cannot hope, however, to portray the character of this many-sided individuality except in so far as it is revealed in those events of his career which I am able to record.

Ancestry, unless one happens to be royalty, is reckoned of little importance nowadays, but to a man of romantic disposition and antiquarian tastes it was a matter of absorbing interest, and "the Udaller"—which was the appellation which suited him best and delighted him most—seized every opportunity in the course of his travels to hunt up old records and note any mention of his name. He found over one hundred variants—from Hollenbourne to Obin. Spelling was of little account, for a man might be christened Howburn, married Holburn, and buried Hoborn, registering his offspring under still other spellings. Whether the name is, like Holburn Head in Caithness derived from the Norse Hellsbiorn (Hell's child), or whether it comes from the Teutonic form meaning hollow or holy burn or boundary, is a matter of conjecture. It is more common in Scotland than in England, where it is very rare indeed. As for pronunciation, my husband used to say that when he reached the Tweed the *r* was dropped, at the Humber he lost the *l*, and at the Thames the *H* disappeared.

At the little village of Holburn on the Border, where the foundations of Holburn Tower may still be seen, David de Houbourne of Holbourne and his descendants lived from the twelfth to the fifteenth century. Branches of the family can be traced drifting gradually southward while another branch appears in Scotland, and is befriended by Edward I. At

Inverkeithing the house of the General Holburne, who fought at the battle of Dunbar, is still standing, as is the castle of Menstrie where there is a comparatively recent memorial to "The last of the Holburnes." By 1530 the southern branch has drifted to Lincolnshire, where they appear as small farmers owning their own land and from John Hobourn, born at Westbie in 1531, to the present day there is no break.

The move to London is romantic. The family had become prosperous when a certain Robert Holbourn as a boy of fifteen was so deeply influenced by the preaching of a famous dissenter, that he persisted in going to hear him in defiance of his father, who accordingly turned him out of the house. The lad tramped to London and offered his services to a grocer. The shopkeeper declined, but on second thoughts allowed him to sweep out the shop for two pence. So thoroughly was the task performed that the boy was engaged to run errands, and was soon promoted to serve behind the counter, eventually becoming a partner. His son, Robert Major Holborn, concentrated upon tea, and founded the firm of Holborn in Mincing Lane, adopting the Metropolitan spelling—which fashion I regret to note has recently been followed by the Border village. He took an interest in public affairs, and the tea trade of London presented him with two silver salvers, costing one hundred guineas, "as a token of respect for his successful exertions in obtaining the removal of an unjust tax." Two of his sons—Robert Major and William— entered the tea trade, and the younger, the last of the Holborn tea merchants, died childless, leaving £183,000 mainly to charities. The youngest, Alfred, who was my husband's father, inherited much of the religious enthusiasm but little of the wealth of his ancestor and became a Congregational minister.

Robert Browning, who says "I want to know a butcher paints, A baker rhymes for his pursuit," would have been agreeably surprised by a peep into the house of a London tea merchant of seventy years ago. Writing of his son, who died before he was twenty, the second Robert Major says:

> There are many besides his mother, brothers and sisters
> who know how he could keep the whole circle in jocund
> mood by the hour, enlivening it with trite sayings,
> anecdotes, aphorisms, descriptions and poetry from authors
> ancient and living, Classic and modern, mingled with
> incidents of the day and hour, for he was a keen and close
> observer, had read generally and very widely, was gifted
> with a good memory, and drew his epigrams for our delight
> from Plato, Schiller or Dickens: I not infrequently found
> him with one of his Greek authors and dictionary, German
> curry night, and a week never passed without my having to
> summon one or other of the four volumes of Thackeray's
> *Miscellanies* back to my book-case.

This same promising youth wrote begging his father to recall
him from his travels on the Continent so that he might start
"learning tea and coffee" as "I don't want to be at nineteen and a
half a great hulking lout living on my father." "When I return
home," he continues, "I shall have received at Reading and Mill
Hill a good solid education together with a little German, the
groundwork of music, and the general polish which travelling
and seeing a little of the world gives. What more do I want to
become a respectable Merchant such as you and Uncle and
Grandpapa have been?

"... Every day I am getting more studentlike and less
businesslike, every succeeding week of study renders me more
likely to take honours at the University and to make a fool of
myself in Mincing Lane." At the age of seventeen and a half he
wrote, "I have lately been reading Skeat's *History of the Free
Churches of England*; I never felt proud of being a dissenter
before, but from this time forth I certainly shall; their being
always on the side of civil as well as religious liberty, and the

injuries and oppressions they have for hundreds of years received at the hands of the ruling sect would prevent me from ever thinking of joining our state Church, even though I might considerably prefer its form of worship and Church government."

It is a far cry from this respectable bourgeois family to the romantic Border chief, but my husband had no doubt that both the English and Scottish branches sprang from this same source and this is confirmed by the similarity in the coats of arms.

Alfred Holborn, my father-in-law, was a man of outstanding ability. His career at Mill Hill School and New College, London, embraces first class Honours in Mathematics, Classics and Philosophy, with an imposing list of scholarships and prizes. He was modest to a fault, and it has been said that he lacked ambition. It is truer to say that "his ambition was to make people good," and in this he was singularly successful.

The following tribute to his memory appeared in *The Congregational Year Book*, 1917: "In heaven the record of what he wrought and suffered for men will be preserved when the sun has grown old and the stars have ceased to shine. For long and strong was the furrow he ploughed for Christ's sake."

His longest term of ministry was at College Chapel, Bradford. I quote a few sentences from letters from some of those who came under his influence. "To me he was the absolute personification of what Christ wished us to be on earth." "I never saw him without wanting to be better." "He lived a beautiful and most useful life." "A saint who lived a while on earth." "O, the beauty of his soul!" I remember him as a charming little old gentleman, for whom the word "self" appeared to have no meaning.

Sons do not always appreciate their fathers, but his eldest son's admiration for his father was unbounded. He spoke of him as possessing in a remarkable degree the Athenian type of mind, not only with regard to his philosophic outlook, but on account of his extraordinary openmindedness—his willingness, indeed his eagerness, to listen to those who differed from him, and his anxiety to do justice to their opinions. Until one has come into contact with such a mind one can hardly appreciate its rarity or its peculiar charm. He married Mary Jane, daughter of John Stoughton, DD, a celebrated Congregational minister and preacher, and ecclesiastical historian. On several occasions he preached before Queen Victoria, by command, and was reckoned one of the three best speakers in the country. When he retired from the charge of Kensington the congregation gave him a silver inkstand and a purse containing £3,000. Mary Jane had considerable artistic talent, and was a beautiful needle woman. Her portrait shows a face of exceptional spiritual beauty, sensitive and thoughtful. When she died after barely three years of married life, her heartbroken husband inscribed on her tombstone the simple words, "Mary, who sat at the feet of Jesus and heard His word." (The inscription was altered in later years). Two motherless babies were left. The elder, John Bernard, was at first called by his second name. In college days he was more often known as John, and this was gradually changed to the Scots equivalent Ian, by which name I shall refer to him. He also adopted his mother's maiden name.

November was the birthday month in the Holbourn family—father, mother, two children, and an aunt all having their birthdays in this dreary month, which was accordingly looked forward to as a season of rejoicing. The 5th, Ian's birthday, was a day of special festivity, for it was also Guy Fawkes' day, and for years the little fellow imagined that the bonfires and fireworks were in his honour, and thought how kind everyone was to celebrate it with such enthusiasm.

Soon after his wife's death the father broke down in health and the children were brought up by their aunt Augusta, who "ruled with a rod of iron," until his second marriage. Rearing other people's children is a difficult and often thankless task, and it is small wonder that neither maiden aunt nor stepmother were able to fill the place of the gentle creature whose letters are overflowing with tender love for her two babies—particularly, perhaps, for the little boy who at two years old "has learnt to kiss so prettily" and who can blow a trumpet, "Blow, not *suck*, as so many children do."

The unhappiness of the period following their mother's death was increased in Ian's case by physical infirmity. Owing to neglect on the part of a nurse, a scratch on the little boy's hand became septic, and ultimately the bone was infected. For four years he carried his hand in a sling, and was seldom free from pain. From time to time the abscesses were lanced and the bone scraped. He was often sent to the house of his Uncle William in London, so as to receive the best medical attention—visits to which he looked forward with the utmost dread. For the first of these operations he was given chloroform, but was so ill for days afterwards that on the next occasion he implored the doctors to operate without an anaesthetic, and promised to remain quite still. Argument with the four-year-old patient proving unavailing, the uncle's wife was consulted. "If he says he will be quiet he will be quiet," was the aunt's comment. It was on a similar occasion that the small boy suffered one of the unfortunate little disappointments of his childhood. He was promised a much coveted toy—a beautiful model of a bath ingeniously filled by means of a syphon—on condition that he made no sound during the operation. At the first shock of pain a cry escaped him, but was instantly stifled, and the remainder of the lengthy and agonizing operation was endured in silence. But, alas, the conditions had not been fulfilled, and the prize was bestowed upon a girl cousin. In the wakeful nights of pain that always followed these operations, grief for the lost toy outweighed physical suffering. Another story of his childhood is very typical. He and his little sister had been invited to lunch with Mrs Milnes, an old family friend. Knowing that the children were not strong, the hostess thought it would be wise to provide a milk pudding, and chose sago as being less common than rice. Unfortunately, it was the bête noir of her little guests, and Ian remarked quite cheerfully, to his sister, "Nasty pudding today, Elsie!" The distressed hostess begged him to leave it, but her four-year-old visitor replied, "It's very *rude* to leave anything on your plate," and manfully finished every scrap.

Until the age of ten Ian attended the Bradford Grammar School, where amongst other subjects, he received a thorough grounding in Latin. He often lamented that he had not been so well grounded in Greek, for when he went to Mill Hill, having done no Greek, but being well advanced in other subjects, he was placed in the second year of Greek, and he found his ignorance of the elements of the language a severe handicap, both then and later. His school record was good, and his library is stored with prizes for many subjects, mainly perhaps classical, but including the Mill Hill School mathematical prize. When he left he was senior monitor and head of the school, and the winner of the Bousefield Scholarship. Though he played games tolerably well he was not a brilliant athlete. But his leisure hours were far from idle, for he was editor of the school magazine, and an office-bearer in several societies, such as the natural history and the photographic. His greatest friend, both here and at Oxford was Henry Child Carter (now chairman of the Congregational Union). When the latter visited us when he came to Edinburgh for the world's Missionary Conference in 1910, he told us some anecdotes of their school days. It happened to be his birthday and we provided a birthday cake with "Henry" written on it in sugar, for which the confectioner charged an extra shilling. It stood on a silver salver surrounded by candles—one for each year of his age. They made a noble blaze, but had to be hastily extinguished before the cake melted.

Amongst the tales of Mill Hill, he told us of a certain master (whom we will call Johnson), who was an Irishman, and inclined to be funny—sometimes brutally so. His jokes were repeated over and over again, and gained in familiarity. When a new boy was expected the whole class waited eagerly for the inevitable joke. When Smith tremblingly entered the classroom for the first time, Johnson would gaze intently at him saying, "Is your name Smith?" "Yes, sir." "Have you a mole on your left arm?" "No, sir." "Then you are my long lost brother"; whereupon the big Irishman would seize the terrified new boy in his arms and lift him from the ground in a frenzied embrace, to the delight of the beholders. Again, he would suddenly pounce on some new boy, Ian perhaps, and say, "Holbourn, it is your birthday." "Please sir, no it isn't." "Would you dare to contradict me! I tell you it is your birthday, and you will stand the class sausages." The unfortunate boy would be sent across to the tuck shop to buy a tin of sausages, which the boys were compelled to eat cold in the fingers, without bread. Sometimes Henry would receive the command, "Carter, come and fight me." Then nothing would satisfy this strange man but that Henry, who was tall and strong for his age, should stand up and pummel the burly Irishman, who passively enjoyed the performance. On one occasion, when the headmaster suddenly appeared upon the scene, Johnson thundered—"Back to your place, sir," and, turning apologetically to the headmaster remarked— "Obstreperous boy that." The only course open to the head-master (Dr McClure) was to call the boy to him afterwards and give him a severe lecture, which Carter meekly received in silence—not for worlds would he have breathed a word against his master. His loyalty was appreciated by Johnson, who was exceedingly kind to him ever afterwards. In spite of his peculiarities, Johnson was a splendid disciplinarian. In the space of a few seconds he could transform his uproarious boys into a silent industrious class, hardly daring to breathe or raise their eyes from their work. But, unfortunately, the headmaster began to see that all was not quite as it should be; "And the last I heard of Johnson," said Henry Carter, "was that he had emigrated to Australia and been converted by the Salvation Army. I always did say that the Salvation Army was a wonderful body."

The Bousefield Scholarship took Ian to London University to study for honours in mathematics, which had been his best subject. Now, however, the call of art became insistent. From the age of four it had been his delight to make little pictures, and present them in little paper frames to his friends, and sketching was the favourite occupation of his spare time. In spite of the fact that his father was a remarkably cultured man, with a gift for drawing and a keen love of nature, and of poetry, the absence of beauty, which almost formed part of the religion of the middle-class Victorian Nonconformist household, filled Ian with a restless sense of loss. "The Need for Art in Life," which became the subject of lectures later in his career, was his own intense experience at this period. Accordingly he transferred his scholarship to the Slade School of Art, where he studied for five years under the directorship of Le Gros and Frederick Brown. The technique of painting was always a trouble to him, and he was supremely dissatisfied with his achievements as an artist. I may, however, venture to quote the remark of the late Professor Sir Patrick Geddes, who wrote: "Holbourn's pictures have an arresting quality of high poetic order—weird scenes in his own romantic island of Foula, Narcissus gazing into the stream or dancing dreamland children. He is far too modest about them."

It was, however, the fundamental principles underlying all the arts—whether of painting, sculpture, architecture, poetry, or music—which now began to claim his attention. He began to develop a philosophic turn of mind, and at the age of eighteen, had written a long and quite profound essay on "The Pursuit of the Ideal". While at the Slade he founded and edited *The Quarto*, a periodical whose aim was to bring before the public the work of young and unknown artists. The result was a production of considerable literary and artistic merit which is now sought by collectors.

The beginning of the development of a gift for teaching showed itself in his conducting of a Sunday school class at Ealing. He was given what was known as "the bad boys' class"; but in a short time he succeeded in arresting their attention so that the class of half a dozen difficult boys grew to a group of over thirty serious students.

As an art student he fell in love, with all the ardour of a romantic nature, with a remarkably clever and beautiful fellow-student of seventeen. They were constantly together, reading Browning and discussing the deeper problems of life; she invited him to her home and wrote to him frequently—"every letter a poem." This intimate friendship was brought to a sudden close by her revealing to him that she had been engaged for two years to another man. To the onlooker it appeared that she had trifled with his affection, but he himself, neither then nor later, ever breathed a word of complaint:

> Lose who may, I still can say
> Those who win Heaven blest are they.

Nevertheless it is no exaggeration to say that he never fully recovered, and to this unhappy incident is traceable much of the sadness of his poetry.

During his training he became very much alive to the lack of cultural background afforded by the art school curriculum. The artist has no contact with the university and is usually lacking in scholarship. Thus the art world has tended to become a Bohemia, separated from the life of the community as a whole, often tending to mere eccentricity. The Slade might as well have been at Timbuctoo as far as the advantages of university scholarship and learning were concerned. The converse was equally true, as he was afterwards to discover. Materialism, and *mere* learning, have lost touch with art and beauty, and vainly hope to build up a civilization without any knowledge of the principles of design. The result is disastrous both to art and to civilization. In order to acquire a sounder knowledge of the history and meaning of art he went, on leaving the Slade, to Oxford University, where he took an honours degree in literae humaniores. This was by no means simple, as it meant reviving Greek and Latin, which had been dropped on leaving school. For his special subject he studied Greek art and archaeology, in which he took first class honours, going out to the British School at Athens for the purpose. Greece cast her spell over him, and he became in the end so steeped in Athenian culture that his friends used laughingly to declare that he was an ancient Greek reincarnate. "The inspiration of Greece—the greatest factor in modern civilization" was the title of a favourite course of lectures; it was also the greatest factor in his own mental outlook. Like the ancient Greeks he derived great pleasure from intellectual conversation and discussion. At Merton College in those days it was the custom for little groups of undergraduates to meet in each other's rooms for tea and, in Ian's set at any rate, for philosophical discussion. To him the value of an Oxford education lay in this interchange of ideas as much as in the routine of lectures, and he regarded an interest in philosophy as one of the essential characteristics of "the Oxford mind."

He was particularly fortunate in his associates, all of whom were men of outstanding ability, and nearly all of whom distinguished themselves in after life. After Henry Child Carter, his most intimate friend was James Alfred Dale, afterwards professor of education at Montreal and Toronto Universities. Amongst those acquaintances whose names have impressed themselves upon my memory were G. E. Chesterton, Augustus John, Sir John Simon, John Buchan, Governor General of Canada, T. Edmond Harvey MP, R. C. K Ensor, Sir Ian MacAlister, secretary of the Royal Institute of British Architects, Sir Richard Livingstone, president of Corpus

Christi, A. D. Lindsay, master of Balliol, The Right Hon. H. B. Lees-Smith, J. Hamilton Fyfe, principal of Aberdeen University, F. A. Barrett and several others.

One of the above recently wrote to me, "It is a sad thing for his Oxford friends to feel that he is gone. I always had such vivid memories of those days when he was one of the most striking figures among us. He had indeed in some ways a tragic life. The one thing that *never* came to him—in his working life I mean—was good fortune. And now it is too late." Another remarked—"He used to think about all manner of things that none of the rest of us ever imagined *could* be thought about!"

With Mr Lees-Smith he was associated in helping to found the Ruskin College for working men, and was on the correspondence and examining staff of the college for a number of years. Throughout his life he was specially interested in the adult education of the weekly wage earners, and always took extra pains to be of as much assistance as possible to any whom he met in the course of his work and of his travels.

In recalling incidents of the Oxford days mention was often made of Mr Stone, the College "scout," who has now served two generations of Holbourns and MacAlisters and probably other sons of Old Mertonians. Although retired, he reappeared this year at the degree-taking ceremony to assist in the gowning of our youngest son.

The Old Parsonage—that delightful old house where some of the undergraduates lodged after moving out of the college—was the happy possessor of "the perfect maid." Her Christian name, I remember, was Alice, and her surname is of no consequence as I have no doubt that that has been changed long ago. "Jimmie" Dale used to describe a scene when Henry Carter, in a fit of exuberance of animal spirits, turned somersaults over the end of Ian's bed until, to his consternation, it collapsed under his not inconsiderable weight. The imperturbable Alice was summoned and listened demurely while the contrite Henry, turning his back to conceal his embarrassment, faltered out his confession.

"Alice, I'm afraid . . . that is . . . er . . . I've broken a bed."

"Yes, Sir."

"Alice, would you . . . could you . . . er . . . I wonder if you would mind . . . er . . . could you get it mended?"

"Yes, Sir."

"And . . . er . . . Alice. Please send the bill to me."

"Yes, Sir."

In 1899 Ian and Mr Barrett joined with Mr F. W. W. Howell in an expedition to Iceland when they made the first crossing of the hitherto unexplored Láng Yökull—a great ridge with vast icefields. It was agreed that Mr Howell as leader of the party should write the account of the expedition, but he lost his life the following year and so no record remains other than Ian's brief pencilled diary. The monotonous entry "Rain all day" becomes abbreviated to "R. A. D." The sledges had to be pulled by hand over the snow and ice and progress was very slow. At one stage they borrowed a pony from a farmer who instructed them to send the little beast back by itself when they reached the steep ground. The pony however had become attached to them and persisted in following them up the hill and they had difficulty in persuading it to return home. The entry for that night is "Worn out, we camp after having pulled the sledge only some three or four miles"; and for the next three days, "Pull, pull, pull. Necks and faces burnt, tortured by thirst, mouth and nose inflamed by snow, blisters on lips . . . Magnificent views, fine snow precipices."

On descending from the ridge the food and fuel supplied ran short but tea and soup were made with water from the hot springs. In spite of some hardship the expedition was looked back upon with delight. The matchless grandeur of the scenery with its sharp contrasts of white snowfields and black basalt rocks, the fiery volcanoes and lurid sunsets, the roaring waterfalls and deep gorges with great overhanging rocks, were unforgetable. Several examples of beautiful iron and silver work provided an additional interest, and the travellers were impressed by the charm and extraordinary hospitality of the Icelanders. Perhaps the hospitality was not always appreciated to the full, for on one occasion a peculiarly penetrating and extremely unpleasant odour pervaded the house where they were staying. After much speculation as to the cause of the nuisance they learnt that a "special treat" was in store for them at lunchtime, in the form of boiled whale blubber. Ian, who always made a point of eating what was set before him, was the only one of the party who ventured to taste a mouthful. The consistenly was like very tough gristle and the taste was if possible even more disagreeable than the smell.

On the way to Iceland the island of Foula was sighted and Ian determined to become better acquainted with its rugged peaks—indeed from the point of view of pure sentiment he dated his ownership of the island from this year, although the actual purchase was not made till about a year later.

At Oxford he was president of four literary and debating societies and was sub-librarian of the Union. A favourite pastime was sculling on the river in a "tooth-pick," but rifle-shooting was his more serious pursuit. He became captain of the Oxford University shooting eight in 1902, and in the same year shot for Scotland against England and Ireland at Bisley. As an art student he had been a member of the artists' corps of the 8th Middlesex, and was in charge of the ambulance unit, and at Oxford he joined the volunteers. In this capacity he formed part of the guard of honour stationed on the steps of St George's Chapel, Windsor, at the funeral of Queen Victoria. He considered this one of the most impressive things he had ever seen.

A passion for the hills dating from an early walking tour with his father in Yorkshire led Ian to spend most of his vacation in the Highlands. He lodged at the Lagganliadh, near Kincraig, with a delightful crofting family of the good old type. Old

Mr Ross was a remarkably intelligent man, whose articles occasionally appeared in *The Times*, and his wife was equally interesting in her own way. Ian's respect for this old couple amounted almost to reverence, and he was very proud of the fact that Mrs Ross referred to him as her "second son." Carpentry was one of his hobbies, and he greatly enjoyed planning and helping to build an annex to their little cottage.

The lure of the hills can only be equalled by sea-fever, and Ian was infected with both. In 1900 he visited Foula, and although he had only a few hours in the island he climbed the Sneug and the Kame and then dropped down to see the North Bay in the glow of a marvellous sunset. The unique combination of mountain and sea was irresistible, and from that date he possessed the isle.

The mundane side of the transaction had yet to be considered. The property had recently been purchased by Mr Ewing Gilmour and he was willing to sell if a sufficiently tempting offer were forthcoming. Ian had inherited a little money from his mother, and with this plus a mortgage from a wealthy and generous cousin he was able to raise about half the required price. Gilmour was a wealthy man who loved the game of bargaining for its own sake and a desperate battle ensued between the level-headed business man and the romantic young artist. The final stages were transacted by telegrams, splitting and resplitting the "absolutely final" difference, and eventually Foula passed to the hands of her lover. Needless to say his sober-minded relatives strongly disapproved of the hare-brained investment, but it would have taken more than an army of bourgeois Victorians to separate him from the island of his dreams.

Through a common interest in rifle shooting a friendship, which had rather far-reaching results, sprang up between Ian and my brother, Laurence Archer-Shepherd, who was also at Oxford. On my brother's mantelpiece there stood a photograph of his only sister at the age of seven, and Ian was amused and interested by her "funny little face." When Laurence invited his friend to stay at Avenbury, Herefordshire, where our father was vicar, Ian, who, in spite of his conversational powers was always intensely shy, was on the point of declining when he remembered the photograph, and yielded to a curiosity to see how the little girl had grown up. As we met in the darkness of a January night there flashed across him the conviction that here was the girl he could marry. After three days he confided this to my brother and at the end of a week spoke to my mother. I was just eighteen and was considered too young to make up my mind on so important a question. In March my mother took me to visit my brother at Oxford for a few days and on the third day of the third month of the third year we became engaged. Although he had had several previous opportunities of making the proposal he was determined, characteristically, that such an event should take place under ideal conditions. So accordingly we climbed to the top of Merton Tower and he showed me the wonderful panorama of Oxford from the four sides, enquiring which I considered the best view. I was undecided, so he took me round the tower again—for it seemed of vital importance to him that I should select the best view. Fortunately my choice coincided with his.

The next day, I remember, we walked to the charming little village of Iffly and he expounded to me his reasons for choosing me for a wife. The only reason which I can recall was my interest in music and his hope that I would supply a branch of art in which he was deficient. I suspect it was a case of "Love disguised as Reason." On returning to the Old Parsonage he felt so elated that he vaulted over the palings, and the landlady demanded "What had come over him!" Years afterwards I called with my eldest son, then entering Merton, and supplied the explanation for which she said she had waited for twenty-eight years. Sitting in this lovely old house during the following days Ian and I corrected together the proofs of his book on Tintoretto, which Messrs Geo. Bell & Sons had commissioned him to write for their Old Master series, and for which purpose he had visited Italy—though I have since wondered to what my assistance amounted in view of my very limited education.

My father was inclined to disapprove of the match on the grounds that Ian was not a member of the Established Church; the fact that he had a very slender and uncertain income did not appear to concern my parents in the least. He had, on the day of our engagment, been appointed a class B lecturer to Oxford University Extension Delegacy, and later in the same year to Cambridge Syndicate, but this did not carry with it the guarantee of any lecture engagements, and he had yet to prove his powers in this field.

In April of this year, when I was very run down after an attack of influenza, Ian asked the doctor to suggest a sea-voyage, and then persuaded my father to allow me to visit Foula accompanied by Ian's aunt, Mrs Georgina King Lewis. We were detained in Walls by snow storms for three weeks and had to return without crossing to the island. I was introduced to the mail-boat crew, and Magnus Manson and I walked together, each politely endeavouring to conceal the fact that neither could understand a word that the other was saying. Mrs Lewis remarked: "What fine fellows they are—no wonder Our Lord chose such for His disciples." This well known old Quaker lady was a picturesque figure in her voluminous black silk dress, and white cap over her dark ringlets. One day when I was confined to bed with a cold, Ian took her to visit Mr Andrew, the parish minister, who assumed that this was the bride to be! On leaving, Ian made some mention of his fiancée and they exclaimed, "But isn't *this* your fianceé?" In the laughter and explanations which followed Ian said, "But did you think I would be travelling alone with a young lady?" The minister's wife looked puzzled, and then said, "Perhaps in the south it would not be considered the thing, but I am afraid we know nothing about etiquette up here."

In the following spring Ian landed on the island with his bride of a few weeks' standing. The Congregational minister, a white-haired old gentleman with the courtly manners of a vanished age, invited us to meet the islanders in the chapel, where he presented us with an eloquent address of welcome. While I sat rather overwhelmed by the proceedings the laird replied, and I remember his saying that whereas formerly the islanders had one friend at the Ha' in future they would have two. This was the first time I had heard our "glorified cottage" referred to as the Ha'. Some of the women addressed me as "Lady," others as "peerie jewel." Most of them louted, or curtsied, while the men stood bare-headed while they spoke to us, or even when they sighted us on the road. (Perhaps the ancient royal tradition accounted for the courtly manners of the islanders). Magnus the Good, as he is called in my husband's notes, invariably backed out of our little sitting room with all the ease and grace of a practised courtier. Yet there was no hint of servility in his manner, and when, after dropping in on our way home from the Sunday evening service to enjoy his discourse on religious or other subjects, he escorted us to the gate of his croft—flinging it open with a flourish as he wished us "Happy Night"—we came away much more impressed with our host's dignity than with our own importance. Indeed we must often have appeared cheap and ill-bred to our regal-minded subjects! Perhaps it was well for me that I had been brought up in a county where we all stood up when the squire entered his private chapel, and where I was curtsied to as the vicar's daughter. Never before, however, had I heard myself publicly prayed for—the prayer for the laird and lady of this island being followed by one for the king and queen of the larger neighbouring islands.

Returning south in the autumn we started married life in two partially-furnished rooms in London. Our relatives and friends thought we were mad, but I had implicit faith in my husband's powers of eventually making his way in the world, and I look back on those days as particularly care free. I continued my studies at the Royal College of Music, while Ian read at the British Museum and lectured for Oxford, Cambridge and London. Our income for the first year was £300, out of which we managed to put by £100—and it was just as well, for in the following year Ian caught a severe chill and consequently had to cancel a number of his engagements. From now onward his life became extremely busy. A full-time programme of lecture engagements at such far-flung places as Ramsgate, Malvern, and Berwick-on-Tweed often necessitated eight hours in the train in addition to one or two lectures and classes. He wrote his lectures in full, although he seldom looked at his notes. Careful preparation of new subjects, revision, wide reading to keep abreast of recent thought, and the correction of students' essays occupied every moment, even in the train, and "work for return journey" was one of the items on his list of "things to pack." Added to this, being entertained in a strange house every day, with strange people, strange beds, and strange meals, was a considerable nervous strain, in spite of the unfailing kindness and hospitality of his numerous hosts and hostesses. Only once did he fall between two stools and leave one house *before* their supper and arrive at the next *after* their high tea! On one occasion in a strange house in Sunderland he sat up talking with his host until long after his hostess had retired. He was shown to his room and got into a bed in which there was a stone hot-water bottle. He gave it a vigorous kick which was followed by a crash and the sound of many waters pouring on to the floor. There had been two hot-water bottles! He removed the sheets, blankets, and mattress, and draped them round the room to dry. Then he folded up towels, curtains, and hearth-rug, and every suitable article he could find, to form a mattress. Just as he had finished there came a knock at the door and his host entered to ask * * * * * it will never be known what . . . and asterisks alone can express the consternation of both host and guest. It is only fair to add that, like the majority of those who entertain wanderers, his host was kindness itself, and refused rest until his guest had been supplied with fresh bedclothes.

His fields of study for his lectures might be grouped as follows:

1. Archaeology and Art-history, especially Greek, Celtic, Mediaeval and Renaissance.
2. Architectural history and design.
3. The Principles and interrelations of the different arts.
4. Plato, Aristotle and Plotinus, and the Greek concept of beauty.
5. The philosophy of beauty.
6. Art and beauty as applied to education, life, character, and civilization.
7. The laws of design, particularly in their mathematical aspects.
8. Civilization—Greek: Middle Ages: Renaissance.
9. Poetry—The theory; The technique of verse: comparative prosody; the poets, mainly English, Greek, and Icelandic.
10. Social and ethical problems. (These were approached partly from the historical but mainly from the artistic viewpoint, as problems of beauty and design). Individualism and socialism; Aristocracy and Democracy; Education; Love and Marriage; Religion.

His versatility and wide mental grip was of course the most remarkable thing about him. On his way from a lecture on, I think, Socrates, he met a member of his audience who remarked, "I have often wondered whether you who know your own special subject so thoroughly can know anything of other subjects." He was astonished to hear that the lectures he had so much admired were not on what the lecturer considered his special subject.

The attempt to make ridiculous questions sound intelligent was part of his work. When lecturing on the Elgin Marbles in the British Museum a passing lady asked, "Can you tell me if these statues ever had heads?" "Oh, no," replied the lecturer. "They were all in this sadly mutilated condition when they were discovered."

The long vacations enabled us to spend several months of the year in Foula, which we looked upon as our real home. The following is taken from my notebook of 1905:

There was no sign of the mail-boat when we reached Walls so I climbed a hill to get a view of the open sea. Below me stretched the smooth waters of the Sound encircling the green isle of Vaila, and, as I ascended, the distant ocean gradually came into sight and I could see the line where the smooth water was met by the waves of the open sea. Suddenly in the west where sea and sky met there sprang into view three sharp peaks—towering despite their distance above the near cliffs of Vaila purple and cloud-capped, watching like some gigantic Sphinx the little ships that come and go upon the eternal ocean.

"Do you see the Foula mail-boat?" said a voice behind me, as a crofter stepped through "a slap in the dyke." "Yon's she just coming into the Sound; she has had a fine run but she'll no' get back this night with the wind against her."

When I explained that I was hoping to visit the distant isle he looked me up and down and exclaimed, "Well, you must have some pluck in you, anyway!" and added: "It's a wild, wild place."

The first day there was too much wind, the second too much sea; on the third day the sea was smooth but the wind, though light, was in the wrong direction. We grew careless, and gradually the contents of our trunks crept out and spread themselves over the room. One morning, soon after dawn, we were aroused by a knock at the bedroom door: "If you please the mail-boat is thinking to make a start today."

"When will she be leaving?"

"Oh, not yet, not yet; there's plenty of time."

I turned over and ruminated, and then, remembering the state of the luggage, decided to get up. When I was half dressed our kind landlady reappeared to ask if we would take some breakfast before starting.

"Oh yes, *please.*"

"We thought that, and have made something ready."

"But you don't mean it is ready *now?*"

"Oh well, not quite. There's plenty of time."

"I'll be down in about ten minutes," said I, resolving to breakfast first and pack afterwards.

While we were enjoying our porridge, and wondering when we should taste food again, we heard the skipper's voice outside the door. His question was inaudible but we caught the reply in a stage whisper, "About half way through their porridge."

"Well, well," and retreating footsteps.

We had nearly finished breakfast when the skipper entered, with his kindly smile and deferential air, but seeing us at table turned with an apologetic gesture to the door. "I'm disturbing you, I'll come back."

"No, no. Come in, Magnus. What do you think of the day?"

"The day is not so very bad."

"When do you think of starting?"

"Oh well, we're making ready—and no doubt you will be having some luggage—bye and bye."

Our next visitor was "Doddie," the strongest though the youngest of the crew. "If you please have you any boxes that we could take down to the boat for you?"

"We have one ready and several others not yet packed. When do you think of starting?"

"Oh well, we're making ready."

"But how long will you be?"

"Oh, take your time, take your time," and he strode away shouldering a big box.

Packing was a weary business, but we were cheered by another visit from Doddie, who went down on his knees and strapped bags and boxes.

"You are not nearly ready, are you, Doddie?"

He glanced round the room, strewn with half-packed bags. "Not yet," he said, returning to a refractory bundle of wraps, "No, no; take your time."

Then the skipper came and I asked him if he would soon be starting.

"If you please," he said, ignoring the question, "Have you anything more forbyes this?"

"That is the last, Magnus, and are *you* nearly ready?"

"Well, yes, I think the men should be coming on for ready by about now."

We strolled down to the pier and found that they *were* ready. They were sitting smoking, but on our appearance they sprang to their feet and, putting away their pipes, handed us in with the utmost solicitude. We skimmed up the Sound under the cliffs of Vaila, past the little stack that stands sentinel at the mouth of the Sound, and from which the length of the passage is reckoned.

"You took the time, Doddie?"

"Twenty past eight."

Scott Henry jerked at the halyards to see if there was any slack, and Magnus at the helm recalled his gaze from the far-away horizon to ascertain if his passengers were comfortable and then, satisfied, relapsed into that expression of straining desire to focus the unseen distance so characteristic of the practised seaman. Pipes and twist were brought out, but though the men smoked there was an air of expectancy about the crew. Little was said beyond an occasional comment on some newly appearing landmark which marked the course or the distance from the land as the cliffs receded and the inland hills appeared behind them.

"I see the Gaads," said Laurence when we had sailed about an hour. Magnus smiled, and told me that meant that we were a third of the way over. The Mainland was growing faint, and the billows hid it from sight when the boat lay in the trough of the waves. Away to the south could be seen the smoke of a trawler, and a herring-boat was beating up to the north. Otherwise our little vessel was alone in the deep waters. Soon Doddie stood up with his face to the west and stretched himself restlessly. Then he moved forward and, with a foot on the gunwale and a hand on the stay, leaned out towards the west.

"What do you see?" enquired the skipper; but there was no reply.

Ten minutes later he asked again, "Are ye seeing anything?" Doddie turned his head, "I think I do."

A little later the question was again repeated. "Yes, yes," replied Doddie, as he returned to his seat with a contented smile. The men looked pleased, their isle had been sighted. True it was but one dark peak above a bank of cloud, but it was enough. A fulmar petrel circled above us with his straight little wings outstretched, and Laurence smiled up at him: "Half road over; we never see them further from home than this."

The men still puffed at their pipes, but in the eyes of each the expression of restless expectation had faded into one of dreamy satisfaction. I, too, felt drowsy, and snuggled down amongst the sails, while Doddie covered me up with the gentleness of a woman.

"Her head is no' very comfartable," said Magnus, taking off his coat, "Roll this up . . . I'm o'er hot e'en noo."

I do not know how long I dozed but I found myself listening to the soft voices of the men and the lapping of the water against our sides. The motion of the boat had changed; she rocked more and I heard the sail flap.

"I doubt it's a pulling job," said a voice.

"Ay, 'tis a pity that—and the tide against us."

"Ay, if we could ha' gotten started twa hoors sooner—"

"Well for that," broke in the cheery voice of the skipper, "If we could ha' gotten started twa hours sooner we'd ha' gotten a fine sailing wind all the way and never heeded the tide."

I stretched myself impatiently beneath the sails and wondered why they did not start two hours earlier. In a flash Doddie was leaning over me to enquire if I was feeling sick.

"No, thank you. Have we stopped?"

"Very nearly; we have lost the wind and I doubt we shall have to pull."

"Would it have been better if we had started earlier?"

"Perhaps—a little—one can never tell."

"Were you ready to start before we came down to the pier?"

"Oh no, no!"

"If we had not been coming could you have started earlier?"

"Well—perhaps—a little."

The truth dawned. "How long did you wait for us?" "Oh, no time; no time at all."

"An hour?"

"Well, really—I could not say."

"An hour and a half?"

"I never noticed."

"More?"

"Oh no, not more! not a minute more, I'm sure."

I was silent; then I lifted my head and addressed the skipper. He was standing beside the tiller which was now powerless to steer a boat that flopped about in the oily swell, and his eyes were straining to catch a glimpse of three sharp peaks and a rounded hill. "Magnus, I'm truly sorry. I believe we kept you waiting today."

"Me? Waiting?"—looking in reproachful enquiry all round the crew till his eyes rested on Doddie whose glance fell—"What nonsense is this boys? I'm sure you never kept us a minute longer than we wanted to stay—not that it would have been of any consequence if you had."

"It is of very great consequence, Magnus, for it means that you have a long pull in front of you."

"Oh for *that*! I'm sure we are none of us caring for that. All we are thinking about is you having such a disagreeable passage; but if you can make yourself anyways comfortable, why then *we* are all right."

"Yes, yes, that are we," chanted the crew in chorus.

For several years Ian was a member of the Zetland County Council and never missed a meeting when in the North. This was no joke, as it entailed a sea voyage of twenty miles and a walk of twenty-seven each way, but he considered himself rewarded when he obtained a grant of three pounds to extend the existing road over a bog—for which work he employed four needy old men. In those pre-pension days even a few shillings made a difference in the simple lives of the islanders.

In 1906, thanks to the generosity of his cousin Annie Freeman, we were able to purchase a small yacht, a strongly built nine-ton cutter, which hailed from the Clyde. Her original name was the *Pirate* but Ian, with his love of all things Greek, renamed her the *Paralos* after one of the twin state triremes of Athens. It will be remembered that when the inhabitants of Mitylene rebelled against Athens the trireme *Salaminia* was dispatched with the edict that all the men of the island were to be killed. Next day the Athenians repented of their harshness and dispatched the Paralos with a reprieve. The rowers of the second ship took no rest and ate at their oars and so succeeded in overtaking the somewhat reluctant *Salaminia*.

The problem of conveying our little yacht from her anchorage at Greenock to Foula was a knotty one. We invited our friend Alan Menzies, at that time professor of chemistry at Glasgow University, to act as skipper, which he consented to do. The voyage occupied three weeks, and we had many small adventures. At Plockton we took on board a fisher lad, and the four of us proceeded merrily on our way. Off Cape Wrath we were becalmed in a fog, and took it in turns to steer by the sound of the breakers on the shore. Through the darkness the foghorn of some other vessel replied to ours, and now and again a curious seal came and peeped at us. At 4 a.m. a light breeze sprang up and we ran before it. But very soon it increased in violence until it reached gale force, and the barometer suddenly dropped right off the scale. We had no charts of the harbours along the north coast of Scotland, but we knew they had a bad reputation, so we decided that it would be too risky to beat back in the teeth of the wind. The only course was to run for Orkney, over a hundred miles. Never shall I forget the mountainous seas that broke over the stern and drenched the steersman time after time, but the gallant little vessel plodded bravely forward. The lonely Sule Skerry standing erect in a vast expanse of water out of sight of all land was most impressive.

A collision with a floating log with sharp projecting branches brought all hands on deck in a hurry, but fortunately no harm was done. The wind increased. The jaws of the gaff broke and the mainsail, with gaff and boom, crashed to the deck and rolled about in an unmanageable fashion. To the suggestion that we should hoist the try-sail our skipper calmly replied, "Not at all, we will mend the gaff." So my workbox was ransacked to provide reels for improvised parrel beads, and eventually the mainsail with four reefs was re-hoisted. The decision proved a wise one, for we reached Pierowall in Orkney only just in time. In another hour or two the sea was in such a state that few vessels could have hoped to weather it. We were asked if we had come from Kirkwall. "No," we replied, "From Cape Wrath." "From a lunatic asylum?" was the next question! When the captain of one of the Shetland steamers heard of our exploit he scolded us violently with an amusing display of temper. I am inclined to think we deserved it.

The *Paralos* was on many occasions the means of revealing the helpfulness and courtesy of the islanders. One night, after being becalmed for many hours, we neared the isle in darkness. We decided to beat about outside till dawn rather than attempt to pick up our moorings in the little creek where there is no possibility of turning the boat to make a second attempt in case of failure. Our behaviour puzzled the islanders greatly—that anyone could be afraid to enter the narrow rock-bound Voe at night was as inconceivable as that a man should be afraid to step out of his bed in the dark. It was evident that we were in difficulties and might welcome assistance, but on the other hand to put out to the rescue would imply that our seamanship was at fault—an insult that might outweigh any injury that the yacht seemed likely to sustain. At last, urged by our maid, an Orkney girl, who promised to take full responsibility, a diffident crew set out to make enquiries. At first we thought it was a boat going out to the fishing on a very early tide, but as its course appeared somewhat aimless and desultory we requested to be towed to our moorings. When the truth dawned upon our dense understandings I penitently asked if the boat had put out to rescue us. I was assured that they would never think of doing such a thing—it was obvious that we were not in need of help, we were doing splendidly—no, they just thought that as it was such a fine night for a row they would take a little trip and have a word with us. It had cost them a night's sleep and considerable trouble, but that, they assured us, was "a pleasure."

In 1907 we came to live in Edinburgh, and moved into 28 Nile Grove only a few days before our eldest son was born. In the next year we flitted to Mayfield Terrace, where the other two sons were born. Each of the boys was given a Greek, a Highland and a family name, but for simplicity I shall refer to them as Hylas, Alasdair and Philistos—the last being a name which occurs in the *Ajax* and is the superlative of the Greek adjective *beloved*.

About this time Ian was commissioned to write a book, *The Gothic Era*, but before it was completed the publisher failed. In the same year Dr Hastings invited him to contribute a series of articles for his *Dictionary of Religion and Ethics* on *The Architectures of European Religions*, and these were published in the form of a book by Messrs T. and T. Clark in 1908.

Among our Edinburgh friends was that stimulating dreamer of dreams and builder of cities Professor Sir Patrick Geddes, and for several years both Ian and I took an active interest in his scheme for turning the waste rubbish heaps of the city into open spaces and gardens where the children of the crowded areas could play in safety.

While living in Edinburgh Ian used to leave for his round of lectures on Monday morning returning on Saturday.

He was closely associated with the Society of Friends, or Quakers, in Edinburgh. He had been brought up as a Congregationalist, and had indeed at one time been destined for the ministry, but although he had a great respect for his father's denomination, and after his death cherished and frequently read his sermons, his artistic nature craved greater beauty than was to be found in the congregational buildings and services. At Oxford

he came under the influence of the vicar of St Frideswide's, in
which church he used to read the lessons and even received the
sacrament in spite of the fact that he had not been confirmed.
For a while he thought of training for the Anglican ministry,
but the Thirty-nine Articles proved an insuperable barrier.
As a youth he had lived for a time with his aunt, Georgina
King Lewis, a noted Croydon Friend. His grandfather, John
Stoughton, was the son of Sarah Bullard, a Norwich Friend, and
he used to tell his children always to love the Quakers because of
their kindness to him as a fatherless boy. His daughter,
Georgina, joined the Friends, and used to say it was "in the
blood." Perhaps it was in Ian's blood also for he eventually joined
the society with which his sympathies had long lain. He was
attracted by the absence of creeds—always a stumbling-block to
his intensely rational mind—by the doctrine of the inner light,
the direct communion with the creator without any human
intermediary, the belief that the voice of God speaking directly
to the soul was a surer guide than the authority of any Church or
even of the Scriptures, and the quiet seeking in the silence for the
revelation of the divine will. The fruits of this doctrine as seen in
a greater understanding and tolerance, and loving kindness unto
every man, greatly appealed to him. Though not quite an
unqualified pacifist himself, he admired the Quakers' absolute
repudiation of the war spirit. "The Immutable Problems of War"
was one of his lecture subjects. But it was "The Beauty of
Holiness"—another lecture subject as seen in the life and
worship of this little society that drew him within their circle.

Ian was frequently asked to preach in churches of many
denominations all over the world. While still in his early
twenties he happened to visit the neighbouring island of Papa
Stour, some eighteen miles from Foula. A storm delayed him
over the Sunday and the catechist kindly put him up. On his way
to the church this gentleman remarked, "Have you chosen the
hymns?" "Why on earth should I choose the hymns?" exclaimed

Ian. "It is the custom of the man who preaches to choose the hymns," replied the catechist calmly. "But I am not going to preach!" "Oh yes," was the rejoinder, "I have told the people, and they are all coming to hear you." So there was nothing for it but to comply as gracefully as possible.

Many years later Ian again found himself in Papa on a Sunday. He planned to arrive late for service so as to ensure there being no repetition of the former incident. The ruse was unavailing, however, for after reading the lesson the minister paused and said, "I see our friend Professor Holbourn in the congregation. I will now ask him to continue the service." The following account is taken from the *Shetland Times*:

> A pleasant surprise awaited the congregation at Papa Stour Church on Sunday. A small boat containing three men put off from a becalmed sailing yacht in the vicinity, and entered the Church just at the commencement of the service. The visitors were recognised as Professor Holbourn and his sons from the Isle of Foula, and at the request of the resident minister, Rev. T. G. Reed, the Laird took charge and delivered a deeply interesting discourse crammed full of wise thoughts. With apt and felicitous references he illustrated the parable in Matt. 25, 14–30, of the Talents, laying stress on the necessity of recognising and developing the true, the beautiful, and the good both without and within in order to truly worship God. There was a large and attentive congregation, who greatly appreciated the kindly interest and help of the visitors. Just afterwards a fine favourable wind sprang up and the smart yacht was soon on its way to Foula.

Brought up in the puritanical belief that theatres were evil, Ian was over forty before he was persuaded to depart from his custom and go to see Martin Harvey in *Oedipus Rex*. All the way

to the theatre he suffered from qualms, and half thought of
turning back. As we alighted from the tram-car a small boy ran
up and handed to Ian a card on which was printed in large type:
BE SURE YOUR SIN WILL FIND YOU OUT.

This restored his sense of humour and he exclaimed "That
settles it; now I *shall* go!" and great was his enjoyment. After the
performance we were invited to meet Mr (now Sir John) Martin
Harvey at the house of Dr and Mrs Cumming, and Ian was
much impressed by the great actor's appreciation of the Greek
mind. Afterwards though he seldom went to the theatre he
always enjoyed it especially a Barrie play or a Gilbert and
Sullivan opera. His power of visualizing what he read was
illustrated on one occasion when he saw a play and remarked as
the curtain rose, "Oh, they have arranged the stage in the reverse
order from when I saw it before." A moment later he realised
that he had not seen it before but had merely read it.

In addition to his lecture engagements in Britain, Ian
received invitations to lecture in France, Spain, Germany,
Austria, Switzerland, and Canada, and in 1913 he received an
invitation from the Lecturers' Association of New York to tour
the United States. In America he gave over a thousand public
lectures in the universities of Harvard, Illinois, Yale, California,
Leland, Stanford, Pennsylvania, Minnesota and Columbia, as
well as the art institutes of Chicago, Detroit, the National Art
Federation, and so on. He held the record for the largest Oxford
University Extension audiences since the movement was started,
while at California he lectured to an audience of over ten
thousand in the great auditorium. The following is a rather
amusing extract from *The Newport Daily News* of 4 January
1914:

A lecturer on such a theme as Socrates rarely has the
satisfaction of having the crowds leaving the hall at the
close mistaken for the gathering at a fire . . . A passenger on

the Fall River car was rushing excitedly toward the rear door when he met Mr Holbourn entering and enquired the reason for the crowds pouring from the Rogers High School entrance. Whether Mr Holbourn's answer, that he had just been delivering a lecture on Greek Thought was a disappointment to his questioner, it highly amused the other passengers, many of whom had attended the lecture. Mr Holbourn would probably say that such occurrences were the common thing in ancient Athens.

Amusing in a different way is a letter from a little girl who wrote:

I felt I must write and tell you how much I enjoyed your wonderful lecture. I never heard anything like it before and would love to hear more. It will help me so with my music . . . I shall be going back to school next term so I shall miss the rest of your lovely lectures unless I can persuade mother to let me come down from London for one.

He was a great lover of children and they of him—partly, I think, because of his insight into the child mind. I remember when a number of less imaginative grownups were peering at a baby over the rail of a nursery playground Ian stepped over the barrier and sat down on the floor beside the delighted infant. Many are the tiny children who have sat upon his knee investigating the contents of his thirteen pockets, stored with gadgets of every description, and crowned by a magic watch with a spring case that would open only when blown upon by the wondering baby. A little girl, now herself a mother, writes to me:

He used to get down on the floor with us and build castles out of blocks; but before the 'faery' game was finished everything, from the books for roofs to statuettes of Alice in Wonderland bordering the pools, everything, including jelly-moulds for silvery towers, made a perfect Magic Castle. But he put life into the creatures, and Beauty everywhere. I remember when the castle was finished it obstructed the front stairway. Do you think we'd allow it to be taken down? Oh, no! We used the back stairway for weeks, and finally, being forced to remove it, had it immortalized by photographing it.

I know that many a family still cherishes his letters to the children, usually illustrated by drawing in inks of many colours.

When lecturing at the court of Saxony an official kept trotting to and fro with instructions—"Will Prof. Holbourn remember to do this and that." Finally came the request, "Will Prof. Holbourn remember to begin his lecture, 'May it please your Royal Highness . . .' " The lecturer promised, and added aside to his sister—"I shall begin . . . 'May it please your Royal Highness the date of Turner's birth was 1850; if this date does not please you kindly supply another.' " One of the instructions was that he must kiss the hand of the princess. At this he demurred and was permitted to substitute a very low bow. When I scolded him afterwards he said, "Well she was old and fat; if she had been young and beautiful I would have kissed her hand. I don't mind doing homage to youth and beauty but I'm bothered if I will to mere rank!" The princess proved a gushing little lady who rushed across the room and nearly embraced him in her enthusiasm for his "divine lecture," until she was recalled to a sense of dignity by a withering look from her brother, Prince Johann Georg, who was, both in appearance and bearing, "every inch a king."

The above was hardly a serious expression of Ian's attitude to rank, for which, especially in later years, he had considerable respect. He paid no homage to wealth but attached a good deal of importance to heredity and training, and he thought that good blood coupled with the stricter discipline and ancient traditions of noblesse oblige did tend to produce the true aristocrat. When American journalists, finding it difficult to grasp the intricate question of udal tenure, made sensational statements to the effect that the king of Foula refused to recognize the king of England he took pains to correct the ridiculous misapprehension and said that king George V had no more loyal subject than the laird of Foula. He added that no one who had lived through the upheaval of an American presidential election could doubt that a limited monarchy was the simplest, the most efficient, and by far the cheapest form of government.

With party politics he was very little concerned and used to say that the counting of cabbage heads did not interest him in the least. He desired a government by to *ariston*, "the best." At Oxford, as president of the Fabian Society, he was a modified socialist, but eventually he voted conservative. Writing to his brother, with the characteristic vehemence with which he loved to hammer home a point of view, he says:

I am not a democrat and I never believed in the extension of the franchise or any of the ordinary so-called reforms. What we need is a narrowing of the franchise, and that applies just as much to the blethering old whisky drinkers at the swell clubs as to the ignorant tradesmen and artisans. Of the two evils I prefer the Tory party—they have always been a minute fraction less selfish, a minute fraction more far-seeing and a minute fraction better educated. But it is a poor choice I grant you. What I want is a good system of testing and discovering who are the lower. Then if they are lower they should be lower. I would then try to breed families of four children from the upper and two from the lower, grading 1, 2, 3 and 4. This would keep the population about level and steadily improving . . . instead of breeding mainly from the worst and then giving them the leadership.

In 1916, at the request of some of his audiences, Ian published in book form a lecture on *The Need for Art in Life*. This *The Boston Transcript* described as "one of the greatest little books of the Age, if it is not epoch making it should be." Ian firmly believed that the lack of art and beauty was the main cause of what is wrong with our civilisation—not the only cause by any means, but the most fundamental. To indicate his attitude to beauty I will quote a paragraph:

> Beauty is the excellence of the thing itself, contemplated in itself for itself and by itself. It is fundamentally unrelated to us as far as its end is concerned. The attitude of the artist is the contemplation of a thing for its own excellence . . . I do not contemplate the beautiful because it pleases me . . . it pleases me because it is beautiful . . . But even then the function of the beautiful is not to give pleasure; its end is in itself. This is the difficulty of the modern age. It lacks the power to appreciate anything that does not minister to the self. The question it always asks is—what use is it? It is not any use; that is just the point. If it were any use it would not be beautiful; it would be useful for some end; its end would not be in itself. But the modern age wants to know, how am I benefitted, or at most, with a limited altruism, how are my kith and kin benefitted, my fellow creatures, my species, my kind? . . . What a curious piece of colossal conceit it is to think that everything must have reference to ourselves and that our criterion of things is to be whether they act, whether they work out, whether they answer, for us. Surely the solar system is excellent in itself, whether we be here or not! Surely the great universe is excellent in itself apart from man's use or even understanding thereof! We need to cultivate a little humility, a little meekness, a little of the artist spirit of reverent admiration, and then he can grasp the beauty of the world.

He was preparing for publication in the same year the result of twenty years of research into the fundamental theory of beauty —an endeavour to prove that the principle of design is the correct relation of the parts to the whole and the whole to the parts, and that this problem forms the basis not only of all the arts whether of painting, sculpture, poetry, architecture, drama or music, but of the art of living and of civilization itself. Up till now his work had gone smoothly, but in May 1915 he was the victim of a disaster which involved the loss of manuscripts representing his life work and also wrought irreparable mental and physical havoc. He was returning from his third lecture tour in the United States on the *Lusitania* when she was torpedoed by the Germans. To one with an intense love of children the experience was rendered all the more horrible by the fact that the great ship was carrying a record number of children. They had indeed been the life and charm of the voyage. They had had their own sports and games, and only a short time before the ship was torpedoed a fascinating little girl of eight years old had been proudly displaying the four prizes which she had won. There was a pathetic story of one small boy, who, having said his prayers and asked that they might be kept safe, got out of his bunk a second time and prayed, "Please God, *do* keep the nasty submarines away." But he lies beneath the sea with his little brother and the rest.

Amongst the passengers was a little girl of twelve whose father had died from the effects of the Boer War and whose mother was sending her over to her grandparents to be educated in this country. Ian had noticed her lying overcome with seasickness and loneliness, and by taking her on deck and distracting her thoughts had enabled her to recover. His own children being safe on land, he resolved to make the child his special care in case of disaster. He had not been warned of the German threat, but had misgivings and, knowing the perils of the sea and the need for taking precautions, he advised a number of the passengers to try on their lifebelts. So far from welcoming the advice they actually resented it, and a deputation waited upon him to ask him not to frighten the women passengers. He christened them the Ostrich Club. Poor things, they paid dearly for it, for he himself saw numbers of people drowned by their own lifebelts which they had put on so as to hold up the middle of the body and throw the head under water.

The ship was unusually crowded so that the second cabin passengers had to have their meals in two sittings and even then tables had to be placed in the passages. Coffee had just been served after the second lunch when there was a terrific explosion, and the ship listed so violently that the dishes crashed to the floor. The stewards shouted, "No danger, keep your seats!" and, except for a few screams, there was almost absolute calm. Ian waited till the worst rush was over and then made his way to where the little girl, Avis Dolphin, had been seated about twenty feet away. He took her to his own cabin, as hers was on a lower leck, and put on her a lifebelt belonging to a fellow passenger who assisted in adjusting it. Ian then gathered a few of his most valuable manuscripts and, carrying his own lifebelt, they went on deck and found the two ladies in whose charge the little girl was travelling. Only one of them had a lifebelt and he offered his own to the other. She refused, saying that his life was of more value than hers as he had a wife and children. It was agreed that if he could place her in a boat he should keep the lifebelt. Afterwards he commented strongly on the necessity for having a duplicate set of lifebelts in the seat lockers on the upper deck. He attempted to get them into a boat on the port side but one was smashed in launching, and another was launched empty and some men stripped and swam after it. The only chance therefore was on the starboard side. He took Avis and the two ladies forward and, kissing the child, told her to find his wife and children and kiss them goodbye from him, and placed the three of them in a boat. It was now twelve or fifteen minutes since the ship was struck and she was very low in the water, so he put on the lifebelt, tucked his precious manuscripts into it, and went forward to find a clear space to jump in. As he jumped he had the horrible shock of seeing the child's boat swamp and capsize, but it was impossible to reach it through the mass of wreckage and people. For years afterwards he was haunted by nightmares and would wake up screaming that the boat had capsized. He struck out to get clear of the ship, swimming with some difficulty through a tangle ot ropes, and then looking back he saw the vessel take her last plunge. He made for the nearest boat, intending to hold on to it, and took with him a man who was floating, but when he reached the boat the man appeared to be already dead and the sailors would not take him in. He threw his manuscripts, many of which had been washed away, into the boat and then held on to a line which happened to be trailing from the stern. Numbers of people were picked up and crowded into the boat, and this so impeded the rowing that it was only possible to crawl along. The empty boat mentioned above had drifted about a mile and a half astern and towards this they slowly made their way. Ian, being towed through the bitterly cold water could not see what progress was being made, and when he asked if they were getting near was always told to hold on for another five minutes. After what seemed to him an interminable age, but was probably about three-quarters of an hour, he became numb and exhausted and begged some of the men who were sitting in the boat to hold on to his hand. So deadening however is the sight of wholesale horror that they actually refused to do so as it was "uncomfortable." He was hauled aboard the second boat but climbed back into the first which contained the remnant of his manuscripts. The sight and sound of the people drowning all around made a scene too ghastly to describe. After a long time they sighted a sailing boat that had put out from Queenstown to the rescue. She was already packed with survivors but took on board the passengers from these two boats. They were huddled together in the tiny hold, dripping wet, many seriously injured—a man with his leg broken, an expectant mother with her ribs crushed, and so on—and all distracted by anxiety for their missing friends. One woman kept moaning, "My baby, my little baby!" She had actually tied the little one to her but when she was sucked down by the sinking ship she came up without the child.

After several hours they were transferred to a small steamer and taken ashore. Ian thought he was able to walk but found that his limbs refused to work, so he was supported by two soldiers and taken to the Cunard office and afterwards to a hotel where he was put to bed. The kindness of the people of Queenstown was beyond all praise. Their means of coping with a disaster on so huge a scale was of course totally inadequate, but everyone did all within their power until some of them began to look worse than the survivors themselves. Ian asked for news of the little girl from everybody who came to him, until at about two in the morning news was brought to him that she was safe. Her two friends had been drowned but she, being lighter, had come to the surface and been lifted into another boat and eventually landed at the same hotel about two hours before Ian himself. He took her to her grandparents in England and afterwards she made her home with us until shortly before her marriage.

I remember that when I met them at Birmingham Ian handed to me a wet pair of trousers which he was carrying over his arm. A porter watched in unconcealed astonishment as I put them into my trunk, so I explained that I had just met my husband who was on the *Lusitania*. But the West countryman's wits were not bright that day. "O—oh?" he drawled, "Was 'ee drownded then?"

It was considered rather extraordinary that on the night before the disaster about eleven o'clock when, though in bed, I was wide awake, I "saw" the deck of a huge vessel with a big dip from stem to stern and so great a list that the people were sliding across the deck and dropping into the water. I had the assurance that my husband was safe, and I said to myself, "It is very selfish of me to be unaffected by all this horror just because my own husband is saved." When I asked Avis' grandfather when he first knew of the disaster he replied that at eleven o'clock on the evening before it took place he had seen the small boat upset and a little girl rise to the surface, and he said, "Depend upon it that's our Avis."

When Henry Carter told his brother that their old school friend had gone down on the *Lusitania* he interrupted his exclamation of horror to add, "But he came up again; he's the kind of person that would!"

One day when Avis complained that girls' books were always so very dull Ian promised to write one for her that should be as thrilling as any boys' adventure story. And so *The Child of the Moat* was created bit by bit, written mostly in trains and read at the weekends to the four youngsters at bedtime. As a mother I did not entirely approve, as the younger ones were wrought up to such a pitch of excitement that they could not sleep—Alasdair especially refusing to close an eye until his father had promised faithfully to deliver the heroine with all speed from the perils that beset her. The book was published in the United States in 1916 and sold out of the first edition immediately, but with the bad luck that seemed to pursue all Ian's writings the publisher failed before a second edition appeared.

In the same year was published *Children of Fancy*, a volume of poems some of which had been with difficulty deciphered from the torn and sodden remnant of the lost manuscripts. It was part of Ian's fundamental principle that no teacher could teach the history of an art, and still less the theory, without a practical knowledge. When excessive travelling—and he completed his million miles in 1928—made painting impossible he turned his attention to poetry and there is a volume of poetry amongst his unpublished work. This is of a very different type from the earlier volume. *Children of Fancy* inclines to the "pretty" whereas an American professor of English wrote, "I have met a number of poets here in New York, highly modernistic and blasé all, and have tried your poem on them . . . It bit them like an east wind and left them gasping." Ian was fond of experimenting in exotic forms of verse, and translated Sophocles' *Antigone* in the original Greek metres. When this was performed in America the rhythm of the choruses was felt to be particularly telling. Other metres in which he, and later the students in his poetry class, experimented were Latin, Arabic, Persian, Turkish, Provençal, Old Northern French, Icelandic, Anglo-Saxon and Celtic.

In the course of his travels Ian visited Japan and wrote his impressions to his brother.

As to Japan it was fascinating. I do not know what struck me most—perhaps their houses, with their absolute taste and entire absence of any furniture—I had not realised the literal truth of this—no chairs, no tables, no beds, no sideboards, sofas, wardrobes, or washstands, no nothing. Perhaps their women—they do not seem like real people and yet they are not like dolls. Perhaps they are best described as perfectly behaved children. Their politeness, their grace, their thoughtfulness, their absolute devotion to—one might almost say worship of—their husbands is unbelievable. It must be appallingly bad for the husbands, but I never saw anything so pretty. Get your wife to try it and see the effect upon yourself. When you travel she will carry a travelling rug and spread it out for you upon the seat. You will both take off your shoes, and you will lie down upon the rug. She will climb up on to the seat and sit on the little scrap of rug left by your feet. She will sit on her toes in exquisitely graceful and charming attitudes (this will require endless practice). She will fan you to sleep, also with inimitable grace (more practice). She will then proceed to do her hair (many years of arduous practice)—every single hair must be in its right place, they are done more or less separately. From time to time she will glance anxiously at you, will brush away flies, arrange your clothes if they slip, and fan you occasionally if she thinks you look hot. She will warn you in time for the station, and will adjust her garments with consummate grace and climb down like a child and put on her tiny shoes. She will wrap up the rugs and carry all the parcels if they are light. If they are really heavy you will carry them, but not otherwise. You will walk out first and she will walk behind. You will take care always to speak of her as Kania—that is "my foolish wife"—other people's wives you call "inside," that is "the one inside." You must be very fond of her but be very careful not to show it either to her or to anyone else. The instance of the heavy and light luggage will help you to understand the principle of the thing. If under any circumstances you were angry with her or raised your voice you would be disgraced for ever. You will find it safer to learn Japanese; then as there are no expletives of any kind in the language you will be relieved from any temptation to use them. Moreover abuse of any kind is more or less impossible. There are no persons in the Japanese language; the only way to express "I" and "You" is "the inferior and contemptible one" as contrasted with "the august and honourable." In any attempt to be abusive, therefore, you will merely be assumed to be alluding to yourself. Admirable Country!

While visiting the Barbadoes he sheltered from a storm of rain under a tree along with a number of native children on their way to school. He overcame the language difficulty by borrowing a slate and drawing a portrait of one of the little girls, which her companions recognised with evident amusement.

In 1918 he was appointed professor in the extension

department of the University of California, in art and architecture, and from that year he spent six months in America and six months in this country. He was in the same year appointed lecturer to the United States Federal Government Committee on Public Information in order to assist in establishing a better understanding between Britain and America.

In the following year he received an invitation to go to Minnesota to build up an art department at Carleton College. (In America a college corresponds to our university, and confers degrees, both ordinary and postgraduate.) Some years previously his idea of founding a university art department as distinct from an art school had been taken up in Manchester. The scheme was well advanced, the money had actually been promised, when the war broke out; the principal promotor was interned in Germany and the proposal was abandoned. Carleton, however, had heard of it, and appointed him to do for America what he had hoped to do for his own country. The results were in their way remarkable—indeed "phenomenal." The aim was to train all students—art and other—"first to know what is; secondly to assess, to value and to appreciate; thirdly to create what is not. Knowledge per se is not creative and will never create a civilization or complete an education . . . The Carleton Art Department is based on the linking up of the principles of design with every other University study." It had two divisions theoretical and practical. All art students specializing on the theoretical or historical side must take courses in the practical, and vice versa. Further, any student in any subject (mathematics, chemistry and so on) is encouraged to take courses in both the theory and ths practice of art.

When he went out single-handed there was nothing at all. Before long the number of whole or part time instructors increased to 6, while the single room seating 130 spread to 6 with offices; the college had the largest percentage of students taking art courses of any university or college in the world, and on an average all BA students, reading every kind of subject, voluntarily took two art courses per head in addition to studio work. The college was selected, along with Swarthmore, by the American Board of Education as one of the two best and most progressive colleges in the United States. In spite of lack of money owing to the agricultural depression in the Middle West, "All this," in the words of the president, "Professor Holbourn has done not only without straw but without bricks."

He found the work intensely interesting and the American people extremely responsive. To illustrate the relation between the students and their professor I may quote from a local journal: "Once more Prof. Holbourn is in our midst rumbling away his diatribes against modern civilization . . . but we love you, dear Professor, and you make us *think*." That indeed was what he set out to do. The following are typical of his comments written on students' essays. "Too much of an echo, not enough of yourself." "That is what *I* think and does not interest me in the least; what I want to know is what *you* think." "I do not mind if you contradict me and prove me wrong; what I do *not* want is my own lecture dished up again." "But that," remarked a student plaintively, "is just what most of the other professors do want!"

His periodical addresses in the college chapel sometimes provoked discussions which lasted for weeks. Perhaps modern American youth was a little startled by an address from the text— "The eye that mocketh at his father and despiseth to obey his mother, the ravens of the valley shall pick it out and the young eagles shall eat it!" Both in public and private he possessed a caustic tongue, but a heart free from malice. He never took offence himself and could not understand why others should do so. His habit of mind, and largely of conversation, was Socratic. Question was met by question. To the query "Which would be better?" would come the rejoinder "What do you mean by *better*?" His power of seeing all sides of a question made it very difficult for him to make up his mind; yet he was often vehemently emphatic, and would give his opinion as to artistic merit with devastating frankness. Any action which might damage a thing of beauty aroused a burst of indignation, while wanton destruction enraged him. He was fond of using paradoxes to enforce his meaning, and one day he happened to see displayed for sale in a shop post cards with the following characteristic quotation from one of his lectures: "Never be satisfied with doing what CAN be done—any fool can do *that*. Strive to do the thing that CAN'T be done."

Discussing phonetic spelling he writes:

> I want us to pronounce as we spell not spell as we pronounce—and I want us to spell according to roots and fundamental meaning. As it is (as I tell my students) we merely bark at each other and no dog knows what the other dog's bark means. That is one of the main causes of the failure of our civilization.

He used to refuse to raise his hat to his girl students if he encountered them in male attire, and said that if they dressed in trousers with Eton crops they must not object to being treated as men—for who could be expected to tell the difference? He had no objection, he told them, to their wearing no clothes at all— provided their figures were beautiful and well cared for—but he failed to see why they should choose to adopt the ugliest costume that had ever been invented, and especially when it looks even worse on women than on men.

His own habit of wearing the kilt was due to a desire to escape from the ugliness of modern costume, and was as far as he dared to go in the direction of dress reform—though he would have rejoiced in trunk hose or a Greek tunic. Those who did not understand his passion for beauty imagined that he wished to be conspicuous, or to pose as a Highland chieftain. But such was not the case. He loved the kilt and maintained that it was not only picturesque but comfortable—being warm in winter and cool in summer.

During the fifteen years we lived in Edinburgh we spent many an hour in house hunting—looking for "a ruined castle in a glen three minutes walk from a mainline railway station!" We had gathered a collection of antique furniture, his students had presented him with a fine carved oak Charles I memorial four-post bedstead, and he longed for a house to suit his treasures. One of the many ruins he thought of restoring was Granton Castle—I am thankful that he did not live to know that this beautiful old building has completely disappeared. Another suggestion was Otterston Castle, which was at one time owned by the Holburnes of Menstrie. One day when I was running my finger down *The Scotsman*'s list of houses for sale Ian remarked, "Of course the house I would *really* like is Fountainhall." "Oh, said I, arresting the moving finger, "*That* is for sale." Ian had seen only pictures of the house and had read the description in MacGibbon and Ross: "A more charming example of an old Scottish residence it would be difficult to imagine." We visited the old place and fell in love with it despite the fact that it was verging on the ruinous. In 1922 we bought it from Sir George Dick-Lauder, and much of Ian's time and limited financial resources were devoted to restoring the house and grounds while preserving the ancient character as far as possible. The name, which had been Penkeith, then its English equivalent Woodhead, and later Fountainhall, we restored to Penkaet to put an end to the perpetual confusion with the other Fountainhall. Its situation—as the name "wooded hill" implies—provided what, after mountains and sea, Ian loved most in nature. He used to say that anyone who cut down a tree without planting another in its place should be hanged! Fortunately the Dick-Lauders had been of the same opinion, and it is said that a former owner, Sir George Dick-Lauder, when advised to fell a tree that was breaking down a wall replied, "No; two men could rebuild the wall in a week but it took God eighty years to grow that tree." The task of rebuilding the wall fell to us, and we were indeed thankful that the tree had been spared to compensate us with its beauty for the labour.

His love of trees led to a funny coincidence. He was walking near Montreal when he noticed in a garden a tree of a kind unknown to him, and, characteristically, he stopped to gaze and wonder. The owner of the tree came out and invited him to walk round the garden. In the course of conversation Ian asked if his new acquaintance were a Canadian. "No," he replied, "I am a Scotsman, but I come from a tiny little village of which you will never have heard—Elphinston in East Lothian." "Why," said Ian, "I see your home from my windows every day!" The Scotsman then went in and brought out some photographs of our own house.

In flowers Ian was less interested, indeed he always showed a greater appreciation of form than of colour. Some of his friends thought that he was unfortunate in his choice of a medium when at the Slade School of Art and that if he had practised sculpture or architecture he would have found it easier to express himself. Gothic architecture was one of his favourite lecture subjects, as also was garden design and the planning of "the perfect city." He had the unique experience of planning the layout of an entire city in Illinois, and the main street bears his name. At Brighouse a lady teacher, inspired by a lecture, converted a rubbish heap into Holborn Garden—a beauty spot designed as "a haven for tired mothers." I like to think that, in spite of apparent failure, there may be scattered up and down the world a few trees, a few open spaces, a few fine old buildings, which but for his teaching would have been swept away, even if it is an exaggeration to say that "the awakening to the value of beauty and the revolt against the sordid ugliness of the past generation is largely due to the inspiration of this Ruskin returned to earth."

With his passion for beauty he combined a love of exact

thinking and correct information. He was never satisfied to leave a question unanswered, and the mention of an unknown place or unfamiliar word would set him hunting up dictionaries and gazeteers. He possessed five different encyclopaedias, and great was his satisfaction if he found that one of these gave some additional scrap of information. Reading at meals was recognised as unsociable but an exception was made in the case of books of reference "for public edification," and often the close of a meal would see the table piled high with encyclopaedias and lexicons.

He was meticulously neat and particular in everything he did. Slap-dash was the last term that could be applied to anything he undertook. Yet the number of his interests and activities—which I do not propose to enumerate was amazing. He writes casually, "There is no book in English on Egyptian sculpture so I have prepared one of three hundred pages to put in our Carleton Library for the students . . . One of the biggest labours was making a map that contained every name I mention. The badness of maps is beyond belief. I had the greatest difficulty in finding the places—some took hours of research. Of course it is what is known as paste and scissors work and not what is called scholarship; but I think it should be useful."

In later years he allowed himself no leisure at all but spent every spare moment in writing, often till a late hour, the philosophy which he felt to be of such supreme importance. He took a daily walk for the sake of health, and spent it in hurrying from one viewpoint on his estate to another. I have never known him saunter. Indeed he seemed to be consumed with some inward fire as he felt time closing in upon him and his message not yet delivered.

But before I draw my tale to a close I will recount one more adventure. An astrologer in New York once informed Ian that all his life he would be threatened by Neptune, but that other powers would intervene on his behalf. The old sea-king's final effort was in 1929 when the Udaller in the words of a friend "tied with St Paul" and was shipwrecked for the third time in his life. The following account is taken from a letter:

It is difficult to give an account of an adventure which will convey to the reader any impression of the feelings of those engaged in it. For excitement, and at times utter hopelessness, this escapade was not far from being a really terrifying experience. My son, Hylas, and I set out from the Voe intending to make a short trial sail—the first of the season. It was not a very nice day, the wind was south-south-east fresh, with rain off and on, the sky was dirty and there was mist on the hills. We tacked southward, and managed to avoid the Hoevdi in spite of mist on the landmarks. We did not take the dinghy on board as we were short-handed and it is heavy work for a crew of two. Passing through the six-knot rank off the South Ness, there was "a bit of a jumbly." There was one big lump, and coming down the far side she dipped her bowsprit right up to the bitts, but the dinghy followed unperturbed by our antics, like a little eider-duck following its mother, and did not ship a drop. We then decided that even though the isle would not look its brightest it was a pity to waste a good breeze, and we should sail round the island. We kept far out in order to avoid the squalls off the great cliffs. I have never seen the island looking so grand. The mist was pouring off the cliffs in angry swirls. With its black walls coming sheer into the water it looked even more pitiless than usual.

We soon got into the hard wind in the lee of the isle. We eased the sheet and took down the staysail, but she still carried too much sail. Hylas pulled in two reefs by hand as far as he could and went below for the reef tackle. He then made the somewhat disconcerting discovery that the yacht was leaking and the water was over the floorboards. He got the reefs snugged down, and we tried to get in the dinghy as she was rapidly filling, and we thought we might have to take to her if the yacht foundered. By this time the wind was so heavy that it was carrying the sea. We thought that this was only because we were at the back of the isle, but we learnt afterwards that a gale had been predicted and that this was the beginning of it. We had noticed that the boat was sluggish when running, but now, when reaching, she sailed very badly, and we knew that this would get worse as she became more waterlogged. We pulled the dinghy up to the side of the boat, but the moment we lifted her bow the water came over the stern and filled her. We tired ourselves out trying to pull her aboard in this condition, but were quite unequal to it. After a futile attempt at baling her out we had another attempt at getting her aboard. The only result this time was that one of the oars floated out of her and we did not dare go back for it; we hoped to do as we had done once before and use the boat-hook as an oar in the case of a desperate emergency. As he did not trust the strength of the dinghy's ring-bolt Hylas fastened another rope to the for'ard taft, but directly he started to pull on this it came out and floated away. He then fastened the reef tackle to the ring-bolt, but the strop of the tackle carried away and that hope too was dashed. Hylas next brought up the trysail tackle, hoping that he might be able to perform the difficult task of shackling it into the bows of the dinghy, but as it was anything but calm, he dropped the shackle-pin overboard. While we rested, gloomily thinking, my glengarry, bearing the family crest in silver, blew overboard. We took this as an omen of disaster, for the Fates seemed to be fighting against us.

Then I had the one inspiration of the day. Why not make the boat haul the dinghy on board herself? I got Hylas to fasten the staysail halyard to her bows and lift them right up in the air, and by going over on the other tack the dinghy would be pulled over by the fall of the then weather-runner as she heeled over the other way. The boom also would strike the halyard and bring it over, providing that everything stood the strain. We went about and the dinghy came aboard like a ton of bricks, pinning both of us underneath her. We struggled out and felt comforted by having our one-oared dinghy aboard again.

Soon the mist came down and hid the isle completely. I went below for the compass, but as the boat lurched violently, I dropped and broke it. We next tried the rather hopeless task of pumping, but a pump like ours is of little use when the mattresses on the lee side are floating in water. We thought of trying a bucket, but found that our only one had hardly any bottom, so we baled for five minutes with a saucepan. Of course it made no visible difference, but might have kept her afloat a few minutes longer. Hylas then had a shot at pumping, holding on to the reef pennant, which was tied to the boom. The tying gave way and he fell into the sea, fortunately still holding the pennant. I tried to help him aboard, but our strength was gone. We struggled for a few moments that seemed years, and at last, with my help, he managed to hook his leg over the head of the rudder and levered himself up in that way. As he crawled aboard a heavy sea swept over us carrying away our boat-hook, and with it went a potential oar and our hopes of picking up the mooring. Our fortunes had about touched bottom now. The mist lifted and we found ourselves off the Strem Ness. Still it was not pleasant to go down and see the water swishing up to the lee side when she rolled. However, now we knew we could pile her up in the North Bay and attempt to find a landing on the boulders before we were dashed to pieces.

About this time I noticed a good deal of blood about the deck but did not discover until afterwards that I had a cut on the knee two and a half inches long and half an inch deep. I soon became weak through loss of blood.

We made lots of little tacks, always keeping close to the shore as we never knew when the yacht might founder. There was a six-knot tide against us, but by means of the strong wind we were able to gain a little on each tack. Eventually we managed to beat up against tide and wind to the mouth of the Voe and thought of sounding SOS on the bugle, but could not find it. It was somewhere under two feet of water and floating floorboards, mattresses, drawers, ropes, sails, etc., etc. This did not mean that we were in harbour—far from it. The mooring is almost certainly the worst of any boat in the world. It is merely a very heavy mooring chain practically in mid-Atlantic, with hardly any shelter, and dangerous rocks on either side of the narrow creek. The bottom is strewn with the lost anchors of boats that have been compelled to cut and run. We were surprised to find heavy breakers on the rocks. As our boat-hook was gone, we could not pick up the moorings, so our first intention was to run her aground and trust to salving her afterwards, but Hylas thought he could manage the anchor. Unfortunately he dropped it too soon and it did not hold. He let the jib fly as he had no strength to take it aboard. We launched the dinghy and tried to get down the mainsail, but it jammed. While struggling with it I was knocked overboard, but managed to climb into the dinghy. A few seconds later Hylas was also knocked into the sea for the second time. He climbed into the dinghy and together we ignominiously shouted for help.

At this juncture I take up the narrative from the point of view of "wives and mithers maist despairing." From the pier I watched the yacht come limping home, sailing remarkably badly. Suddenly first one and then another of the crew was swept overboard. While the island men were dragging down a boat to the water's edge, the women gathered on the banks, some holding their breath, others wailing, and one or two begging their menfolk not to put to sea. I told the islanders not to risk their lives for my men, and they replied, "There is no risk, but if there were it would make no difference." As the dinghy's painter had been cut she could not be towed, and the occupants had to hold on to the boat in front. The wind was now blowing out of the Voe and progress was slow. It was with great relief that we saw the boats appear round the end of the pier, but the next moment they disappeared from sight. The wails rose to shrieks. A "humbliband" had broken and while it was being mended the boats were swept back. The yacht was abandoned to her fate and everyone expected that she would funder shortly. The *Paralos*, however, had other notions. She drifted some few hundred yards, neatly anchored herself, and gracefully rode out the gale with only five fathoms of anchor chain. Next day it was discovered that the ring in the anchor had been bent by the strain from a circle into an ellipse. The dazed and exhausted voyagers were put to bed and restoratives were administered to the overwrought women. Hylas was able to get up the next day, but the injured leg necessitated prolonged treatment in hospital and never completely recovered.

Ian's work in America was after his own heart both within the college and in lecturing and organizing exhibitions, etc., in a wider field, and as a member of the governing board of the state art society. Yet he longed to return to his own country and devote himself to its needs. He was intensely homesick and was consumed by "a kind of spiritual loneliness that is almost a disease." His ideal of happiness, he told a friend, was to spend three months in his own home. Yet even this modest demand was not to be realized. Above all things he desired time to put into publishable form his vast work, extending to twenty-five thousand pages of manuscript, on the theory of art. With this end in view he applied for the Watson Gordon professorship of Fine Art at Edinburgh, but though on the short leet he was not successful. He had intended to retire at the age of sixty, but his savings were involved in the Wall Street crash so that this became impossible. Like most of those who offer to the world something of which the public does not realise its need, he was hampered all his life by the necessity for earning bread and butter, aggravated in his case by interminable travelling, and also his desire to surround himself with beautiful things. He was extremely abstemious in his habits, and had no patience with people who indulged in likes and dislikes in regard to food. A craving for tobacco caused him much trouble. Following his father's excellent example he never smoked till after lunch. But even moderate smoking was injurious to his delicate throat, and time after time he was ordered to cut down his smoking until at last he was reduced to three cigarettes a day. Although he made a point of giving it up entirely for several weeks every year so as to insure that the habit should not gain the mastery over his will, he never conquered the craving, and he strongly dissuaded young men from starting the habit.

Although tolerant of moral failure—with the possible exception of dishonety—he was not one who "suffered fools gladly." He had a horror of taking animal life, but this did not apply to flies, against which he waged ruthless warfare; he said that their aimless buzzing round and round was unpleasantly suggestive of human life. One Sunday in Foula during the sermon he caused amusement by a sudden noisy attack with a hymn book upon a bluebottle that was climbing up the window pane. When remarks were passed afterwards he said, "Well it was so *stupid*. It had crawled up that pane and buzzed down dozens of times; it must have *known* it couldn't get out that way—and the window was open all the time. Stupid thing!"

He never shot for sport and there is a tale in this connection which I took down verbatim from an islander:

One day a visitor was leaving the isle and the laird thought he would fire a salute; so he went and fetched a thing he had then, and that is a rifle, and someone asked if he could hit one of two cormorants some distance outside, and he said, "Yes, but it would serve no purpose." But as they were very close together he offered to put a shot between them. He asked what range it would be, and they guessed three hundred yards, so he just put it at what he thought it might be, and fired, and the shot landed exactly between the birds and splashed up the water over them—a thing of which you would not often see the like, and there was not another man who could have done it. So there was no doubt he could have hit them if he had wanted, but it would have served no purpose as himself said—which was a thing that was true.

He disliked officials as such and was always pleased if he could penetrate to the individuality beneath. I remember his triumph when he succeeded in eliciting a friendly remark from a station-master who "had been an official so long that he had forgotten he had ever been human." He was particularly fond of the keepers of the ancient monuments, many of whom showed a real affection for the buildings in their charge. When visiting Register House in search of information relating to Penkaet an official asked him "for what purpose" he desired to look at the ancient documents. "Oh, pure curiosity," said Ian, with a shrug. The shocked official explained that they *never* gave permission for such frivolous reasons. Needless to say before long they were both deep in the intricacies of obsolete Latin.

Having property in more than one district caused confusion in regard to income tax, and at one time he was bothered by repeated applications from one office for a tax which had already been paid through another. Explanations having had no effect, at last he wrote two letters. To A. he wrote, "Dear Sir, As I have already stated, I have paid my taxes through B." To B. he said, "Dear Sir, Can't you explain to those asses at A. that I pay my tax through you?" By accident he placed the letters in the wrong envelopes. B. returned the letter intended for A., but from "the asses" at A. there was complete and lasting silence!

Like so many artists and poets, he combined a light-hearted gaiety and whimsical humour with a profound melancholy amounting at times almost to despair—the dread lest the good should be fighting a losing battle and that the powers of evil, folly and ugliness might ultimately oust those of beauty and wisdom. He shared with the Greeks the fear that

> Man, albeit with justice on his side,
> Fights in the dark against a secret power
> Not to be conquered, and how pacified?

He loved spring, with its promise of beauty, but detested autumn, with its depressing reminders of death and decay. Like the Greeks he dreaded the deterioration of old age, and amongst the current papers left on his writing board was the adage "If it's age you're looking for it's aye coming." I am almost glad he was spared the horrors of conscious degeneration. With the likelihood of an operation hanging over him he became increasingly concerned with the question of immortality, and would startle a casual acquaintance by demanding, "Do you believe in a future life?" He would report a favourable reply to me with great satisfaction, and would add, "If that is true then nothing else matters." When an operation was decided upon no one but the patient anticipated disaster, and although he knew there was no cause for apprehension he was unable to free his mind from the gloomiest forebodings. To distract his thoughts we made, along with our youngest son, a delightful tour of the Border district and visited Holbourn village. He was greatly cheered, too, by the news that the experiment in research physics upon which our eldest son, Hylas, had been engaged almost day and night for four and a half years was now "practically certain to succeed."

On the day before his departure to hospital he told me that he thought he had really made an epoch-making discovery in his philosophy, and hoped he would be able to write it out. Whether he did so or not I do not know—if so it lies with the rest of his monumental pile of manuscripts. His writing is as clear as print and I cherish the hope that some day some student will come forward and complete the work. When the car arrived to take him to the nursing home he took a hurried farewell of his favourite spots in the garden—the rockery, the parterre and the lily pond, all of which he had planned with such affectionate care. The operation went well and by the third day we congratulated ourselves that the danger was over. Nevertheless I went to bed on the night of 13 September 1935, weighed down by a sense of impending disaster, and I was scarcely surprised when at 5 a.m. a messenger arrived to tell me to go immediately to the nursing home. I found Ian quite conscious and not very unlike his old self. Hylas arrived from Oxford a few hours before the end, but as the patient seemed inclined to sleep it was thought unwise to disturb him. The other two boys were in Foula and could not be informed of their father's serious condition until the day of his funeral. Throughout the day he frequently appeared to be writing in imagination—his face wearing the familiar absorbed expression as he traced words with his finger on the coverlet. Almost his last words to me were—"I think my philosophy may be counted as a *real* contribution." Receiving no reply for a moment, he turned to me with an impulsive gesture and asked quickly—"Don't you agree?" When I assured him that I did he looked satisfied and settled into a peaceful repose. At midnight he breathed his last, at the age of sixty-two, paying in the words of his surgeon, "the penalty of an over-sensitive nature."

When the news reached Carleton College his assistant, Mr Hyslop, "was overwhelmed, and dismissed his class with the most beautiful words in reverence to Professor Holbourn and his ideals." A memorial service was held and the flag was flown at half-mast. The president informed me that "a student loan memorial fund was established in his honour." A colleague wrote, "It is impossible to over estimate what he did out here—I often marvelled that one rather frail man could accomplish so much."

Perhaps in conclusion I may venture to quote a poem that was given to him as expressing his personality— but for the fact that in this case the poet *did* write "lines."

### A POET WITHOUT A LINE

One poet I knew
Who wrote not a line
Yet lived his life through
In a meter divine.

He walked with his own
Though his own knew him not;
His soul dwelt alone—
He was one men forgot.

But the deeps of his eyes
Burned with music and song;
He roamed in the skies
Though he moved with the throng.

When he spoke, 'twas with calm,
In tones soft and low,
That soothed like a balm
Or an eventide glow.

And when he passed on
Men woke with unrest
Knowing something had gone
That had touched them and blest.

(JPG in *The Harp*)

# APPENDIX

# APPENDIX
# JOHN SANDS

ARISING out of the several references by the author to John Sands, the archaeologist, notably on pages 119 and 120, the following article was contributed to the *Shetland Times* of July 3, 1937, in which the late Professor Holbourn's articles were then appearing serially. The article was written by Mr John Nicolson, JP, the well-known Shetland writer, by whose kind permission it is reprinted. (MCSH)

John Sands belonged to Edinburgh. He was a fully qualified lawyer, but apparently never practised his profession. He found in journalism a career much more to his liking. Sands took a particular delight in frequenting out-of-the-way corners, and spent lengthy periods, living more or less as a recluse, at Tiree in the Inner Hebrides, Vaila, Foula and Papa Stour in Shetland. He spent also some time in Faroe, and the writer met several elderly people in Thorshavn who recollected his visit to these northern islands, and his interest in archaeology and folklore. He was twice in St Kilda. On the last occasion he was a prisoner on the outpost for fully eight months. For some reason the smack which usually visited the island in August or September with the necessary winter supplies failed to arrive. As no other vessel called at the place, Sands was unable to get away. To complicate matters a shipwrecked crew of Austrian sailors landed in the bay one bleak morning in January. Their boat was smashed on the rocks in landing. A time of great privation followed. The small stock of provisions was soon exhausted, and latterly the poor, kind-hearted natives had perforce to grind the corn that had been set apart for seed. In the midst of these trying circumstances Sands thought of a method whereby their situation might be broadcast. The result was the dispatch of a rudely-formed little boat carrying an appeal for help. A fortnight afterwards the boat was found at Poolewe in Ross-shire. In this way was the sad plight of St Kilda made known to the world outside. For many years Sands' "mail-boat" was a recognised form of communication with the St Kildeans.

I do not know when Sands first came to Shetland. He lived for some time in the lovely little island of Vaila, earning a livelihood by means of the pen. In addition to freelance journalism, he had outstanding ability as an artist, and was a frequent contributor to the pages of *Punch*. He wrote many letters to the *Shetland Times* of that period, meetly scathing indictments of local injustice and oppression. The statement that he "sailed close to the rocks but never struck," is certainly correct. His legal training stood him in good stead in the polemics in which he engaged. Sands wrote an extremely interesting story of his stay in St Kilda, entitled *Out of the World*. The illustrations in the book were from etchings on copper which he had done himself.

He never claimed to be a poet, but the book which he published, *King James' Wedding and Other Rhymes*, contained some jolly good verse. There was humour, there was satire, and biting criticism of existing conditions in Shetland and elsewhere. One humorous touch which comes to my mind was "The Aberdeen Tailor's Apology." A tailor in the Granite City on one occasion secured the contract to supply the Shetland RNR with trousers. When these were delivered, however, they were found to be too small for the stalwart Shetland men. But how was the tailor to know?

> When at the skule, there at the tap,
> A tattered portion on the map;
> I judged them by their sheep an' shelties [Shetland ponies],
> Which should account for a' my faulties.

There is no doubt that Sands had a deep love for Shetland, and that its solitude appealed to his nature. This was revealed very clearly in verses written after a brief sojourn in the south. I am quoting from memory:

> No mortal this world beneath
> Ever felt so happy at flittin',
> For I sail in the *Norna* from Leith,
> God willing and weather permittin'.
> So farewell to your puffing of steam,
> To your engines for ploughing and threshing,
> And give me the kittiwake's scream,
> Where the billows are rolling and dashing.

Similar sentiments were expressed in his verses on Vaila, one or two of which I can recall:

> The population is but small,
> In numbers, twenty-two in all,
> One man and many maids are tall,
> But all are kind in Vaila.

> No Sabbath bell this island reaches,
> No preacher ever comes and preaches;
> Some shift their shirts, and some their breeches
> To mark the day in Vaila.

Here let me live, and when I die
Beneath the sea pinks let me lie.

At the time of which the professor speaks when Sands was championing the cause of the Foula folk in their struggle against landlordism, and the pernicious system of Truck that prevailed, he produced some striking cartoons. One of these represented Foula as a beautiful maiden. Entwined round the body was an ugly boa constrictor, its deadly fangs poised over the maiden's head as if it were about to strike. The serpent was labelled "Landlordism." Lesser-sized, but equally formidable in appearance were the reptiles that wound round the arms and legs. The former were styled "L—s" and "J—s." The latter "Missionary" and "Truck."

Another of his cartoons depicted "The Grinding of the Foula Man's Nose." A crofter fisherman was shown with his nose to a grindstone, which the bearded merchant was manipulating. At his side stood the missionary, who was saying: "Grind it well, P—r, and if anyone says you did it, I'll call him a liar." Another poor victim was seen moving away with his hands to his face, and bemoaning the fact that "they had not even left him a stump."

It must be upwards of forty years since Sands left Shetland. His destination at that time I do not know, but I have reason to believe that he died not many years afterwards in Argyllshire.

Following the publication of the foregoing article by Mr Nicolson in the *Shetland Times*, a correspondent to that journal quoted the complete verses on Vaila, which are as follows:

Come let me sing in homely style
The praises of this little isle,
In length and breadth about a mile
	Yet large enough is Vaila.

The people in it are but few,
In number only twenty-two,
But kindlier souls I never knew
    Than those who dwell in Vaila.

Though all the men can use the spade
And help by it to win their bread,
Yet fishing is the favourite trade
    When weather suits in Vaila.

But weather does not always suit,
And then they patch or sole a boot,
Or make a rivlin for their foot,
    Or mend their lines in Vaila.

But when the weather it does suit
Then bolder men are not afloat
Than those who launch a six-oared boat
    And rush to sea from Vaila.

Though wind be strong and billows high
Across the tumbling tide they fly,
Whilst calm but watchful is the eye
    Of every man from Vaila.

They luff her up or keep away
And with the raging surges play,
While o'er the gunwale pours the spray
    But scares no man from Vaila.

Here none a doctor need employ,
For all the best of health enjoy
Old Christopher eats like a boy
    Thanks to the air of Vaila.

Although eight years beyond four-score,
And rather stiff to pull an oar
He still can work upon the shore
    With flail or spade in Vaila.

No Sabbath bell this island reaches,
No parson ever comes and preaches,
Some shift their shirt and some their breeches
    To mark the day in Vaila.

Let others seek the crowded town
Where faces wear a frigid frown,
But I would rather settle down
    In some retreat like Vaila.

I've dwelt in places in my time
Where grew the orange and the lime,
But I prefer the chilly clime
    And treeless cliffs of Vaila.

What splendid views by sea and land
The wild indented crags command,
The isle of Foula, peaked and grand,
    Delights the eye from Vaila.

The lofty far famed Fitful Head,
Of which when boys we all have read
Though pleasures keen now mixed with dread
    Is visible from Vaila.

The ruined Brough of Culswick too,
The stronghold of some Pictish crew
Upon a crag appears in view
    Across the sound from Vaila.

Here let me live, and when I die
Beneath the salt turf let me lie,
Where billows break and sea fowls cry
    Upon the rocks in Vaila.